Praise for

Understory

"*Understory* is a powerful look at one conservationist's life of discovery, anger, pain, and reconciliation. Van Tighem's soulful and entertaining remembrances chronicle the shifts in Alberta and explore the potential for positive change if we remember we are bonded to Earth, not aloof from it. Don't read this book – put it under your pillow and, through osmosis, let its contents energize you to think about what's important in your life."

—**Lorne Fitch**, biologist and author of *Streams of Consequence: Dispatches from the Conservation World* and *Travels Up the Creek: A Biologist's Search for a Paddle*

"A very well written book based on real-life experiences. Van Tighem's inclusion of the Blackfoot Peoples gives the story a holistic perspective from the standpoint of Native Peoples."

—**Harley Bastien**, Piikani Elder, Buffalo Rock Tipi Camp

"*Understory* – the darkness and the light, a voyage of self-discovery through the prisms of nature, family, and some hard knocks along the way. Van Tighem confronts our abuse of both nature and people, contrasting the sensibility of nature against the imperfection of humankind, including the bureaucracies and economic systems trying to shackle us. But he offers a glimmer of hope and sage advice – the losses are offset by the gains – reuniting with old friends, embarking on new adventures, and revisiting familiar haunts in mountains, forests, prairies, and streams."

—**Cliff Wallis**, Member of the Order of Canada and past president of the Alberta Wilderness Association

"Kevin Van Tighem's *Understory: An Ecologist's Memoir of Loss and Hope* is a powerful, deeply moving read. It is a coming of age for both the man he would become and the west he would treasure and protect. Beautifully written and at times brutally honest, it is the inner song of a man and his place."

—**Roy MacGregor**, author of books including *Paper Trails: From the Backwoods to the Front Page, a Life in Stories*, *Original Highways: Travelling the Great Rivers of Canada*, and *Canoe Country: The Making of Canada*

"In this searingly honest and lyrical reckoning, Kevin Van Tighem unearths the tangled legacy of colonial institutions – religion, Western science, and even our beloved national parks – and how they've shaped our identity and relationship with land, wildlife, watersheds, and one another. Both an ecologist's lament and a love letter to the wounded wild landscapes that endure, *Understory* asks: How do you see the land, and how does the land see you? It is an illuminating offering for these urgent times."

—**Trina Moyles**, author of *Lookout: Love, Solitude, and Searching for Wildfire in the Boreal Forest*

Understory

Understory

An Ecologist's Memoir of Loss and Hope

Kevin Van Tighem

RMB

Copyright © 2025 by Kevin Van Tighem
First Edition

For information on purchasing bulk quantities of this book, or to obtain media excerpts or invite the author to speak at an event, please visit rmbooks.com and select the "Contact" tab.

RMB | Rocky Mountain Books Ltd.
rmbooks.com
@rm_books
facebook.com/rmbooks

Cataloguing data available from Library and Archives Canada
ISBN 9781771607452 (paperback)
ISBN 9781771607469 (electronic)

Copy editor: Peter Enman
Cover photo: iStock.com/mashuk

Printed and bound in Canada

We would like to take this opportunity to acknowledge the Traditional Territories upon which we live and work. In Calgary, Alberta, we acknowledge the Niitsítapi (Blackfoot) and the people of the Treaty 7 region in Southern Alberta, which includes the Siksika, the Piikuni, the Kainai, the Tsuut'ina, and the Stoney Nakoda First Nations, including Chiniki, Bearpaw, and Wesley First Nations. The City of Calgary is also home to Métis Nation of Alberta, Region III. In Victoria, British Columbia, we acknowledge the Traditional Territories of the Lkwungen (Esquimalt and Songhees), Malahat, Pacheedaht, Scia'new, T'Sou-ke, and W̱SÁNEĆ (Pauquachin, Tsartlip, Tsawout, Tseycum) Peoples.

All rights reserved. No part of this publication may be reproduced, stored in a retrieval system, or transmitted in any form or by any means – electronic, mechanical, audio recording, or otherwise, including those for text and data mining, AI training, and similar technologies – without the written permission of the publisher or a photocopying licence from Access Copyright. Permissions and licensing contribute to a secure and vibrant book industry by helping to support writers and publishers through the purchase of authorized editions and excerpts. To obtain an official licence, please visit accesscopyright.ca.

We acknowledge the financial support of the Government of Canada through the Canada Book Fund and the Canada Council for the Arts, and of the province of British Columbia through the British Columbia Arts Council and the Book Publishing Tax Credit.

Canadä  Canada Council   Conseil des arts
for the Arts   du Canada

 BRITISH COLUMBIA | BRITISH COLUMBIA ARTS COUNCIL
An agency of the Province of British Columbia

Disclaimer
The views expressed in this book are those of the author and do not necessarily reflect those of the publishing company, its staff, or its affiliates.

Our land is more valuable than your money. It will last forever. It will not perish as long as the sun shines and the rivers flow and, through all of the years, it will give life to men and beasts...You can count your money and burn it with the nod of a buffalo's head, but only the Great Spirit can count the grains of sand and the blades of grass on these plains. As a present to you, we will give you anything we have that you can take with you. The land we cannot give.

—Is'sapomahksika (Chief Crowfoot)
at the signing of Treaty 7

You can't go back and make a new start, but you can start right now and make a brand new ending.

—James R. Sherman, *Rejection*

It's not enough to recognize the landscape; does the landscape recognize you?

—Tatsikiistamik (Narcisse Blood),
Kainai Elder, teacher, and scholar

Contents

Introduction	1
1. Origins	3
2. Calgary	19
3. Trout	35
4. Pheasants	49
5. Off-Trail	59
6. Mountains	83
7. Lines and Limits	103
8. Rivers	117
9. Grey Ghosts	137
10. Transitions	161
11. Paahtómahksikimi	185
12. The Road to Banff	211
13. Imposter in the Executive Suite	231
14. Spirits and Stories	249
15. Home	277
Notes	297
Selected References	299
About the Author	305

Introduction

In 2011 I retired from a lifetime career spent in western Canada's national parks. Free at last from bureaucratic constraints, I joined the boards of conservation groups, wrote books, and even ventured briefly into politics as an Alberta NDP candidate in the rural southwestern riding of Livingstone-Macleod. There was a certain feeling of desperation involved; time was running out and there were things that still needed care and attention. It wasn't that I had any surviving illusions about saving the world, or even my corner of it; it was more a matter of duty. I felt I owed it to the things I loved never to turn away. I still feel that way, but time is no longer my friend.

Inevitably, as one does during the autumn years, I also spent a lot of time reflecting on what, if anything, was the meaning of a long life journey immersed in the nature of my home place. Why, in a world that has blessed me so richly, was I so beset with grief? Is there a good way forward? Finally, I decided to write a book and see if the act of writing it would help me find some answers. To my surprise, it did. Writing can be funny that way; it's really just another form of thinking. But I'm merely the author; readers will judge for themselves.

I would like to thank Wink Bedard, Lorne Fitch, Bill Hunt, Irene Kerr, Leroy Little Bear, Brian Van Tighem, Gail Van Tighem, Gordon Van Tighem, and Margaret Van Tighem for reviewing parts of the text and providing helpful commentary. Harvey Locke and Marie-Eve Marchand offered important insights at a key juncture. I owe particular gratitude to Naomi Lewis, who critiqued and edited the entire manuscript; her expertise and advice proved essential in polishing and shaping the book you hold in your hand today. And, as always, thanks to Don Gorman and the whole team at Rocky Mountain Books for trusting in me and working so hard to send this work out into the world.

Gail shared many of these experiences, while giving me the gift of over four decades of love and companionship, as well as three now-grown children who each, in their own ways, have made everything worthwhile. I deliberately kept their presence in these pages to a minimum not because they weren't there, but because their stories are theirs to tell in their own ways. Nonetheless I dedicate this book to those three fine humans: Corey, Katie, and Brian.

Finally, thanks to friends and colleagues who made this book possible by sharing the experiences it chronicles. Many are named in the text and others aren't, but I cherish them all. They made the stories and, to a humbling and gratifying degree, they helped make me.

***

The book's title is *Understory*. Every forest has one. What seems like a green and welcoming place on first sight can prove disconcerting when one steps past the forest fringe and into the shadows it hides. There is light in the understory, but darkness too. There are unexpected holes and awkward tangles, shy flowers hiding in hollows, plants and insects that sting, birds that sing – it's not at all what it appeared to be at first sight. One never walks out of the same woods one walked into. Or, perhaps more accurately, it is still the same woods, but one's illusions about it are gone. You can't really know the forest until you've forced your way into its understory, and back out again.

There are parts of the understory I wish I had never seen. Even so, exploring it was worth every living moment. It still is. And that's good, because I'm still lost in there.

1. Origins

The Calgary in which I grew up seemed a perfect place, far from the ugliness that populated the pages of the papers my parents read. In the 1960s most kids still lived outdoor lives free from constraints, other than the injunction to be home before dark.

I used that freedom, and my bicycle, to seek out wild places and explore them. It was still a small city and nature was never far away. Cottonwood forests filled the floodplain of the Bow River. Where the pavement gave way to gravel, prairie grassland and brush-filled valleys receded off to where the Rocky Mountains shimmered on the horizon. My childhood passion for birdwatching kept me searching for rarities, and that search opened up more and more of what seemed, to me, like a perfect foothills paradise. In memory, it was a golden age.

Brewer's blackbirds would rise from their nest sites in the tangles of buckbrush that lined those prairie back roads, scolding with sharp, clacking calls. They dove at me as I pedalled earnestly past in search of more exotic discoveries.

One of those roadside blackbirds, however, introduced me to the darker side of my imagined Eden. Half a century later, its memory still haunts me. I was 12 years old when I found the little bird struggling in the dirt beside the road leading into the Inglewood Bird Sanctuary. The water in the ditch was covered with the viscous stain of oil that had seeped from the adjacent Imperial Oil Refinery. Somehow the blackbird had managed to get fouled by it. I held its fragile body in my hand until it stopped struggling. It was smeared from head to tail, pink flesh showing through the oil-caked plumage, panting for breath.

In those days one didn't rescue sick creatures; one put them out of their misery. There was no hope for the little bird. Choked with sudden grief, I pulled its head off and, horrified by what I had done, threw the little carcass away from me. It splashed down into the puddle.

I have never been able to rid myself of the image of that plume of bright red blood spilling into the oil-stained ditch, under the fading blue promise of that vast western sky. Years later, I recognize that moment as the beginning of the end of innocence, and the start of a search that led, decades later, to a better way of knowing, and living in, a world defiled by unacknowledged abuse.

***

Our family home was at 315 Sharon Avenue, in Calgary. It was a diagonal street that ran along the bottom of a hill, tucked between the wealthy homes of Scarboro that lined stately roads in the neighbourhood beyond the top of that hill, and the humbler, more crowded working-class homes of the Sunalta district that stretched between us and the Beltline, an even older neighbourhood closer to downtown. At one end of our street was the Calgary Tennis Club with its dark green fences and red clay courts. The tok-tok of balls bouncing against the practice backboard was a common accompaniment to my daily walks to Sacred Heart Catholic school, three blocks away.

The back hill was wild, with rough fescue prairie and a tangle of willows, saskatoons, and other native shrubs. Like other kids in the neighbourhood, we brought Mom sweaty handfuls of prairie crocus from that hill each spring, until finally there were no crocuses left. We built improvised forts of branches and grass in the shrub tangle. Sometimes, briefly, a spring would emerge among the willows and seep downslope to the road that ran along the foot of the hill behind Sharon Avenue's yards. We even had springs emerge at the top end of our yard once or twice, but as the city grew, and more and more of the snowmelt and spring rains got diverted into storm sewers, the shallow foothills aquifers dried up and so did the springs.

The native wildness of our back hill vanished too; some urban planner must have decided it was too great a fire hazard. More than one spring prairie fire had scorched all or part of that hill black over the years. It was probably just a matter of time before a grass fire would jump the alley at the top of the hill and take out a house or two. One year, big machines appeared and cleared away the bushes, broke up the soil, and planted the whole thing down to a tame grass mix. Nature had been banished. It was a bitter blow to the neighbourhood's feral child population and perhaps especially to me, given the obsession with nature, especially birds, that I had developed at a very early age. Fortunately, by then I had gotten old enough to travel farther afield in search of wilder places and new birds to check off in my bird guide.

Still, it was one of my first encounters with the blithe ease with which the society into which I was growing could wipe out the character and life of a home place – something that became a source of recurring grief.

One day, returning home from a fishing trip, Dad pointed out the oil refinery at Turner Valley. He said that it was polluting the Sheep River. That made no sense. This was our Alberta – a place of clean, sweet-smelling skies, pristine streams, birdsong, and endless miles of wild forest, prairie, and freedom. Pollution was something that happened in other places. We lived in a *good* place.

Over the years that followed I began to realize that part of growing up is learning to see through that sort of comfortable illusion. Still, in those early years I fought hard to hang on to my belief that the grown-ups running my world could never really compromise the wonder of the place.

A baby boomer in Alberta, I grew up amid both growing prosperity and the long, sad decline in the living beauty of my home landscapes. They were two sides of the same coin. The Turner Valley refinery is closed now, the land beneath it permanently fouled. Abandoned oil and gas wells, some leaching toxins into groundwater, litter the province. Bold blackbirds no longer rise from roadside tangles in the places where I once rode, because an expanding city has devoured the whole landscape. Wounds, everywhere. Wealth, pocketed.

In the Christian Bible the apostle Mark recounts Jesus asking, "What shall it profit a man, if he gains the whole world and loses his soul?" One might equally ask: What does it profit a society if it gains material prosperity but sacrifices the Creation that gave rise to it?

***

Solastalgia is the darkness that floods the soul when one's home ceases to be. The solution to homesickness might be to go home, but that option doesn't exist if one has never left home in the first place, yet it's gone. Back when I was sure all was perfect in my world, such grief-filled longing was unimaginable. As the decades passed, however, its shadows engulfed me. I think this species of angst is peculiar to this time in history, at least so far as it relates to the natural environment. I know I am far from alone in feeling it, and far from alone in looking for a way through it.

That's what this book is about – that, and hope for a better way forward, because there is one.

Even in spite of the human tendency to resist change and indulge in nostalgia, throughout most of Western history, people looked forward in hope to the future because they believed that better days lay ahead. That no longer seems to be the case. From a material point of view the optimism of past generations seems to have been warranted; everything is available today. Even so, and perhaps for the first time in history, whole generations look with dread at what lies ahead. We seem beset by wicked problems that defy resolution: accelerating climate change, biodiversity loss and extinctions, a legacy of colonialism that has filled the globe with nation-states constantly in conflict and frequently at war. Democracy seems like a failed dream. Angry nostalgia fuels populist movements that despise those who care and reward those who don't.

I spent the first decades of my life convinced of my good fortune in having enjoyed the perfect childhood in the finest of places among the best of people. Then I became aware of the dark shadows cast by all those bright things. The places I loved were as often as not degraded remnants of lands and waters that had been richer, wilder, and certainly more sustainable before I knew them. I love them still, because they are the places of my life, but I can't pretend not to see the wounds. My family story turns out to have been poisoned by betrayal and denial. We are only beginning to acknowledge a collective failure to respect the Treaty relationships that made our home place possible. But that failure is just a part of a greater failure to recognize, or even acknowledge, the respectful relationships we were meant to have with other creatures, with the rivers, the prairies, and the forests, and with the living spirit of this place we occupy – and consume. The society in which I have lived my life is to an uncomfortable degree a culture of abuse.

Once one sees that abuse, one can no longer look away from it; it's everywhere.

What do you do when you realize that many of the things you love most deeply are the products of harm? What do you do when things you knew for certain turn out to have been wrong? How deep must one's roots be before one truly belongs to a new home place? There is a great deal written about the damage done to the Indigenous Peoples whose homelands were colonized by newcomer peoples like my family. That's all true. What needs equally serious consideration, however, is the harm we more recently arrived people did, and continue to do, to ourselves. Reconciliation is a far more profound challenge than it might seem, because at its heart it demands that we abandon a culture of exploitation that just seems normal to most of us.

The easiest response, perhaps, might be simply not to worry about it. It's easy enough to live mindlessly. There are so many diversions, so many entertainments and distractions, things to look at on our cellphones and television screens. We could choose to lose ourselves in the moment and leave the hard questions for others to worry about. Everywhere, prophets and true believers of the consumer economy assure us there is no real price to pay for living the way we do. If that's not enough, religious leaders have scriptures with which to justify our abuse of Creation, and are always available to absolve us of our excesses. Scientists and experts have taken over the powers of destruction and creation from God; we have faith that, with enough money and power, they can fix anything. Why worry?

But I talk to people half my age who tell me they can't bring themselves to have children because they have no hope for tomorrow. They look at the future and see only the certainty of failure. They live on the edge of existential despair. Like Kurt Vonnegut, they can't shake the belief that "things are going to get unimaginably worse, and they are never, ever, going to get better." If things are so great, why does everything seem to be turning out wrong?

Like many others, I spend too much time ruminating over regrets and grappling with grief. Even so, I wouldn't change a thing. The experiences that gave rise to my darker reckonings helped make me who I am, every bit as much as the love, joy, and brilliant moments that have also filled my years. In spite of everything – perhaps more accurately, because of everything – I live in hope that we who live today beneath the chinook arch might yet become who we could have been, how we should have been, and what we need to be truly to belong to this place, to one another, and to tomorrow.

I do believe there is a way forward to a future in which we can thrive and find joy. It isn't an easy one, because it demands that we look unflinchingly at things our culture demands that we not acknowledge at all, and then put those things behind us. On the premise that each life is a series of stories, and every story has something to teach, I reflect here on some of the adventures, pivotal moments, and epiphanies that have led me to a way of seeing my story, and our story, through entirely different eyes than the ones that, so many decades ago, gazed in horror at that bright blood spilling from a broken bird.

Origins   9

In this era of consequences, good outcomes are neither easy nor, perhaps, likely. But they're also not impossible. First, we need to look back down the back-trail and consider it more critically. Where did that trail fork, and where might those other forks have led us, had we chosen them?

***

My back-trail begins three-quarters of a century before I was born:

The bunchgrass prairie was fading to brown and the leaves of saskatoons and aspen turning red and yellow when my great-great-uncle Leonard finally arrived at Fort Edmonton on September 5, 1875. He had walked most of the 1300-kilometre distance from the Métis settlements along the Red River to this isolated fur trading post on the south bank of the North Saskatchewan River. The buckbrush was heavy with white fruit. Plump red rosehips adorned the tangled shrubs along the river breaks. The low, clear flows of late summer had made river crossings easy, and thousands of geese and cranes were gathering into noisy flocks, preparing to migrate south.

"Here was the least common denominator of nature," W.O. Mitchell would write nearly a century later, "the skeleton requirements simply, of land and sky…stretching tan to the far line of the sky…and waiting for the unfailing visitation of wind."[1]

Leonard was well out of his element. Barely 24 years old, he had left his family's home near Meulebeke, Belgium, a year earlier for the first time in his life. He had agreed to accompany Bishop Vital Grandin across the Atlantic Ocean to the New World and serve for a few years in distant Roman Catholic missions. Bishop Grandin's Oblate missionary order was devoted to spreading its faith into what it considered the godless peoples of North America. Grandin had made the trip to Europe to raise funds and find new recruits. He brought 15 young men with him when he returned by boat to New York and thence by train to Lachine, on the Saint Lawrence River.

The following year Leonard accompanied Grandin across the

Great Lakes by boat and then by land to St. Boniface, near what is now Winnipeg. They continued west from there in early June – mosquito season in the tall-grass prairie of the Red River lowlands. The days were noisy with the screeching of wood on wood as they followed a train of 80 wagons pulled by oxen and horses.

The Métis of the Red River colony were off to kill bison for the hide trade. Although rutted bison trails still laced the open plains, the animals themselves were already becoming hard to find because of overhunting and a deliberate campaign of extermination south of what the Blackfoot and Cree Peoples called the "Medicine Line" – the invisible border between what were considered to be Britain's colonial holdings and the young United States of America.

Five years later the Métis would do their final, futile hunt; bison had been virtually wiped out. The land lay stunned beneath the prairie sky.

***

The wild roses were in full bloom when the wagon train left St. Boniface. The subtle sweetness of their bouquet permeated the more overwhelming odours of manure, trampled grass, alkali dust, and sweat. Thunderheads dragged curtains of grey rain across the gentle swells of prairie, darkening the ground with shadow, then sailing off into distances so immense as to be almost unfathomable for the skinny young lad marking off each day's miles. Long-billed curlews and marbled godwits came shrieking across the prairie only to veer away at the last moment, beaks open in mock threat, defending hidden nests from the passing travellers. Pronghorn antelope stared, then wheeled and dashed away, flashing their white rumps. During breaks in travel, when the wooden cart wheels finally stopped their shrieking, the thin swirling songs of pipits and horned larks became audible in the sky above and small brown sparrows and longspurs with unfamiliar markings sang from low shrubs and grass tussocks on all sides. It was a land rich with life but, to European eyes, empty of purpose.

Leonard had been raised in a pastoral agricultural landscape outside an ancient town. In his youth, the family estate had been a sprawling parkland – mowed lawns, flowering hedges and borders, Spanish conifers, and summer shelters. Neighbouring farmers grew potatoes and flax for trade and raised livestock and vegetable crops for their families. They sold their produce in nearby towns, each with church spires, cobbled streets, and sombre, settled families. A pastoral and long-civilized country, it was also a place in crisis, its economy suffering from potato blight and competition with agricultural exports from the New World that were flooding Europe and disrupting markets. In the late 1880s optimism and hope were as scarce as francs in the once-prosperous farm country around Meulebeke; that was one reason that Bishop Grandin had such success at finding new recruits from among the devout Catholics of the Flemish Netherlands.

To the young Belgian, this endless prairie landscape must have seemed as devoid of civilization and meaning as it was godless. It was the rawest of raw materials from which settlers would have to fight hard to forge some kind of facsimile of the Europe from which they were fleeing. He and the many thousands of settlers who would follow the young seminarians' footsteps over the ensuing half century were escaping from a continent that had failed them, but determined to help create a new facsimile of it. They could imagine nothing else.

The unbroken plains around Leonard seemed an alien wilderness offering neither reassurance nor certainty. He must have lain awake at night sometimes, under that vast dome of stars, listening to the trill of night insects and the whine of mosquitoes, praying for his religious faith not to abandon him. There was no going back.

The British government considered this western territory to be a hinterland, unceded and still occupied by godless savages. The British had only gone so far as to grant a royal charter to the Hudson's Bay Company that, until it was terminated in 1870, had given the company a monopoly on trading and exploiting the territory's resources. There was no actual government presence in the west until 1874, the year before Leonard finally trudged into the company's fort at Edmonton only to learn that Catholics were no longer wanted there.

"It must be remembered that up to my arrival in the west, 1875, there was no militia nor police protection in these regions," Leonard wrote in his second codex, three decades later. "The fact is that the Catholic priest was generally the guardian of the peace, the magistrate and soldier. All came for protection to him. Hence it was that the famous Hudson's Bay Company was glad to avail itself of this efficacious security; hence it was that the priest was always welcome at the home and at the table of the bourgeois de la company."[2]

But the first detachment of North-West Mounted Police had arrived in the west a few months earlier. As the company was switching its interests from controlling the fur trade to developing land, it no longer felt the need to offer space in its trading posts to Catholic missionaries. The Methodist in charge of the fort, in any case, had little love of papists. Leonard's first job upon his arrival at Fort Edmonton was to help tear down the Catholic chapel inside the fort while Bishop Grandin concluded arrangements to secure a new site a few kilometres away at St. Albert.

***

Those were horrible years for the Indigenous Peoples of the plains, foothills, and northern forests. Although their lives had reached a sort of material peak in the early part of the 1800s, by the end of the century destitution and ruin were everywhere.

Fur traders had brought cooking implements, glass beads, and other previously undreamed-of riches when they began to establish outposts in what is now Alberta a hundred years earlier. Horses and firearms changed bison hunting and travel. Trade for meat and hides turned bison from a central part of plains culture into valuable trade commodities. For a few prosperous decades the western tribes had mobility, hunting success, and material well-being unlike anything they had experienced before.

But they also had diseases they had never experienced before. Their immune systems were not ready for the recurring waves of smallpox, tuberculosis, and other European diseases that swept west across the Great Plains ahead of the white colonizers. Increased mobility meant that tribes who had lived in relative isolation from one another now met more frequently. Horses were valuable, and valuable things are worth stealing. Stealing creates conflict. And the firearms that made hunting easier also made warfare more lethal, even as alcohol made conflicts less rational. Meantime, the profits available from dead bison and beavers led to increased hunting pressure, not only from the Indigenous Peoples of the region but from Métis communities and the growing number of white Europeans.

Worse, south of the invisible Medicine Line along the 49th parallel of latitude, American colonizers had embarked on a deliberate scorched-earth strategy of exterminating the bison, correctly calculating that wiping out the source of their food and their culture would defeat the Indigenous Peoples of the plains faster than genocidal wars. Leonard arrived in the west at a time of terrible transition, unaware he was part of it.

***

The ancient North Trail along the western edge of the Great Plains ran just east of the foothills, where there was good water and abundant food in the form of wintering bison herds, berries, and medicine plants. The trail didn't follow the easiest route from north to south but hung to the west, closer to sacred and storied landforms, glacial erratics, and cottonwood groves. For the Siksikaitsitapi (Blackfoot) and other peoples who used the trail, its alignment connected their culture to places steeped with meaning.[3]

Leonard travelled south to the Highwood River in 1883. His superiors had sent him to help with a residential mission school the Church was building at Dunbow. It wasn't ready yet, however, so he continued farther south along the North Trail to the tiny settlement of Fort Macleod. He never got back to Dunbow – instead he spent the next 20 years as a parish priest for settler communities at Macleod, Lethbridge, and the surrounding area.

The newcomer people had brought with them a strange tradition of naming places not after the stories of those places, but after people. They now called the southern segment of the North Trail the Macleod Trail, after a Scottish-born policeman. The trail was rutted deep with the marks of Indigenous travois and more recent carts and wagons. It followed a braided way across vast plains of ripening bunchgrass, dipped into valleys full of wolf willow and wild rose, and deepened as it cut down into the valleys of the Sheep River, Willow Creek, and finally the Oldman. To the west, the line of the Rockies etched the horizon at first until the long line of the Porcupine Hills obscured the view to what the Siksikaitsitapi know as the Miistakis, the backbone of their world.

For Leonard, it was empty space and scenery through which he must travel before arriving at a lived-in place where there were souls to be saved and chapels to be built. He carried in his gear a jewelled container with a consecrated host at its centre; as a newly ordained priest he was deemed worthy of stewarding his Church's holy sacrament. Steeped since birth in the centuries-old cultural stew of European Christianity, in his mind there was no question he was bringing the sacred to primitive peoples who, in his world view, had no experience of it.

For the Niitsítapi whose home he was traversing, however, this was not scenery; it was their holy sacrament. Everything had a spiritual dimension. Simply to be on that land was to participate in the sacred. Travel, on trails that connected places of deep spiritual meaning, was liturgy. They didn't need to wait for a priest to build a church; they lived in one. Trails like the North Trail were laid out as much as spiritual paths as practical transportation routes. Simply by tracing that ancient trail south across the living plains, Leonard essentially spent his whole journey in church; he just had no way of perceiving it – just as most of his subsequent

Indigenous contacts would struggle to understand the meaning of his European church's rites, relics, and recitations.

**

A decade later, Leonard's older brother Victor traced his brother's footsteps to Canada's northwest territory. Unlike Leonard, who worked mostly among the immigrant community, Victor lived among the Piikani People at Brocket. His first impression of the people native to this far place was one of deep distaste:

> On Saturday we see the first tents of the savages. They are a few poles put together and covered with linen or hides; what poor dwellings! The savages are crawling out. How grubby and dirty are they…They have brown skins, long hairs and are wrapped in a blanket or piece of rug. Unhappy in body and soul![4]

It took many years for Victor to overcome his initial revulsion for Indigenous Peoples. Eventually, he became friends with some who accepted his religious faith, but he frequently expressed exasperation with what he saw as the laziness and disinterest of the people whom he considered his charges. As a European, he knew what a productive life was meant to look like; he could see no virtue in a life of hunting, gathering, and strange ceremonies. He also had no way of recognizing the deep, abiding trauma that many Indigenous Peoples were afflicted with now that the bison were gone, their freedom had been surrendered, and a growing flood of aggressive Europeans was arriving to kill the prairie sod and plant the exposed soil with foreign food crops. He believed he offered them something they lacked: lives with meaning – farming and Catholicism – and was annoyed that for the most part they passively resisted it. It annoyed him right up until his final departure back to his European homeland, where he could be among sensible people again.

The Blackfoot must have been relieved to see him go.

***

Leonard, working mostly among the white colonists, had a healthier attitude towards the original people of his adopted home. When Prime Minister John A. Macdonald embarked upon a policy of starving the plains people to whom his Queen had solemnly committed, by treaty, to provide food, Leonard became a passionate advocate to the Ottawa government on behalf of the desperate Blackfoot. The government stonewalled him. Macdonald thought hunger would force Indigenous Peoples onto the reserves and make the job of agricultural settlement less difficult.

For all that he cared about Indigenous Peoples, Leonard harboured no sentimental feelings for their past, nor for the natural condition of the lands that were the foundation of their culture and the source of their spiritual lives. His world view told him that western Canada was a godless, wasted wilderness; it was natural and right that Christian people should arrive at last to bring their God to the people who lived here, to plough the prairie and convert it to proper farmland, and to bring civilized order to the forests, waters, and wildlife. And so, although his prejudices may have been less overt than those of his brother, they were no less devastating. And he had no way of perceiving them in himself; everything about his mission and the colonial enterprise of the growing European communities of which he was a part seemed normal and right.

Leonard never went back to Belgium. Instead, when another brother's children were left orphaned back home and in the care of an impoverished sister-in-law, Leonard applied for permission to foster the oldest boy. Barely 11 years old, little Joseph travelled halfway around the world to meet his uncle in Calgary in 1893. He grew up in the company of celibate males and constant religion; it can't have been healthy. Leonard came to see his nephew as a kind of successor, but when Joseph went into seminary years later it eventually became clear he was not meant to be a priest. Instead, he went to work for the Union Bank in Okotoks in 1903.

Seven years later he married Janie Kelly, an Irish-Catholic farm girl from nearby De Winton. That was the start of the family into which, 77 years after Leonard's arrival in what became the province of Alberta, I was born.

This recently appropriated place was now my home.

2. Calgary

In 1991, at the age of 39, I became a park warden in Waterton Lakes National Park. I needed a warden hat, but I couldn't get one to fit; they were all too small. Visiting with my mother one day, I mentioned the problem. "My head is too big," I said.

"I know," she said, wryly.

There was a chinook arch over the Rocky Mountains on the day Mom gave birth to me at Calgary's Holy Cross Hospital. My older brother Gordon had arrived four years earlier, but by the time I came along in December 1952, she and Dad had begun to worry about whether there would ever be a second child. My arrival, big head and all, answered that question. After their second child emerged into the organized chaos of an overcrowded maternity ward, at the height of the postwar baby boom, it was as if the floodgates had opened. Mom went on to give birth to eight more children over the following decade and a half. We weren't so much a family as a small colony. We could have fielded our own football team.

Dad was eight years older than Mom. In fact, he once served as a substitute teacher for her Grade 8 class. They had grown up a few doors away from each other in the dry and dusty prairie town of Strathmore, Alberta, but it wasn't until Mom was 21 that they turned their eyes towards each other and then towards the altar.

Dad's father Joseph was the manager of Strathmore's Union Bank. His family was upright and respected – two conservative Roman Catholic parents, four boys and a girl, all of whom adhered strictly to their religious and social responsibilities. Any skeletons they might have had were locked firmly in cupboards that even they never peeked into. They would have admitted to no cupboards.

Mom's dad, Alban McParland, on the other hand, was what I imagine would be called black Irish. He smoked like a chimney, swore like a pirate, was well known at the beer parlour, and could hold me enthralled for hours with his stories and reminiscences. Mom would remember his temper as much as his humour – perhaps a bit more. She had one brother who had a mysterious (at least to me and my siblings) falling out with his family. I encountered him by the old Calgary Tennis Club on my way home from school one day in 1961 or 1962. Uncle Gordon seemed handsome and carefree to my eyes. He greeted me like an old friend, chatted briefly, and then fished around in his pocket until he came up with a nickel, which he gave me in exchange for a promise to say hi to Mom. When I showed the coin to Mom, she tsk-ed annoyedly and said, "What is Gordon doing giving you money when he can't even buy groceries for his own family?"

I would have liked to have known him better, but he lived a different life than ours.

The other uncles played more prominent roles in my life, especially Frank, the youngest of the Strathmore Van Tighems, who shared a home with his older sister, Gerry, in Calgary.

Clarence, the dashing-looking extrovert of the family, was a Canadian consul in foreign places. His wife Noelle had a European accent and austere manner. Their three boys were named, in good Biblical fashion, Paul, Mark, and John.

Leonard, my dad's oldest brother, had the same stern appearance and bushy eyebrows as Dad, but the kind humour in his eyes surfaced more often. Perhaps my cousins saw Dad in a similar way, but with us Dad was stern; we were, after all, his responsibility. And responsibility mattered in our family. Leonard and Delma raised their two children – Ann and Pat – in High River, close enough for holiday visits, but not for the regular contact we had with Gerry and Frank.

I never met my paternal grandparents – they had both died before I came along. I have one memory only of my maternal grandmother Blanche, whom we called Nana. I don't know how old I was – maybe 5 or 6 – when we went to visit her at the Lacombe Home, a grim-looking institutional edifice on the edge of the small town of Midnapore. She was dying of Parkinson's disease. Visiting her was scary and strange. Her old skin was stretched tightly around the bones of her skull. Her mouth was caved in. Her hair was grey and I could see her scalp through it. I suspect the visit was so she could see her grandchildren one last time as she was dying.

Nana smiled with her tired old eyes because her mouth seemed unable to make the shape anymore, and she reached out with a twitching hand that knocked the lid off a porcelain bowl on her bedside table. When she managed to pluck a humbug out with long, thickened yellow nails, she reached out to me, offering the candy with that shuddering hand. Mom made me take it and I put it in my mouth while the strange scary lady I'd been told was my grandmother watched me. It's the desperate kindness in her pale, tired eyes that I remember now, but I was too frightened and awed by her deathly pallor to see it then.

Many years later I sat with my own aged mother in a Calgary hospice as she died from cancer. Her mouth was collapsed, her grey hair thin and her skin pale and blotchy. I watched her take her last shallow inspiration of the earth's living air. She never exhaled it. It was like she wanted to take that last breath with her.

She looked like Nana had looked to me a half century earlier. She was beautiful.

***

I don't know the story of Mom and Dad's courtship. He had served as a Lancaster navigator in the Royal Air Force and then the Royal Canadian Air Force during the Second World War and, after getting home alive in 1945, took teacher training and started work with a posting to a one-room school near Baintree, Alberta. He showed me the spot a couple of times during hunting trips; it was just a corner lot with a spindly hedge of caraganas in what felt like a dry and dusty nowhere. He also told me how he had given into temptation one day and shot a cock pheasant under those caraganas with his .22 rifle. Then he panicked – there was not yet an open season on the recently introduced game birds – and buried the carcass under the bushes. That Friday he dug up his victim and smuggled it home to Strathmore, where his mother helped dispose of the evidence by cooking it. The family ate many pheasants in the years that followed, but only legal ones; he'd learned that there are consequences to poaching, even when you don't get caught.

After Mom graduated high school, she took secretarial training in Calgary in 1944. She got her first job with a small Calgary oil company, Pacific Petroleum. She told me she and the other girls in the office had been called into a meeting where the owners announced the sad news that they were going to have to shut the company down for lack of cash flow. The following day the message was rescinded by the two jubilant managers; Leduc No. 2 had blown in, and the company owned a stake in it.

As it turned out, she didn't stay with the firm much longer anyway. When Dad started working for the Calgary Separate (Catholic) School Board, he asked her to marry him. She was 21, and he was approaching 30. They married in 1947, she soon became pregnant, and she stayed that way for most of the following two decades.

I grew up to the sound of diapers being washed late at night and all the noise and activity of a family of ten kids. Most of us developed a tendency to introversion; that's probably because quiet and privacy were so rare in our home.

Everything was completely normal. It was my childhood, after all, the only childhood I'd ever experienced in the only family I'd ever known in the only corner of the world I had yet seen. So it was entirely normal that I was one of ten children with an exhausted mother who didn't even have a driving licence; who only got out to shop or visit when her husband or sister-in-law was available to drive her there. It was normal to get a spanking on the bare behind on days when Dad got home from work and learned of some egregious misdeed one of us might have committed. It was normal to have an uncle with an almost unmanageable stutter talking down to or bullying us while his humble spinster sister quietly helped mom with errands and babysitting, submitting to the frequent cruelties of the world by "offering them up" to the God she served until her death.

As my world expanded beyond the family home, when I would visit friends at their homes, I discovered that other people had strange families – not at all like our normal one. This illusion lasted for many years until I finally realized that normality is an invention that can lead to dangerous illusions and unhappy outcomes.

***

In the last few years of his life, Dad became my best friend. Sometimes he would ask my opinion or confide in me, inconceivable though that at first seemed, given that it was a side of him I'd never seen or imagined before. He'd always seemed the all-wise patriarch – stern, distant, judging, rarely benevolent, always right. Or at least that had been my experience of him. And now he was an older friend, talking vulnerably to me of things I was almost uncomfortable hearing about. Much as I had spent my adolescence resenting and rebelling against his authority, I found the release from it and the emergence of a more vulnerable, less certain older father disconcerting. Even today, now that I'm the age he was when he died a quarter century ago, I remember and miss the infallible patriarch I remember from childhood – but I am no less grateful for having met that other him at last.

It was on a drive west from Calgary into the mountains when Dad started talking about marriage, and about his thoughts about Mom and their years together. I was startled, then bemused, to hear him reflecting on such intimate matters out loud. I tried to understand where he was going with this awkward discourse and gradually came to understand what I hadn't seen until then – that my parents' relationship had not been easy. Mom's constant pregnancies had become wearing and hard, and she had had scarcely a moment of her own for many years. Dad had been unable to discuss feelings or sexuality, and had embraced his breadwinner role as both an escape and an excuse. Not consciously, of course; they had both been raised into an unquestioned patriarchal world of male authority, in the Church and in the home. Rather than confront some of the most intimate and important issues of a marriage, the expectation was that she, and he, would "offer it up" to their God and carry on. And during that drive he was trying to express his humbling realization, so late in life, that the woman he'd treated simply as a wife and mother was actually a wise, emotionally complex, and deeply moral human being. That in spite of the dominant role he had assumed because of his position and responsibilities in the family, during all those years it was my mother who had been the stronger and better person in their marriage. He was trying to find a safe way for a reticent man to express the love and awe he had for the whole person he was still learning to see in the woman he'd married almost half a century earlier. In a way, he was going to Confession, a particularly difficult one.

I looked at the wrinkled, familiar face of the man beside me and felt like I was seeing him at his best, at last. I wanted to hug him, or cry, or both. Few things have made me feel so grateful as the fact that he lived long enough for us to take that drive together.

If anything, I learned that day it is never too late to find a better version of oneself.

***

Our house had been built in 1919 and, for at least part of its life, it had included a dark little basement suite that would be condemned as unrentable today. I always wondered who had lived in that basement before our family arrived. Their stories left with them.

Dad and Mom moved their growing family into the house in 1957. It seemed huge to me, as most houses do to most kids, but it was just a mid-sized one-storey bungalow. Three bedrooms along the south side gave off to a hall that opened to the living room; Mom and Dad's bedroom opened off to both the living room and the near end of the hall. The living room had an attached dining room with a swinging door to the kitchen. The bathroom was tiny, between the kitchen and the hallway. A sunroom was attached to the living room on the side opposite Mom and Dad's room. The sunroom housed Dad's reference book collection and files and served as a sort of never-used office, being too cold for anything else. Its main attraction for the kids was that it was the Christmas tree room. Each year the tree went up in the sunroom and then Dad unscrewed the doorknob and hid it away so nobody could peek. The door had glass panes, so an old sheet got the job of screening the view into the now-secret and fascinating corner of the house where, we were sure, presents would be piling ever deeper. One Christmas in particular stays in my memory as a peak moment; when we were finally allowed to see inside, there were three shiny new bicycles in there. And one was mine! That bike soon expanded my home range far beyond our little corner of Calgary.

Gordon and I, being the oldest, got our own bedrooms down in the basement. It was dim and dank down there. Between the doors that opened into the main basement from our rooms, an ancient furnace with asbestos-tape-wrapped vents reached octopus-like into the ceiling. A dragon slept in its depths and awoke with a roar at regular intervals all winter long. I fell asleep most nights to the rumbling of the furnace and seemingly constant thumping of the washing machine on the opposite wall where my exhausted mother, after all the kids were finally in bed, washed load after load of cloth diapers and soiled clothing.

Upstairs, Mary and Margaret started out with their own rooms, but the babies kept on coming. Finally, the inevitable could no longer be avoided, and Dad got an addition built onto the back of the house. He planted a dolgo crabapple and a rescue apple-crab outside the back window of the new bedroom, and the trees grew up with us. Crabapple jelly and sugar-pickled apple-crabs became an annual fall tradition. I've abandoned the latter but have had a lifetime addiction to the jelly. It smells and tastes of that childhood home and the parents who centred our lives. Dad, in his old work shoes and garden clothes, teetering on a ladder to pick crabs; Mom skimming foam off the simmering sea of fading, cracking little apples in the turkey roaster on the stove; Dad, again, spooning claret-coloured jelly onto his unbuttered toast while Mom assembled school sandwiches on the side counter.

The garden behind the house was a lifelong project for Dad. It was meant to be good soil but had suffered from house construction. Year after year Dad dug the garden by hand, wheeled the cobbles and stones away with a barrow, worked old leaves into the soil, and built compost in a pit at the back end of the garden where he dumped lawn clippings and leaves. Gradually, the garden became more and more productive, but it never really yielded enough produce to support the size of the family growing inside that home.

One year we did pretty well with potatoes, though. That was the year Dad decided our tired front lawn was in need of renewal. He arranged with a farmer friend to have a load of rotted manure delivered. The manure arrived while Dad was at work, so the truck dumped it out on the lawn and left. When Dad got home he discovered what Mom already knew; the manure had never been allowed to rot. It was fresh from the intestinal tracts of the hogs that had produced it. And pretty soon everyone in the neighbourhood knew that too, because the odour was almost unendurable. Dad quickly rented a rototiller and dug it all in, but the smell lingered.

The next spring, Dad planted the whole front yard with potatoes. With the hog farm stink gone, our neighbours forgave his earlier transgression, but he was probably still considered a bit of an eccentric as the former lawn became a forest of flowering potato plants. We ate a lot of mashed and boiled potatoes that winter: potatoes with every meal. Then he seeded the grass back in, and within a couple of years the lawn was looking tired again because its real problem had nothing to do with soil quality and a lot more to do with too many kids trampling on top of it, and too many poplar roots beneath it.

The poplars growing in the boulevard on each side of the street were part of what gave our quiet little back street its character. They were towering old veterans already when we moved in and had clumpy scars where they had already been pollarded at least once.

The street was an oiled gravel tunnel through arching shade. There were even bigger trees in a neighbour's yard, probably of the same vintage but never trimmed back. Their gargantuan growth had likely been encouraged by the groundwater seeps along the base of the back hill.

Poplars like water. Their roots seek it out. So they stole all they could get from the front lawn but, worse than that, they found their way into the sewer pipes. And in our old inner-city neighbourhood we had the original sewer pipes where both the storm water from the streets and the black water from household drains all ended up in the same pipes and flowed, untreated, down to the Bow River. More than once I woke to find the main basement outside my bedroom had become a shallow lake full of wads of toilet paper, partially dissolved brown lumps, and ugly yellow bubbles. The floor was cement and sloped to a drain hole that led to the sewer, but when the boulevard trees managed to sneak their roots into the underground sewer line it didn't take long before a dense wad of rootlets stopped all movement underground; then the only escape for the sewage was up the drain hole and into the basement. For a day or two Gordon and I would have to sidle along the walls where the slimy mess didn't quite reach to get to and from our rooms. Then the Roto-Rooter man would arrive and grind the line clean again. I imagine Mom or Dad applied some bleach to the mess before it drained, but I can't actually recall that; maybe they didn't. Between the radon gas, of which I'm sure the basement was full, and the coliform bacteria that must have been rampant in the cement floor after all those sewage backups, my having made it to old age relatively intact seems a remarkable achievement. But perhaps it actually helped; my immune system doubtless got a good workout down there.

Eventually, the City brought the sewage system in our old neighbourhood up to more modern standards, but by then I was grown.

***

It was a Catholic home and we went to Catholic schools with other kids who looked like us. I never met a single Indigenous person until I was grown up; what I knew of them came from comic books and cowboy Western movies. We were never taught about the treaties. We learned from textbooks written by people of European descent, taught to us by white people in classrooms with crucifixes on the walls.

For most of his career Dad worked as the superintendent of the Calgary Roman Catholic (Separate) School District #1. Even as he and Mom contributed more than their share to the baby boom, his job involved managing the consequences of that boom at a community level. When he started working for the school board, Calgary had 1,714 students in eight Catholic schools. By his retirement in 1977, he'd overseen the system's growth to 60 schools with 22,000 students in a fast-growing prairie city.

Dad was deeply serious about his work. He'd been raised in a devoutly religious household where duty, service, and self-discipline mattered above all else. So our family didn't spend much time dealing with feelings and doubts; our upbringing was mostly centred around doing what was right, and being punished when caught doing what wasn't. Dad was a provider first, a disciplinarian second, and a counsellor not at all. For the first few years of my life I remember a harried mother, when dealing with misbehaving children, saying, "Wait till your Father gets home." And we waited with trepidation because usually, after a quiet consultation in the kitchen, he would come looking for the errant child, who would be hiding somewhere in the house looking as innocent as possible, and shortly thereafter our pants would be around our knees and we'd be getting a spanking on the bare bottom.

The spankings didn't improve our behaviour, but they probably made us sneakier. They also elevated the level of awe and fear our father inspired in us, at least the older kids. And that might be why they ended by the time I was 9 or 10; we were never privy to the quiet late evening conversations that went on in the living room when we were all supposed to be asleep, but I suspect Mom and

Dad came to the conclusion at some point that the family needed a different approach to the division of disciplinary duties and to the whole idea of spanking. We still got the terse words and lectures from our stern-voiced father, but physical punishments vanished halfway through my childhood. Misbehaviour, of course, didn't.

***

With no driving licence and little spare time, Mom had to assemble her social life mostly out of moments at home. Tea breaks with Mrs. Bogaart, a kindly Dutch woman who helped in the house two days a week, were important to her. So, too, were visits from her aging father, Alban McParland. On those afternoons when they sat together in the kitchen drinking tea and smoking his cigarettes, I often found a way to insinuate myself into the company just to hear him talk of fishing for giant bull trout, hunting grizzly bears, and exploring places whose very names were magic to me. It would be many years before I would visit the upper Highwood River valley, but when I did it was with a sense of awe and mystery because of the myths with which his storytelling had populated that place.

Although Dad had grown up hunting ducks and upland birds near Strathmore, it was Pop Pop who introduced him to trout fishing and the cheery little creeks of the foothills and Front Ranges. Dad told me that the first time Pop Pop took him camping in the Highwood, he had the job of opening the gates along the gravel road up the valley. There were 18 of them.

Mom loved her father; I remember the merry tinkle of her laughter while they visited. But he died in 1974, and his tales went with him. The passion for wild places they had kindled in my imagination lived on. In retrospect now, I can see the importance of his stories in telling me who I was, where I was, and how life was meant to be. Those few visits listening to a family elder shaped my spiritual universe far more than the many more hours I spent in church being instructed by male priests we were meant to venerate.

Growing up in a devoutly Catholic household, there was an expectation that we would be good Christian children. Sin might be something we were all prone to, but the assumption was that it would nonetheless not visit our household. Just in case it did, we had the Catholic sacrament of Confession, where one sits behind a slatted screen and recites one's failures to the shadowed silhouette of the priest on the other side.

At the end of Confession we were told to recite a few prayers, and then we were absolved. Just like that! Magic. And we were sent off with the admonishment to go and sin no more. But there was that problem again: we were not supposed to sin, but we knew we would. It's how we are, especially since Catholicism, like many religions, deems the most human of impulses to be sinful. So I would emerge from the confessional with a clean slate – and the hopeless certainty that I would soon fail again.

It was actually a pretty good racket for the Church; they had us over a barrel.

Sacred Heart Church was dark and austere. Stained glass saints glowed above rows of hard wooden pews. Should a black-robed priest emerge briefly from the sacristy to do something mysterious at the altar, I would hear his shoes rapping sharply on the marbled floors, an empty echoing sound; then he would be gone again into some inner sanctum and the breathless silence restored. It was an empty cavern of stillness and shadows, more like a mausoleum than a place of celebration. There was nothing nurturing about it; it offered neither intimacy nor warmth. It seemed a place of secrets, reserved for grim clerics privy to a distant God's magic words, where the best a small boy might hope for was to be ignored and to escape early. Clearly this was an edifice that had been built to awe, not to welcome.

Pushing the heavy wooden door open to leave, ironically, was like stepping into glory. Here was the brilliant sunshine and the smell of lilacs, green grass growing, the sudden sound of traffic swishing past on 14th Street. Here were the smells of food cooking, lawns newly mowed, and automobile exhaust. Overhead, the wild, plaintive cries of gulls; squint into the brightness and you could see them wheeling high above the city, tiny against the sky where they circled close to heaven.

Emerging from the solemn shadows of Sacred Heart Church felt like stepping back into grace, not away from it.

The church and school both occupied the same city block, three streets away from our family home. On the avenue between, there were young birch trees in among older, but dying, poplars. In the crotch of one of those birches, one year shortly after my first Confession, a pair of robins built a nest. If I stood on tiptoe and reached as high as I could, I could get my fingers over the edge and feel the warmth radiating from four smooth eggs while the adult robins scolded and dove at me. There was a soft smell to that tree when you stood that close, and thin curls of white bark twisting out from the trunk. The sky, in my memory, was blue. Confession, sin, and unattainable ideals were temporarily forgotten; this was the elemental world where wild creatures lived real lives, even here in the inner streets of a hard city. No black-robed priests here; this was between me and the robins and the birch trees and the sun on my crewcut head, like a caress from the Creator, under a sky full of mystery.

***

In those days, as now, new theories of education rose and fell with unfortunate frequency. I hit Grade 1 when there was a big interest in IQ testing and moving smart students along. I was evidently smart, because my parents agreed to have me accelerated, which meant I completed both Grades 2 and 3 in the same year. But my birthday is in December, so I had already started school early, at the age of 5½. The net result was that when I went into Grade 4, many of my classmates were 10, and I was only 7. I was 13 in Grade 10, barely into puberty, surrounded by large teenagers who were always better at everything.

Since I had been smart enough to accelerate, I was naturally expected to excel as a student. But kids aren't just learning machines; they are social creatures. I didn't excel. My marks were generally good, but certainly not in phys. ed. I was a little kid compared to the older classmates to whom I constantly compared myself.

The combination of being smaller and less mature than my class-mates, while yet having higher expectations imposed on me, had a subtle effect that I only recognized many years later. The origins of my lifelong expectation of failure, constant need for approval, and impulse towards self-justification only began to dawn on me after I had retired. During one of our weekly lunch dates in the city around that time, my mother said, "I sometimes think that the one big way your father and I let you down was to have you accelerated in school."

I was taken aback; I couldn't see how that would have been a problem. On reflection, I realized she was probably right.

It wasn't that bad, though, because after school and on the weekends there were places not far from home to explore, bird book in hand, notebook full of lists, and free from the expecta-tions of others. I found birds gradually, perhaps starting with that robin nest, and with each new species that revealed itself to me the wonder and possibilities of the natural world grew.

There was a strange whistle I sometimes heard on my way to and from school. Finally, I spotted the rose-coloured bird high in a poplar and, when the second edition of *Birds of Alberta* came out, it had a photograph that might have been taken in the very spot I first saw it: a pine grosbeak. I hadn't even imagined the world contained such a thing as a pine grosbeak, and here was one in my neighbourhood, virtually part of my family.

Down by the railroad tracks, in summer, I saw a black and white bird on a fence wire. It looked like the illustration of an east-ern kingbird in my book, but it didn't have the little red spike on top of its head. I came home filthy that day from creeping on my hands and knees to get as close to it as I could. My notebook was full of drawings and notes of what I suspected must be a new spe-cies because it definitely didn't have that red crest. Only later did another book explain that the red tuft is usually tucked out of sight. In fact, I've never seen it to this day. But here was another bird to add to the list that made my home city a more exotic and mysteri-ous place than I had ever imagined.

Least flycatchers called in the neighbour's shade trees. Those were yellow warblers and house wrens singing in our hedge. On the Elbow River I saw strange elongated black and white ducks: mergansers. High above the schoolyard, crying forlornly: Franklin's gulls wheeling in the blue. One day a furtive movement in a clump of saskatoon bushes resolved itself into a catbird. After a brief, almost conspiratorial glance, it burrowed back into its secret shrubbery as I fished out my notebook and pencil and recorded yet another discovery.

Alone in the weedy corners of a bustling city, I didn't need to think about being undersized or poor at math or doomed to disappoint my parents and fail my God; I was in a world without judgment, in the moment, among the living things that made this home place more whole with each new discovery.

But, of course, on Monday there would be school.

By high school it had become clear that mathematics and I would never really understand one another. And given our failure to connect, physics and chemistry soon turned up their noses at me too. I began to skip school; why ask for help when I wasn't meant to need it and was privately convinced of my inability to learn? Besides, the wild places were waiting down along the river or up in the hills. Whatever my other failures might be, I always fit in there.

I remember the start of adolescence with a sort of grim nostalgia; it was not easy. Even in the woods and prairies, surrounded by birds and the tracks of wild things in the mud and snow, lost in exploration and discovery, I could feel that yoke of private failure weighing on my shoulders. I was meant to meet a higher standard, and I wasn't doing it.

But as long as I was out there in the wild, I was among friends. Far from church; close to the Creator.

3. Trout

Limestone Mountain was never meant to have a road and endures one only reluctantly. Alberta's main forestry trunk road carves a cautious way up out of pine forest and across steep hillsides, climbing and clinging its way across the mountain's face before arcing back down to the shrubby flats along Radiant and Ten Mile Creek. It's a stretch of road that demands one's careful attention at the best of times, but in the dark and driving rain of a late July night it seemed to defy logic that there should be a road here at all.

I wasn't driving. I was only 9. I huddled in silence on my end of the bench seat, trusting the silent silhouette at the other end to get us safely to where Dad and my brothers waited at their campsite on Elk Creek. The car smelled like cigar smoke and fishing gear. My uncle, Frank, smoked White Owl cigars. Dad had smoked Marguerite cigars until he quit, apparently to set a good example for his growing family. It didn't work; most of us took up smoking in our teens.

But that would be later. I was still too young to be tempted by the forbidden rebellions of adolescence. Gordon, my older brother, was 13. Our lives were still centred on the things the males in our family did, like camping in thunderstorms deep in the Rocky Mountain foothills.

Lightning stabbed across the sky almost continuously as the car began the downward grade, gears whining and gravel crunching beneath the tires. Even when three or four bolts lit up the landscape at once, offering a flashing glimpse of what looked like a brilliant silver engraving of dark hills, pale meadows, and distant water, my uncle made no comment. Like my father, he had a remote and stoic manner when driving. Frank was completing his seminary training to become a priest. I assumed his thoughts must be weightier than mine.

In those childhood years it never occurred to me to try and parse the personalities of the adults in my family. They were who they were, authority figures all. They were my benchmark for normal. And although tonight the sky shuddered with the jagged chaos of almost constant lightning, thunder booming so loudly that it was audible above the frantic lashing of rain against the windshield, it felt comfortable to be here in the front seat of my uncle's old Chevrolet, following its headlights down the muddy stream that spilled ahead of us along the road. We were going camping. There would be fishing. Life was as good as it could get. If I worried at all, it was that all this rain might dirty the streams too much and the fish wouldn't bite.

When we arrived at the roadside campground, Frank drove slowly around the perimeter road until his headlights picked up the pale green bulk of my father's old Pontiac. Rain was streaming down its sides and behind it, partly obscured by trees, was the khaki canvas outline of the tent. Frank stopped the car and turned off the ignition. Without looking at me he said, "Stay put," and let himself out into the rain. The trunk opened. I watched through streaming rain as he went past, now clad in a yellow rain slicker, and pushed his gear through the tent door. A moment later he was back at the trunk, and then the door opened and he thrust my rolled-up sleeping bag into my arms.

"Am I sleeping in the car?"

He gave me a withering look and closed the door on me.

Evidently, I was sleeping in the car.

I would normally have preferred the tent, but when my uncle joined our family camping excursions they took on a different flavour. There would be tension in the air tomorrow as Dad and his younger brother replayed old passive aggressions, we kids suddenly transformed into bit players in a drama we didn't understand. The solitude of the car felt friendly and calm, under the circumstances. I burrowed into my sleeping bag and listened to the patter of rain on the roof and the rush of the creek outside. I was camping again; tomorrow there would be fishing.

The cottonwoods along Sharon Avenue would be bright with new green leaves when the camping urge hit me each year in mid-May. Sidewalks were sticky with poplar buds. In the evenings newly returned robins would perch in the treetops, scolding randomly in their own avian version of the spring fever that infected most of us kids. Walking home from school on rainy days, I'd create imaginary trout streams in the runoff draining along street gutters and go fishing in my imagination, impatient for the real thing.

I watched the Betty Barometer weather cartoons on the front page of the *Calgary Herald* each day; when she predicted a nighttime low above 40°F, I would spread Dad's canvas tarpaulin on the grass at the far end of our backyard, lay out my sleeping bag and a spare blanket or two on one side, fold the tarp over, and go camping. Lying under the big spruce tree with the smell of canvas in my cold little nose, I turned the traffic noise on 12th Avenue, a block away, into the rushing sound of a trout stream and went back to those far foothills in my imagination.

Real camping trips had to wait until summer, but Dad got impatient too, so we usually headed out for an advance session each May long weekend.

Back in the foothills, spring was never as advanced as it was down at the edge of the prairie in Calgary. Green spikes of new grass showed inside last year's weathered thatch, but from a distance the grassy slopes were still a faded brown. Crocuses and powdery little draba mustards might be showing on the sunny slopes, but hardened snowdrifts lingered in the shade of diamond willow thickets and under the spruce trees.

That first weekend trip was never an epic adventure like the summer ones. It was necessarily close to the city – usually a campground like Sandy McNabb west of Turner Valley or Waiparous Creek northwest of Cochrane. From there we would venture out in search of trout along newly wakened streams too cold to wade but full of possibility.

The road up the Sheep River west of Sandy McNabb terminated at a fork in the road near the Gorge Creek research station. Both forks were gated and usually locked. One led farther west into the headwaters of the Sheep, over a remote divide and thence down the Elbow River to Bragg Creek. The other fork followed the rim of the Gorge Creek valley into the forested headwaters of Ware Creek, looping back to Threepoint Creek and the foothills west of Millarville.

None of this geography translated into a map in my young head; it was all mysterious, wild, remote – rich with possibilities. The world was still taking shape in my imagination. When Dad parked the station wagon near the locked gate and we got out into the spring sunshine to organize fishing gear and lunches, the narrow gravelled road winding up into the pines was as good a promise of wilderness adventure as I needed.

We walked in from the gate to the upper reaches of Ware Creek. Dad, like most fishermen in an era when bag limits were large and everyone took their catch home, considered his favourite trout streams to be absolute secrets. We were never allowed to know their names because he didn't want us blabbing about them to our friends. Ware Creek was known to me through all my childhood years as Seven-Mile-Walk Creek. It certainly felt like a seven-mile walk, up the rim of the Gorge Creek valley and into the pine forest, around bend after bend, watching for the first flicker of living water that would promise an end to walking and a start to fishing.

I must have been 7 or 8 the first time I was considered capable of the hike. Gordon was four years older than me, which made him a big kid. I was a tag-along. When we finally reached the large culvert where that newborn creek went chattering under the roadway, I was left there with strict instructions not to stray while Dad and Gordon vanished into the trees on a cow trail that led somewhere secret. I watched enviously, certain they were headed to some fishing paradise, before the stillness of the morning woods and the chatter of running water turned my attention to the little creek.

Below the culvert the creek flickered in and out of sunbeams that penetrated the looming spruce canopy only here and there. Little flies spun and danced above the water, so close they sometimes seemed to be skating along the surface. Small birds flitted through the branches. One day I saw movement in the alders and stood still until a perfect little male Wilson's warbler emerged, picking unseen bugs off the branches, its yellow breast brilliant in the spring sunshine. It felt like a gift of magic to see that living jewel emerge from forest shadows just long enough to fill me with wonder, before flitting back into its secret world of flickering leaves and tangled branches. If birds like this dwelt in such perfect places as these, I felt, I should know them better. They were family I hadn't yet met.

Sneaking along the creek, I found pools where trout hung suspended, their little pale mouths opening and closing as they breathed the water and shifted position to grab passing morsels I couldn't see. They were small fish, but I was a small fisherman; my hands shook with excitement as I tried to toss my spinner or snelled fly through gaps in the overhanging branches. Inevitably, the fish would dart away and hide beneath an undercut bank or in a tangle of roots, leaving me to rescue my lure from the foliage.

Then one day I felt a tug and saw the flash of a struggling trout; I'd hooked my first fish! Frantically, I yanked with all my might and the little trout went shooting past my ear to land in the dried leaves behind me, flipping and jumping in shock at finding itself out so suddenly of its element. I pounced on it and held its cold little body in one hand while I whacked it on its head with a stick as I had seen my father do. The fish quivered briefly and went still.

My slippery little victim was a cutthroat trout, perhaps 15 centimetres long. I held it on my hand and studied it – the sleek, greenish-gold flanks speckled with tiny black spots that grew denser towards the tail, the orange-red slashes beneath its gill rakers, the blush of salmon colour down each side of its white belly. It had dark, bruise-like parr marks along each side. It was perfect.

But my trophy was also dirty from its brief struggle on the forest floor. I took it down to the edge of the water and knelt, almost reverently, to wash the debris off. If I was going to show it to Dad and Gordon, it should be unmarred. I teased the leaves and duff off one side, turned the trout over in my hand…and the slippery little thing squirted out of my grasp and went spinning slowly into the depths. Its belly flashed white, then vanished, then reappeared as the current swept my first fish into a deep hole beneath a partly uprooted tree. A moment later it emerged into the faster water at the tail of the pool, tumbled into a riffle, and disappeared.

I searched down the creek, but my fish was gone for good. I was heartbroken. And although Dad, when he and Gordon finally emerged again from the forest shadows, believed my tale of woe and congratulated me on my first fish, nothing could console me for its loss. Especially when I looked into Dad's wicker creel and saw a shiny pile of much larger trout. He and Gordon had each caught their limits.

Years later, on a whim, my wife Gail and I loaded up our own kids and took them to Seven-Mile-Walk Creek. We didn't leave them alone at the culvert; we took them with us as we explored downstream to see if we could find Dad's secret. And we did – it proved to be the tallest beaver dam I've ever seen, backing up a deep pond into a willow flat full of birdsong. I caught a 43-centimetre cutthroat on my first cast. That would have been a fish worth showing to Dad, but he was long gone by then.

A couple of years later the headwaters of the Bow River got hit with an unprecedentedly intense rainstorm that delivered more than 300 millimetres of rain in less than 36 hours. The giant beaver dam blew out under the force of the flood. Dad's secret beaver pond was a meadow the next time I checked it. A humble little creek snaked its way through tangles of resprouting willows before spilling through the ragged gap in the old dam. The beavers will be back some day, even if I'm gone. Our story will go on.

***

Alberta's oil industry had its legs solidly under it by the 1960s when Dad introduced his sons to those headwaters trout streams.

Seismic crews were carving lines through forests all up and down the Eastern Slopes, setting explosives and recording their subterranean echoes to map the hidden rock layers and drill into those most likely to hold black gold. My older cousin Don Kelly worked for one of the companies exploring what had so recently been the wild foothills home of Indigenous Peoples we never saw there, and could barely imagine. He bequeathed my father a treasure as valuable to us as the Dead Sea Scrolls: a roll of maps covering all the hills and valleys west of Calgary. They were plotter-printed maps that traced the creeks back to their sources and overlaid the landscape with all the most recent seismic lines that had been sliced into it. I imagine they were surplus maps that had been replaced with more current ones, but even if they were a year or two outdated, they were a treasure for a family of anglers hooked on exploration.

On our longer camping trips Dad would load the canvas tent, a big tin box full of cooking supplies and utensils, a few bags of groceries, and all our camping gear into the back of the station wagon and head out of town with a load of whatever kids had been chosen for this particular adventure. The back seat got increasingly crowded as the younger kids grew big enough to join the excursions.

Our road to adventure was the Forestry Trunk Road that headed north from the old Banff Coach Road, Highway 1A, west of Cochrane. It was a slow road, gravelled and winding. In dry weather great plumes of pale dust followed us into the pine-clad hills, seeping into the car through cracks around the doors. One summer Dad had so many kids that he decided to put an old mattress in the back of the station wagon for the ones who wouldn't fit in the tent. He piled the gear, and a couple of kids, on top of it for the long, hot drive north. What he didn't reckon with was the effect the constant swaying and bouncing back there would have on young tummies, especially as the dust grew thicker and the heat became suffocating.

To my younger brother Michael's credit, he gave Dad fair warning: "I feel sick."

To Dad's discredit, he tuned that out as just more juvenile whining.

And to our collective discomfort, the car stank for days. Dad put that mattress out with the trash when we finally got home. Mom, no doubt, quietly rolled her eyes, thankful that her husband had left her and the girls at home, as usual.

But most of our camping trips smelled fine. They smelled of pine resin, fried trout, sweet mountain breezes, and the cold, willow-scented breath of morning trout streams. We fell asleep to the smell of warm canvas, surrounded by the comfortingly familiar lumps of siblings in sleeping bags, and woke up to the hiss of the Coleman stove, the odour of partly burnt pancakes, and thoughts of wilderness adventure and big fish.

Those big fish, we were convinced, would be in deep pools far from the road-accessible stream reaches where other, lesser fishermen wasted their time. So Dad would unroll one of his precious maps, and we'd cluster round arguing about which map squiggle was mostly likely to harbour the monster trout we had no doubt awaited us out there behind those hills. Our suggestions carried little weight; Dad always made the decision. Then we'd load up with rain capes, sandwiches, and fishing gear and head off up a seismic line that the map showed intersecting with a trout stream. We walked ourselves skinny each summer, making those sweet wild places part of our identity.

In the 1960s most foothills streams opened to fishing on alternate years. The left-bank tributaries of a river like the Red Deer or Clearwater would be open one year and the next year the map in the fishing regulations would show them all in red, closed, while the right-bank tributaries would be marked open in black. It was a system intended to ensure each creek's trout population would have a chance to grow up and spawn at least once before being diverted into frying pans, but the effect was also to ensure most of those fish died young. The trout we caught were usually in the 20-to-30-centimetre range. Bigger fish rarely turned up. When they did, they were usually at the end of Dad's line.

Like most anglers in those days, we often had no idea what kind of trout we were actually catching. The fishing regulations didn't require us to identify our catch; the limit was simply ten trout, regardless of species, as if all trout were created equal.

All trout weren't, although it was years later before I learned that.

The native trout of those Eastern Slopes streams are bull trout, a species of char whose lineage extends well back into the days when glaciers covered the land and the rivers that drained them were turbulent, cold, and silty. As the glaciers melted down and retreated – mountain glaciers into the highest, shadiest basins of the Rockies and the continental glaciers into the high Arctic – bull trout spread upstream into the new creeks and rivers that drained the emerging landscape. Aggressive predators once they reach maturity, they grew huge in the lower river reaches that swarmed with prey species like sculpins, mountain whitefish, and minnows. Pop Pop's stories about monster bull trout in the upper Highwood and Elbow would have been about spawners that had made their way up from the lower rivers. Most of those migratory stocks had already been fished to extinction or had their rivers blocked by dams by the time we started lobbing our lures into his storied streams. We didn't know that; we assumed the big ones were still there, in remote pools undiscovered by other anglers.

As the mountain glaciers shrank, all those centuries ago, their drainage streams sometimes changed direction. Creeks that originally drained west of the ice into the headwaters of what is now BC sometimes found easier channels as ice barriers melted away, exposing new terrain. That process of headwater capture brought new trout species over to the Alberta side of the divide 10,000 to 15,000 years ago. Rainbow trout that had worked their way upstream from the Fraser River, for example, found their headwater creeks flowing east into the Athabasca and Peace River drainages. It wasn't until I moved to Jasper in the late 1970s that I first encountered those beautiful little Athabasca rainbow trout in Devona Creek and the Wildhay and Berland Rivers, north of Hinton. They might be geologically recent arrivals, but they seemed perfectly fitted to the little foothills streams that were now their home, and mine.

That first cutthroat trout from Ware Creek, two decades earlier, was also a product of headwaters capture. Westslope cutthroat, as their name implies, are native to the streams draining the western side of the Rockies into the Columbia River drainage. At some point, a few thousand years ago, they too found themselves in creeks that no longer flowed west towards the Pacific, but east into the prairies. From there they spread into all the accessible waters of the South Saskatchewan River drainage, from the Ghost and Bow Rivers south to the Oldman, Waterton, and Belly.

Those three species were Alberta's native stream trout. But they were awfully easy to catch, and delicious to eat. As new roads opened up the hinterland, profligate anglers soon fished the native stocks out. Spoiled by easy fishing and frustrated by how soon it ended, angling groups began as early as 1900 to lobby their governments to refill the depleted streams with hatchery-raised fish.

The federal Department of Marine and Fisheries opened the province's first fish hatchery in Banff National Park in 1913. It was followed by hatcheries in Waterton in 1928 and Jasper in 1941. The national park fish hatcheries, until they closed in the late 1970s, provided the bulk of the fish used to stock waters both inside the parks and in the provincial streams we grew up fishing years later.

The fish culturists who ran the early hatcheries – one of whom was my mother's uncle Bill Cable – had no doubts about the merit of their work. They enthusiastically imported trout from around the world and tried them all out in Alberta waters. German and English brown trout, California golden trout, and Ontario brook trout all found new homes here. Park wardens released thousands of Atlantic salmon into Lake Minnewanka and other large lakes. The Banff hatchery invented a new kind of fish by hybridizing native lake trout with introduced brook trout. They called the result splake, and released them into lakes to the enthusiastic plaudits of outdoor columnists and fishing clubs. Not to be outdone, other hatcheries crossed brown and brook trout and turned the resultant "tiger" trout loose into Alberta waters.

Anglers wanted trout – they got trout. But invader trout, not the ones that belonged here. Some of the newcomers thrived – especially rainbow, eastern brook trout, and European brown trout. These were the trout Gordon and I read about in outdoor magazines, where famous anglers fished famous waters. Now we had those fish too, instead of what many anglers considered the second-rate species the place had come equipped with. A lot of fishermen considered bull trout vermin and killed all they could because they saw them as an unattractive predator that preyed on the more desirable introduced species.

Most of the fish my family brought home were cutthroat and bull trout because the headwater streams we preferred to fish were still relatively pristine. It wasn't until I was 11 or 12 that I caught my first brook trout, in the James River. I was entranced by its intricate pale markings, orange fins with black and white stripes on the edges, and little red spots, each with a blue halo, speckling their sides. I'd never imagined a trout could be so pretty. Unaware of the devastation the species was wreaking on native trout species with whom it competes for food and often hybridizes, I became an instant member of the brook trout fan club.

One early spring day in 1968 my father told us that a colleague of his had told Dad about some huge fish he'd caught in a small foothills river. We'd never fished there before because we preferred the small creeks in the public forest reserve farther west; this stream flowed through farm country. We decided to give it a try anyway.

That weekend found us walking down a wooded road allowance between two barley fields into a valley full of birdsong. Dad's old binoculars were around my neck because I was skeptical of the fishing prospects but hopeful of some new birds.

Snowmelt runoff had partly discoloured the stream but the spring floods had yet to arrive. The river felt too large for my taste, and its bottom too muddy. The only gravelly bits were in the fast runs at the heads of the long pools that stretched between willow swamps and spruce groves. Bank swallows coursed back and forth above the water and kingfishers flew chattering from pool to pool. The woods were full of the songs of Tennessee warblers, vireos, and ruby-crowned kinglets, and there seemed always to be a red-tailed hawk or two screaming overhead.

As always, we split up. Gordon and I went downstream and Dad headed upstream. I soon tired of casting and retrieving my spinner through empty pools. Instead, I wandered into the woods along cow trails, tracking down birds whose songs I didn't recognize. It was a glorious day, full of new discoveries – Tennessee warbler, rose-breasted grosbeak, ovenbird; all these new members of my wild Alberta family. At length I headed back to our rendezvous spot to wait for Gordon and Dad.

Gordon was as fishless as me. Dad, on the other hand, arrived with two huge trout hanging from a willow branch and slapping against his leg as he walked. Both were more than half a metre long.

Those were our first brown trout, and just as had been the case with those pretty little brook trout, I was an instant fan of these great, yellow-sided salmon-like creatures. We fished that river for several seasons, always before the spring flood. It was hard fishing – we rarely went home with more than three or four fish among us – but the fish were always big. Sometimes we found them against cutbanks at the edges of pools; sometimes they churned out of the fast water at the heads of pools to grab a spinner retrieved downstream. Inevitably, each strike from fish so big nearly stopped one's heart. The largest brown trout we ever killed was, predictably, Dad's. It was 81 centimetres long.

***

Fishing became an obsession for Gordon and me; we lived for those excursions to the meadow streams of the high foothills and the small rivers draining out into farming country farther east.

When I was old enough to have my own newspaper route, I finally had my own money. My first purchase was *Birds of Alberta* by Salt and Wilk. While browsing the nearby shelves at the Evelyn de Mille bookstore in downtown Calgary, I espied a much larger tome titled *McClane's Standard Fishing Encyclopedia*. If *Birds of Alberta* was a treasure, that illustrated fishing encyclopedia seemed a gold mine – it covered everything imaginable about fish and fishing anywhere in North America. But it cost as much as a gold mine too, at least to a kid earning only a couple of dollars a week. When I finally had enough saved up I was sure the book would be gone, but I was wrong. I hugged it all the way home on the bus and spent the next few days in my bedroom, reading it from cover to cover.

That book, and the used outdoor magazines Gordon and I bought from a bookstore in Hillhurst, spawned my initial interest in becoming a fly fisherman. During my 13th summer my parents allowed me to bicycle from youth hostel to youth hostel through Banff National Park; on the second day of that adventure I watched, awestruck, as the first fly angler I'd ever seen executed one perfect cast after another on the wide channel connecting first and second Vermilion Lakes. But my ambition to cast flies had to wait until I was in high school and finally earning enough money from a part-time job to acquire better gear. Even then, I couldn't afford a fly rod. Gerry, my aunt, made the mistake of asking what I would like for Christmas one year and, when I said I really wanted a fly rod, she made the further mistake of promising to get me one. She hadn't costed them out first. I remember her paling a little at the price tags when she finally drove me down to Russell's Sporting Goods to shop for one, but to her credit she stuck to her promise. With the reel and line I bought with my own money, I was finally equipped to fish like the anglers I'd read about.

Flies remained a problem. They cost money and they were easy to lose. A budding fly angler spends a lot of time snapping flies off on mistimed casts or tangling his line in streamside shrubbery where the only way to rescue it is to break the leader and leave the fly dangling out of reach.

We had acquired a dog, Tim, by the time I got my first fly rod. His mother had been mostly border collie, but his father was unknown. Poor Tim learned to loathe the sight of fingernail scissors, because when he saw me approaching with them he knew his beautiful fluffy tail was about be defaced again. I manufactured my lures with Gordon's model airplane cement, old Christmas tree tinsel, Mom's sewing thread, feathers I'd found outside or salvaged from Dad's pheasants, and furry bits of Tim's tail. The ratty little flies I produced were surprisingly good at catching fish.

After school I would walk a few blocks and cross the railway tracks to the Bow River, where I fished beside the Crowchild Bridge until after dark. The small rainbow trout there seemed particularly easily fooled by my handmade flies. As the sun set behind the cottonwoods of Lawrey Gardens, I worked at perfecting my casting technique or sat and watched the traffic stream by on Memorial Drive across the water. The river was soft-spoken and steady, slipping out of its golden evening glow into the gloom beneath the bridge, then emerging into paleness as it coursed its way towards the towers and lights of downtown Calgary. While the growing city hummed around me, oblivious to a young boy picking his way along the rip-rapped bank of its river, I listened to the water and wondered which bits of it came from the upper Jumpingpound; which from Meadow Creek where Dad once saw a giant bull trout; which from Johnson Creek with its abundant little cutthroats and bird-filled meadows. Some of the river came from Banff National Park's glaciers and snowfields. This wide urban river held all those streams, was born in all those wild places, and yet it was utterly unlike them as it carried its gathered histories through that oblivious city.

That river was in some ways like the males of my family; aloof, distracted, seemingly more concerned with its own business than with a boy who chose its company and longed to know it better. Like them, it was full of stories that were meant to be part of me. But I knew even then I would only ever get to know some of those stories, parts of others, and some not at all. There would be some I would never understand. Others will trouble me to my resting place.

4. Pheasants

The first pheasant flushed as the kitchen door slammed. Dad and his cousin Albert Desmet, whose farm we were visiting, scrambled to slide shotgun shells into their double-barrels as Gordon and I raised a chorus of excited shouts.

"There's one, Dad!" I yelled. I guess I assumed that since he was more than 9 he must be blind.

"There's two more!"

"Holy! Look at them all!"

Dad gestured furiously for his loud-mouthed kids to pipe down. Too late: at least 50 pheasants exploded from the side of the coulee below the house. Albert just shook his head.

A few independent-minded birds were still in there, fortunately. By the time the dog had worked to the head of the coulee Dad was well on his way to another limit of ring-necked pheasants.

That was 1962. Alberta's Western Irrigation District seemed like a paradise for those who hunted pheasants and Hungarian partridges each fall. Originally rolling mixed-grass prairies, the landscape had been reshaped into a patchwork of flood-irrigated hay fields, leaky ditches lined by big poplars, tangles of buckbrush and rose, and sloughs full of cattail and sedge. It was almost perfect pheasant habitat, and an idyllic place for Dad and his young sons to hunt through the long autumn seasons into late November when the snow began to drift.

Driving home in the evening, Dad sometimes talked about his youth. He described clouds of ducks darkening the sky and sharp-tailed grouse sailing above the shrubby sand hills north of Strathmore. I would watch the shimmering lines of northern mallards strung out like shifting signatures on the sky and feel deeply, fervently, a part of this vast and beautiful landscape and the prairie heritage into which I had been born.

Those days afield taught me to see land as habitat and to try to figure out why wild things lived where they did; hunting was the start of many things. And yet the land I was learning to love was not the land it was meant to be; it was a hybrid place where two stories had collided and the trajectory and pace of change got knocked off kilter. Its accidental wealth of habitat and wildlife was too good to last, and it didn't.

***

The Desmet farm is at the head of a long draw that drains into Crowfoot Creek, a small wetland stream too humble for its name. Crowfoot (Is'sapomahksika) is remembered as a great 19th-century Siksika Chief. It was his strategic thinking and pragmatic realism that helped bring Treaty 7 into being. Crowfoot used his diplomatic skills to persuade other Blackfoot, Tsuut'ina, and Stoney Chiefs to put aside their differences and doubts long enough to sign onto a treaty that helped make this place called Alberta possible. Alberta was never the product of conquest; it came into being through what was meant to be a sacred accord among equal peoples.

It didn't turn out that way. At least, it hasn't yet.

The alkaline creek winding its way east from the coulee behind Desmet's farm has lost the memory of the bison herds and cranes that once foraged in its floodplain, but it carries the name of a great man into the future of a province that might never have existed were it not for him, and the heartbreaking clarity of his understanding of how hard a turn his people's world was taking.

Treaty 7 was signed in 1877 beside the Bow River at Blackfoot Crossing, half an hour east of the farms my family would hunt a century later. Only two years earlier, Leonard Van Tighem and his companions had hiked across hundreds of kilometres of unbroken native prairie. And, barely five years later, work crews completed Canada's first national railway across those same plains. The Canadian Pacific Railway enabled families escaping economic depression, landlessness, and agricultural disasters in Europe to acquire land here and take up irrigation farming. When Is'sapomahksika succumbed a few years later to tuberculosis – one of the alien diseases those new arrivals brought with them from Europe – he died in a place where, for the first time in centuries, the future would no longer resemble the past.

Canada was more of an optimistic notion than an actual nation in those days. The founding fathers were in a race to keep British Columbia in British hands rather than lose it to aggressive Americans who had convinced themselves it was their manifest destiny to control the whole continent. Lacking public funds to build a railroad linking the country from coast to coast, the Canadian government turned to its wealthy friends. The Canadian Pacific Railway was financed mostly by Montreal capitalists who speculated that the project would make them wealthy if they could just stay solvent long enough to get it built.

They drove a hard bargain; part of the deal was that they would be given ownership of large tracts of land that could later be sold at a profit. One of the largest such blocks of land lay east of Calgary. To maximize its profits, the CPR built canals and dams to divert Bow River water for irrigation. The company offered "ready-made farms" to hopeful settlers – including our relatives – in what came to be known as the Western Irrigation District.

The original irrigation canals were simple dirt ditches that traced circuitous lines along topographic contours. Lacking waterproof linings, they leaked, especially on their downhill sides. The leakage enabled tangles of buckbrush, rose, willows, and poplars to grow up into thickets that sheltered the pheasants we hunted. Hunting along those ditches was less a prairie experience than a riparian one. The pheasants sneaked out into adjacent grain fields to feed on spillage from harvesting operations, and then retreated into their brushy jungles where other creatures foreign to the original mixed-grass prairie were also finding new homes: great horned owls, chickadees, woodpeckers, red foxes, blue jays, and migrating flocks of tree and white-throated sparrows. We saw our first mule deer in 1963. By the 1970s white-tailed deer, a species that was virtually unknown in the province for most of the 20th century, had become common. The seeming permanence of that landscape to my young eyes was an illusion; all was in a state of rapid evolution.

One of those WID canals cut across the west end of the Desmet property. Seepage from the ditch sustained not just the weedy habitat where we hunted but also the family's drinking water supply. The water from their shallow well was barely potable because of the alkali salts it absorbed from the soil. To my pampered urban taste buds it was less like drinking water than something that might seep out of the edge of a hog pen; certainly nothing like the sweet, cold springs we found along foothills trout streams in summer. When we stopped at the farm for lunch or, more rarely, dinner, we kids knew we were about to face the ordeal of getting that water down our throats without gagging.

Albert's wife Florice did her best to hide the alkaline taste by serving flavoured Kool-Aid or lemonade, but it didn't really help. The Desmet kids seemed fine with it; it was one of the things that made them feel a bit alien to me, even if we were related.

Albert's father had been second cousin to my grandfather. Our family relationship to Bill and Mary Louise Praeker, whose farm was about a mile southwest, was closer; Mary Louise had been born a Van Tighem. Most of our hunting took place on those two properties. Growing up in the small farming town of Strathmore had made Dad half a town kid and half a farm kid. He went to school with kids who now operated these farms. As a teen, he had earned spending money stooking wheat. We kids were just tagging along with Dad and hoping for pheasants to flush; we didn't understand the degree to which each bird hunting season gave Dad a chance to reconnect with old friends and old memories.

***

My childhood obsession with birds and nature expressed itself in numerous ways, including the scrapbooks into which I glued nature-related stories from the local newspapers or that were sent to me by friends of my mom who knew about my passion. I still have the scrapbooks; one has the dried-up claws of a pheasant, a partridge, and a mallard I salvaged from our hunts.

The news clippings from 1967 include several describing the growing consternation of fish and game clubs and farmers as the prairies got hit with an exceptionally severe winter. The snow grew deep and drifted. Brief chinooks were only enough to form frozen crusts on the drifts, not to melt them away. By mid-winter it was clear we were witnessing a pheasant apocalypse.

Those birds had been introduced from populations in England and China that rarely cope with deep snow. As hardened drifts covered over their coverts, the birds simply froze to death in their sleep. Halfway through the winter the provincial government, in a misguided effort to save game birds, cancelled legal protections for hawks and owls. That made it a lethal winter not just for introduced game birds but also for native raptors. A lot of great horned and snowy owls, rough-legged hawks, and eagles got delivered to taxidermy shops that year.

The pheasants died off anyway. Their problem had never been winged predators and it wasn't just winter; it was habitat loss. Although subsequent winters were less severe, the decline continued. If the native prairie fauna had mostly vanished by the time I was old enough to tag along on Dad's hunts, by the time I was old enough to carry my own shotgun those upland riparian habitats and mixed farm fields, and their new communities of more exotic species, were fading into history too. They lasted just long enough for me to make them a part of myself, and to grieve their loss.

Cliff Wallis shook his head in bewilderment when I expressed that grief to him one day during the summer of 1973. Cliff and I were sharing a tiny one-room cabin on the north shore of Sturgeon Lake near Valleyview while we documented the ecosystems of a new protected area for Alberta's park planning department.

Like me, Cliff was born and raised in Calgary, but, unlike me, he had no family hunting or fishing traditions. He found his clear-eyed love for the original nature of our part of the world on his own. He could see nothing even remotely appealing in the sight of a quarter section of wheat stubble, or in the flush of introduced pheasants or partridges from a weedy drainage draw below an irrigation ditch.

"It's all trashed," he said. "How can you be sentimental over a place that's been so abused? It's all crop monocultures, chemicals, non-native plants, and eroding soil! Pheasants don't even belong here."

I had no ready answer. There was no way I could refute what he was saying. It was one of those questions I chose to avoid, because I didn't want to face the implications of the answer. The implications were not just about the landscape and its wildlife, after all; they were about my very sense of who I was. But he'd asked it, and it stayed with me like a scab that kept wanting to be scratched.

If what I loved was the product of abuse, then who was I?

***

Even as we built our family stories out of long walks in pheasant country, irrigation and its associated agri-foods industry were well on the way to turning large parts of Alberta into a biological wasteland.

When the CPR had made all the money it could from selling land to hopeful farmers and there was no more profit for its shareholders in continuing to run the irrigation system, it handed its responsibilities over to the provincial government. In doing so, the CPR was an early adopter of what became an Alberta business model: privatize the profits and socialize the liabilities. Other private irrigation ventures farther south and east followed suit. Taxpayers have been subsidizing the industry ever since. During the 1950s the federal Prairie Farm Rehabilitation Administration built several large dams and canal systems. In the 1970s Alberta's environment department took over irrigation development. Southern Alberta now has two-thirds of Canada's irrigated farmland. Irrigated farms cover almost 700,000 hectares.

Irrigation is a godsend to farmers dealing with sparse rainfall on Canada's western prairies. Dams and weirs divert water from prairie and foothills rivers, especially during spring floods, into large canals. Elaborate water supply systems store the diverted water in reservoirs, then feed it out through canal networks to the farmers' fields during the hot, dry summer. Some canals put return flows back into rivers at their downstream ends. Others drain into the open prairie, spilling leftover water into natural lowlands. Most of the water just vanishes – consumed by crops or evaporated into the dry winds.

Politicians see value in subsidizing those reservoirs and canals, both because the dollars they spend aren't theirs, and because those dollars generate votes. The billions of dollars of public money government water agencies have spent on building and maintaining that irrigation infrastructure today sustains Alberta's agri-foods industry. Subsidized water is a sweet deal for the corporations that now dominate much of the landscape, but it also represents a massive public subsidy to both the destruction of prairie nature and the hollowing out of rural society as small farms disappear.

Starting in the 1970s, mostly to reduce water losses, Alberta Environment pumped billions of public dollars into irrigation projects that replace wildlife habitat with more crops. Water engineers lined canals with plastic or cement to reduce seepage. They bulldozed down poplar stands and closed hundreds of kilometres of secondary ditches, replacing them with buried pipes. In southern Alberta they dammed the Oldman River, Willow Creek, and the Little Bow River while expanding off-stream storage reservoirs too.

The big new centre-pivot irrigation systems require big fields. Buying the expensive pipes and pumps forced many farmers into debt. Their need for cash flow drove them to farm more intensively and eliminate any unproductive corners that were not helping to pay off those loans. Farmers created space by tearing out fence lines and filling small wetlands: more habitat loss.

It all made economic sense, but it also represented a second wave of ecological loss. The first had wiped out the native prairie.

The second continues to erase the hybrid diversity that developed during that earlier, less-efficient irrigation era.

Pheasant populations crashed after that hard 1967 winter and continued to decline through the ensuing decades. The Alberta government, responding to hunters' concerns about habitat loss, tacked a surcharge onto hunting and fishing licences, and created a new Bucks for Wildlife Fund. The government spent the money on postage stamp-sized habitat restoration projects where they release captive-raised pheasants on public shooting grounds. There the confused creatures die quick deaths under the guns of modern hunters who have never seen a wild pheasant, or real prairie.

It's not just the ghosts of bison that haunt the plains today.

**

Most of this, however, passed my family by. Each fall we just headed east to hunt those old familiar corners. Sometimes we'd arrive to find a brushy swale we'd always hunted gone, ploughed under and incorporated into the surrounding grain field. But on our relatives' farms, at least, there were other good places that persisted from year to year. The Desmets' land gradually changed as farming efficiency took priority over retaining pheasant cover, but the Praekers held onto their network of brushy draws and drainages. We noticed when tangles of buckbrush began to turn into meadows of smooth brome and other grasses, evidently having fallen victim to herbicide drift from adjacent fields. Even so, it was still the familiar geography of home; we walked among memories and stories from autumns gone by, and sometimes, even now, a pheasant would erupt cackling from the willows to the sudden crack of a shotgun, and once more it would be everything we remembered.

Even on the slow days it was good to be out there because we could renew our connections with relatives whose home place this was too. We all might live different lives, and their roots here might reach deeper than those of Dad's offspring, but each of us was part of this place and its new, emerging story. We were threads in the same fabric.

I remember the way Bill Praeker would look at Dad as we stood in the farmyard under that vast prairie sky, cats winding around ankles and house sparrows jabbering in the caragana hedge, breathing those old familiar scents of livestock manure and damp straw. It was a comfortable look from a weathered, friendly face; the look of a man who had no doubts about his connections to this piece of earth and to this visiting relative – joined to both by the webs of memory and relationship that hold the world together. A kindred look; his son Herman looks at me the same way each fall, now that Bill and Dad are both gone. I wonder if he sees the gratitude in how I look back at him. It's there.

"Well," Bill would say to Dad, gesturing past the gravel grid road to the poplar-lined irrigation canal winding through golden stubble fields, "there's not as many birds down there as there used to be, but I guess you can try to find them."

There aren't. I still do. I can't help it; it's part of who I am too.

5. Off-Trail

The news media were full of images of young Americans protesting a war in Vietnam. The postwar baby boom had produced a bumper crop of restless teenage idealists. The very air seemed to smell of revolution and renewal, even in our isolated corner of what was still known as the Bible belt. As seemed always to have been my lot in life, I was running to catch up. I was younger than the much cooler faces I saw in the news stories, and stuck in high school while others were on the road. And I lived in a dusty little city called Calgary rather than a happening place.

I was 15 that summer of 1968, and still a geeky birdwatcher painfully conscious of the fact that none of the cool kids ran around with binoculars around their necks. Even my Vancouver birder pen pal, Errol Anderson, was cooler than me. For one thing, he came from Vancouver, one of the only places worth being in Canada if you wanted to be part of this hippie generation. And he seemed to live with few constraints. One morning early that year Margaret had gone out the back door on her way to church, only to turn around again and announce to Mom: "There's somebody sleeping in the backyard."

Errol had hitched his way to Calgary and arrived at our house late at night. Not wanting to wake anyone up, he unrolled his sleeping bag and went to sleep on the dry space under the dryer vent. Lucky for him that the house was seething with youngsters and their laundry; it was actually quite comfortable there. Mom fed him breakfast, and then he and I went birding. I was in serious awe of this nonchalantly cool older kid who could hitchhike a thousand kilometres to hang out with a friend.

His letters later that spring told me he'd landed a summer job as a naturalist at a provincial park on Vancouver Island; it seemed his ability to inspire awe and envy in me was without limit. He suggested I visit him there. We could borrow a motorboat and look for seabirds. It was as if he simply assumed I was as free as he seemed to be. I knew there was no point in seeking permission to make such a trip, but maybe I could fake my parents out. And so my plan was born.

It was a shameful bit of deceit on my part, and the beginning of a serious breakdown in trust between me and my father that caused us both a lot of torment over the subsequent years. But I had no crystal ball, only teenage obsessions. And so I started talking up my desire to do a solo backpack trip from Calgary to Banff. And because, I now realize, my parents had always been impressed by both my passion for nature and independence of spirit, and wanted to nurture both, they put up only a mild and token resistance designed more to ensure I planned things thoroughly than to discourage me. I didn't plan a thing.

In retrospect, I still can't quite understand where they found the faith or confidence to let some of us range so widely and take such chances. But the day came when Dad backed the old station wagon out of the driveway and drove his 15-year-old son and a loaded backpack to the city limits. He dropped me off near the Bow River, and I promised to phone when I got to Banff. We figured that should take a week or so. I'm not joking: they let me do this. They trusted me. I still shake my head, but with ten kids maybe they didn't have much time to think about it. No map, no discussion of things like private property, the Stoney Indian Reserve, stream crossings, or any of the other possible impediments to my solo expedition: I was let loose to work it out on my own.

Not that any of those impediments really mattered, because as soon as Dad's tail lights vanished over the hill, I stuck out my thumb and hitched my first ride ever. I had seven dollars in my pocket but lots of Kraft Dinner in my pack and no experience of disaster in my lifetime to inspire doubts that all would work out fine. Even so, it felt a bit unnerving to find myself in a stranger's car, speeding into the near-unknown.

It proved easy. One after another I got into strangers' cars, went through the ritual of introducing myself and getting the feel for how much conversation the driver wanted, and then watched western Canada roll past the window as the hum of asphalt under tires took me steadily further from my trusting parents and that familiar former life of home and siblings. I wasn't part of that now, in my eager young mind; I was part of the hippie generation. Free and feral and finding my own way.

***

A year or two previously I had attended a week-long summer camp for aspiring young naturalists near Peachland, in the Okanagan. That was where I had met Errol. So although the Trans-Canada Highway went west towards a place called Kamloops, I decided to head south from Sicamous into terrain that felt, at least vaguely, more familiar.

Near Vernon I got a ride from a man in his late twenties. He was friendlier than most of my previous rides and asked a lot of questions. How old was I? Why was I on the road? Where was I planning on staying that night? He had a cooler full of beer and offered me one. So now I was driving through the Okanagan, drinking cold beer from a brown bottle with a short neck, watching water and beaches go by, visiting with a friendly stranger. This was the life; it was a heady feeling. Then it became a strange one. My upbringing was one in which there were more things one did not discuss than there were things that one did, so I was exceptionally naive. It had never occurred to me before that some men might have unsavoury reasons for befriending young boys, but I still had that intuitive sense of danger with which every creature is born. I realized gradually that something was off, and that this beer wasn't a gift. I had told the driver that I was headed for Vancouver, and he had said he could get me as far as Osoyoos, but as we passed the welcome sign for Penticton and he handed me a second beer, I finally decided to heed the growing unease.

As we slowed into the town traffic, I announced that I liked the look of the place and wanted to spend some time there, so thank you very much but I'd just get off here. He argued, telling me how hard it was to hitch rides south from Penticton, getting a little assertive, but I knew for sure now that I had to get out of that car, although I still wasn't sure exactly why. I thanked him innocently, grabbed my pack, and hopped out at the next red light. I could tell he was mad at me, but I didn't know why. Weird, spooky guy, was all I thought.

I walked a couple of blocks to a sandy beach and sat on my pack in the Okanagan heat, watching families play and sun sparkle on the water, the low mountains hazy across the way, and the pleasant buzz of mild intoxication very quickly helped me put the whole thing out of my head. I was on an Okanagan beach, alone, one of a new cadre of adventuring teens. It felt amazing.

That night I slept under some weeping willows near the town beach, reassured by the knowledge that there were real hippies camped nearby and so this was clearly the right place to be. In the morning I caught a ride south and saw sagebrush and semi-desert and then the Similkameen River flickering in and out of sight among its cottonwood groves in a scorching and strange new landscape. What I could see of it made me think it must be a great trout stream, and that triggered the first moment of regret and homesickness; if I were still in Calgary this would be the season for fishing and camping with Dad and my siblings. But that was only an ephemeral thing; I was gripped by the headiness of freedom and the open road ahead.

The lower mainland was not the urban chaos it is today, but it was still a long series of short drives from one turnoff to the next as I caught rides with strangers who were doing short local trips. It was dark by the time I caught my last ride in Burnaby. No problem there, I figured, because in Vancouver I could go to Errol's house. Somebody would probably be up, because his dad worked nights. .

This driver was a small, soft man with fat fingers and an apologetic smile. He was quietly friendly, inquisitive like some of my previous rides rather than aloof or distracted like others. I explained about Errol's dad but he said that their address was quite a bit out of his way and if Errol's dad had already left for work we'd just be waking up his mom, and anyway he had a spare room so if I wanted to crash at his place for the night he could give me a lift the rest of the way in the morning. That seemed to make sense.

His house had a hollow, lonesome feeling to it. It didn't feel like a home so much as an empty granary. The spare room had a bed and a mattress, and I think he found a sheet for me before I rolled out my sleeping bag and thanked him again. He closed the door and was gone.

Later I woke to the realization that someone else's hand was on a part of me that only I had touched before, at least since I was very young. At first it didn't seem strange, while I was mostly still asleep, but then I was wide awake, shocked and trying to figure out why this was happening. I had never even imagined that a stranger might do something like that. Panicked, I lay still a moment, and then I rolled over and made a big pretend yawn. The room went very still. I rolled back and opened my eyes. There was a dark figure sitting on the side of the bed. In an innocent voice I said, "Oh, good morning. Is it time to get up?"

Fortunately for me, my molester was a timid man, full of shame and self-loathing. He retreated into a phoney cheeriness. He told me he had to go to work soon and offered me breakfast, to which I brightly replied I wasn't really hungry, to which he earnestly replied that was okay, then, he'd go start the car. It was a stiff and stilted drive through the early-morning streets of what was now a frightening and unfamiliar city. I was so far from home. But this tormented soul seemed to have scared himself as much as me, so the danger had passed. We both just wanted this over with. He let me out in front of Errol's house, and we said phoney goodbyes. Then he was gone and my heart went back to normal.

Errol wasn't home. His parents told me that he had started work the week before. His dad, a shy, sad man, drove me to the ferry terminal at Tsawwassen and bought me a return foot passenger fare, waving off my thanks, and the aspiring young hippie, still trying to process the previous night's surreal experience, went to sea. Grey morning water and misty islands, swarms of gulls, and the occasional exotic bird – an auklet or murrelet or a flock of grebes – slipped past as the big ferry threaded its way through Active Pass and the Gulf Islands before easing its way into the slip at Schwartz Bay. I joined the queue of pedestrians heading down the walkway as vehicles streamed past. Shortly after the second sign telling me not to, I stuck out my thumb and caught another ride.

I examined this driver pretty closely – but he was fine.

Still, later that day as I was heading north along the island towards Miracle Beach Provincial Park where I expected to find Errol, I got a ride from another man who took a close interest in me. Unlike in those earlier encounters, however, this man seemed genuinely concerned. He clearly didn't believe it when I assured him I was 17 (which I assumed to be a mature enough age to be on the road), nor that my parents knew where I was. He was a teacher and clearly figured I was in over my naive little head (something I already knew but determinedly chose not to admit to myself) and sure to end up in trouble. He tried earnestly to talk me into staying at his family home, but my belated sense of danger was now hyperactivated and I refused. In the end, when he dropped me off, he handed me a ten-dollar bill and stared me in the eyes as he told me to be careful and to really think about whether it might not be better to go home. I slept in the salal that night alone, safe, scared, and very far from home.

My would-be rescuer would have been happy to know that I soon took his advice, because when I walked into the park office at Miracle Beach Provincial Park the person there said that Errol was on a week-long trip to Mitlenatch Island. There was no way I could wait, as my backpacking trip was due to end in a day or two.

***

Of the trip back, I remember only bits. The stranger's ten-dollar bill came in handy near Mission when nightfall found me walking along a dark highway in driving rain, looking for a place to camp. The rain had brought out dozens of big banana slugs. No way was I going to sleep among those slimy monsters. I walked until I found a motel and used the money to rent a room: another new experience.

The next day brought another disturbing episode near Princeton. Again I was a passenger with a solo driver. This was one of the more taciturn ones; he drove, and I looked out the window watching the afternoon light slant across unfamiliar semi-desert slopes. In those days Highway 3 was a two-lane asphalt highway with a soft gravel shoulder. The dotted lines put passing cars into the path of oncoming traffic. A car passed us and swerved back into our lane to let a westbound vehicle go by. Then he cut out again and passed the next car, and shortly later he passed a third. But this time his right wheel went off the pavement onto the soft shoulder and then the whole vehicle shot into the ditch, sending up a cloud of dust from which the car emerged, rolling sideways until it came to rest upside down beside a cross-fence.

Along with everyone else on the road, we stopped and jumped out. The air smelled of crushed sage, spilled gasoline, and desert dust. Some stood by the highway and gawked, but I followed my driver as he and several others ran out to where the car lay inverted, its engine pinging and water draining from the radiator into the ground. Somebody said we should try and get the car right side up, so we all lined up and hoisted until, with a jarring crash, the vehicle settled back on its bent wheels. Through the shattered windshield glass I briefly saw a man lying along the bench seat beneath the crushed roof. I couldn't tell if he was alive or dead, but I had never seen anyone that shade of ashen white before. I suspect now that he was dead, but if he wasn't, the crowd's well-intentioned act of righting his car probably didn't help.

We drove on from there in silence. I kept picturing that strange moment when the vehicle went tumbling out of its own dust cloud into the sagebrush. The driver kept to the speed limit and did not pass, and for that I was grateful.

When I finally arrived in Banff, I called Dad from a phone

booth and a couple of hours later his station wagon pulled up to the curb in front of the Banff Museum. I think he was proud of me for having made it the whole way to Banff from Calgary, and probably puzzled by how little I had to say about what I'd seen along the way. For my part, I no longer felt connected to my own family in the same way I had been before. I had tasted freedom and adventure on my own terms, and been changed by the experience, perhaps especially by the shocks and close calls. And I had also done it by deceit, which had the effect in its own way of cutting me off from Mom and Dad.

But things returned to normal soon enough; we went camping and fishing, summer ended, school began again. I had gotten away with it.

Or at least I thought I had. Then one day I came home from school and Mom met me at the door with a strange expression on her face. She didn't say much until after Dad had gotten home and we'd all had supper. Then she told me that Errol had called that afternoon to say he was sorry to have missed my visit that summer.

And that was pretty much the end of trust, at least between Dad and me. Only once it was gone did I begin to understand how precious it had been. It was many years later before I fully understood how badly I had betrayed their faith in me and shaken their sense of their own judgment. I still don't really regret that trip and what I learned from it, about others and about myself. I do, however, deeply regret the degree to which it was the product of deceit.

***

Being a product of the baby boom, I reached my late teens as part of a massive wave of other teenagers who were spilling out into a world that seemed made for us and wasted on our parents. It was the flower power generation, the Woodstock era – with Crosby, Stills, Nash, and Young assuring us that we could change the world. And Lucy was in the sky with diamonds; I joined her there for a few months.

A friend introduced me to marijuana in Grade 12. We smoked joints or, when we could afford it and there was a supply in town, little cubes of hashish burned on the end of a pin or squeezed between two red-hot kitchen knives. Mom noticed when some of our knives lost their polish and acquired burn marks, but she never figured out what had made them that way.

The marijuana phase coincided with a rapid decline in my school grades and attendance, but I don't think it was a cause-and-effect relationship. Both were part of my increased disenchantment with the life I was expected to lead and my yearning for something different. I suppose it was my teenage job to rebel, but I didn't change the world in the process, just mostly my own prospects. The other factor was confusion and fear every time a math teacher walked in the door. By the end of Grade 12, I was in real trouble – the classes kept moving on to new material long after my incomprehension had left me unable to grasp even the basics of algebra and trigonometry. I dropped Math 31 in a fit of utter despair and I was soon skipping most of my Math 30 classes. There was no help available outside of class. Dad tried to walk me through some math concepts at home once or twice, but when I couldn't grasp his explanations, he gave up, frustrated. I had never been good at math anyway, but at least my social studies and English grades were okay. I would have to take my math courses over a second time, having finished with a 55 average and insufficient credits to go on to university.

St. Mary's had a full-year curriculum, which would have required me to waste another full year if I wanted to make up my grades there. The semester system was still new to Calgary, and the nearest Catholic high school on semesters was Bishop Grandin, at the far end of the number 9 bus route in the newer suburbs of south Calgary. That's where I went to try and salvage my education.

Bishop Grandin felt strange, almost foreign, and not just because it was almost an hour's bus ride from home. Unlike St. Mary's, which was tucked into the riparian edge of the well-forested Elbow River valley in Calgary's oldest Catholic district, Bishop Grandin stood out in the prairie sun on what used to be the Burns Ranch before the city reached out and engulfed it.

St. Mary's Boys School had been built in the 1950s and was already tired when I attended – worn linoleum floors and low ceilings, dusty blackboards, scuffed-looking wooden bleachers in the gym. Half the teachers were Catholic priests. The students crowding the halls between class were a mix of kids bused in from the working-class suburbs of Ogden, Forest Lawn, and Bowness and the well-off children of old Calgary families, from Mount Royal and Scarboro – old neighbourhoods with green, curving streets whose cracked sidewalks were shaded by huge poplars, elms, and spruce trees. It was a melting pot of an inner-city school, with roots as deep as the old trees surrounding it.

Grandin, on the other hand, was faced with a pale, reflective brick that might almost have been chosen to emphasize its intrusion into the bright prairie landscape that had existed there until only a few years before. It was like the surrounding neighbourhoods: new and out of place. This part of the city was no longer of a piece with the original town at the confluence of two foothills river valleys; this was the part that had overflowed onto the plains above – a process of sprawl that continues to this day. The school and its neighbourhoods were new and different, and so were the students. Most were the children of a new upper middle class growing up around the booming oil and gas industry. Many of their parents had followed that industry from Texas and Oklahoma, bringing American brashness and materialism to Canada's Bible belt. Money was starting to flow into Alberta as it never had before, and it was flowing in no small degree to these new suburbs metastasizing out from the old cowtown. People who had never encountered prosperity before were newly awash with it.

These wealthy kids with their alpaca sweaters and sealskin boots seemed a different species than the St. Mary's crowd I'd known over the previous three years. I still brought my sandwich and apple to school in a brown paper lunch bag, but that put me in the minority. Shortly after I'd settled into this strange new school with its brutalist cement walls, green chalkboards, and shiny new lockers along the halls, a classmate invited me to join him and some others for lunch. We went out to the student parking lot – these kids actually had cars! – and piled into a sedan with four others before heading down to Macleod Trail and into an A&W. I had enough money for a root beer, fortunately, but I felt profoundly out of place with this confident, cheerful bunch who could afford burgers, fries, and shakes for lunch – every day. It was the first time I felt like a stranger in my own city.

I was at Grandin to improve my math and science marks so I could complete matriculation for university. I had only two classes a day. As often as not, it was as easy to skip them as to sit through the long bus rides and cope with the despair and fear of not understanding what the teachers were talking about, while knowing my dad was expecting me to demonstrate the same kind of self-discipline and dedication he expected of all his offspring.

One day, arriving after lunch on a day when I'd missed a morning class (and the whole previous day), the assistant principal, Mr. Coughlin, caught me winding my way through the throng towards my locker. He smiled wryly down on me. "Mr. Van Tighem," he said, in a voice dripping with irony, "it's so kind of you to spare some of your precious time for us."

***

When school ended for me at Christmas I had barely managed passing grades. I needed to find a job so I could afford tuition for university, because it was expected that I would go there next. I'd figure out what to study when I got there.

Meantime: a job. Jobs were scarce in mid-winter, but there was an ad in the *Calgary Herald* for frontline staff at the Banff Springs Hotel. The town of Banff, until then, had been mostly a place for summer visitors. In winter the tourist establishments closed up, and the local ski hills opened, mostly for the benefit of southern Albertans. But this winter of 1969/70 was to be the first winter when the Banff Springs would stay open to host international tourists visiting what were now the big three national park ski resorts – Norquay, Sunshine, and Lake Louise.

I'd never dreamed of working in Banff, but once I started to imagine it the idea became huge. I could be away from home and working in the actual mountains with other people my age. I applied for and was offered the job of night-shift elevator operator. Dad drove me out to Banff and introduced me to a kind widow who had two rental rooms in the upstairs of her house. She had been his landlady years earlier when he had a summer job driving sightseeing buses. She rented me one of the rooms, confident that my father's son would be a good tenant.

Well, I wasn't awful. But I wasn't cut from Dad's cloth either.

The Banff Springs general manager had an obvious problem with alcohol. He and the rest of the hotel management clearly saw the hotel as Canada's answer to the great Swiss resorts. There seemed to be some confusion about the location of those Alps, however, as the hotel had a strong Scots theme happening too. Frontline staff wore tartan; the bellmen even wore kilts. The other night elevator operator, Tom, warned me never to eat at the staff cafeteria because they put saltpetre in the food to suppress our sex drives. As if that were possible. But still, I didn't eat there. At 17, I had high, if unrealistic, hopes with regard to sex.

Tom showed me a particularly convincing magazine article about the benefits of hallucinogens, and I soon decided to try LSD too. My first trip was with a tiny little tablet of what was called Orange Sunshine. It was so tiny I was pretty sure I'd been cheated. Wrong. I dropped it with two girls from Nova Scotia who had come to Banff for their gap year and were working as chambermaids. We bought squirt guns and went wandering through the woods on Tunnel Mountain in our own primitive version of Pokémon GO.

At one point, having gotten separated from them, I lay down beneath an old veteran Douglas fir tree to watch its branches toss in the howling chinook wind that was blowing down the valley. It didn't take long before that tree was growing out of my chest and I could feel the roots pulling as it braced against the wind. Whatever else might be said for our casually irresponsible use of hallucinogens, that was a mystical experience; I still remember with a kind of reverence and gratitude the sensation of becoming one with that ancient tree and the even more ancient earth in which it was rooted.

But I was too young at 17 to be there, and too self-indulgent to use the experience well. By March I had gotten myself fired from the Banff Springs and evicted from my rooming house. Things spiralled downhill that spring, and I was in some danger of ending up living on the street. After my eviction, I shared a little backyard greenhouse that a kindly hippie a couple years older than me was renting. Staff rentals in Banff could be strange, but that greenhouse, barely two metres high in the centre and half a metre at the sides, was among the strangest. It was actually a pretty cozy place to sleep, but there was no room for anything else. When Peter moved on in the spring, I camped out in the willows beside Vermilion Lake for a while. No animals ate me.

One April evening I was walking down Banff Avenue with a friend when a station wagon pulled up to the curb in front of us. It was Dad. He looked cold and grim. I opened the door and got into that familiar vinyl interior with the little plastic statue of the Virgin Mary magnetically attached to the dash. Dad was in his fishing clothes.

"Are you staying here or coming home?" Dad asked. Disappointment and disgust were radiating off him in waves.

"Coming home, I guess."

And I did. He had rescued me from myself. Years later, long after he had died, I said as much to Mom. She fixed me with a wry look and said, "Your dad only went up to look for you because I told him to. He had pretty much given up on you."

It must have been a strange drive for Dad, heading up that long highway into the mountains to track down an errant son in whom he had once had such high hopes. It must have been strange for Mom, waiting at home, wondering whether she would ever see me again. I recently found her letters to me, letters to which I hadn't bothered responding, each carefully worded to keep from triggering teenage rebellion but with an undercurrent of growing desperation only too apparent to me now. As a father myself, I find my heart aching when I think of what they must have been going through.

***

But home was home, just like it had always been, and I was a son and brother again, and Banff was something that had happened but was past. Well, almost.

Dad arranged for a friend to give me a summer job at his engineering company. I was a flagman on surveying crews, and the rest of the time I worked in a soils lab. It was strange having a job and working with people who definitely were not hippies and had no interest in that lifestyle.

Still, I wasn't quite finished with it yet. I don't recall where I got it, but I bought a little square of LSD-impregnated blotting paper somewhere for two dollars. Lacking a plan for it, I decided just to take it one evening and go wander around the city. That evening we had dinner at Gerry's house. She had a two-bedroom suite in an up-and-down duplex. When Frank was in town, he had one of the bedrooms. He was there that night.

Frank by now was an ordained Catholic priest who served in various rural parishes around southern Alberta. When I was little, we had known him as Uncle Frank; now he was Father Frank. In our patriarchal world as a Catholic family, that gave him a unique kind of power and stature, second only to that of our actual father. As one of the grown-ups in the family, it seemed a given that his authority and power were never to be questioned by the younger generation.

Frank kept an ironic kind of emotional distance from everyone around him; he was there, but he wasn't. We didn't recognize his passive aggression and bullying as character flaws because they were what we were used to, but there was no question that his brother's family gave him a constant outlet for asserting his power and crushing ours. He kept a squirt gun beside him at the dinner table. If a kid fussed or refused to eat something or in some other way failed to meet his standard of acceptable behaviour, Frank would squirt us. Even though that seemed normal to us, there had always been a feeling of tension and repression around that table. By now some of us were in our teens, and the squirt gun came into play less often. The bullying continued.

Margaret, now in her early teens, was often a victim of his hectoring. He was being particularly obnoxious to her that evening: little digs, sardonic insults, constantly posing questions to her that were mock-polite but meant to wound. And everyone kept on eating. The dysfunction in my father's family must have been incredible, and the tradition of patriarchy in my elders' faith overwhelming, because they simply let Frank's abusive behaviour go on and on.

Finally, the rebel hippie in me got fed up. "Why don't you just leave her alone?"

As soon as I said it, I was shocked at what I had done, and scared. I waited for the adults all to come down on me at once. In our world, one didn't stand up to grown-ups.

Frank pretended to ignore me, but all went quiet. The tension level around the table hit a new high. But everyone, including the adults, just kept on eating. It was weird. So I sneaked my blotter of LSD under my tongue while dessert was being served, made my excuses shortly later, and slipped out into the evening. I was desperately relieved to escape.

Years later, Margaret told me it was one of the best moments of her life because it was one of the only times anybody ever stood up for her. That broke my heart; what a childhood. But we all remained quite convinced that all was normal; for us, it was. It would still be many years before I came to understand just how wrong we were.

***

I caught the bus downtown. Wandering down the 8th Avenue mall I could feel the buzz start. Things began to get strange. It was that moment where you suddenly know there is no turning back and that you won't be in control of the things about to happen. I found a low cement wall that enclosed a flower bed and sat on it, watching the street scene and the passing pedestrians and traffic, the neon signs above dark windows where stores had closed for the night, the darkening sky – and it dawned on me that I might be in for a very bad time. I couldn't go home, after all.

So it was with great relief that I heard my name called and looked up to see one of the Banff crowd waving to me. Jack asked what I was doing. When I explained I had just dropped acid and had no actual plans for the night, he was shocked and concerned. He insisted I shouldn't be taking my chances alone.

Jack lived in Calgary too, but he was dating a girl in Banff. He planned to visit her there that evening. I gratefully accepted his suggestion that I go with him. Even better, his car had an eight-track stereo. I was soon lost in his music, burrowing through the night back into those welcoming mountains. It was turning out to be a good evening after all.

But when we got there, Jack parked in his girlfriend's backyard and went in, leaving me in the silent car. It was dark and windy. The shadows of branches danced in the streetlight glow against the back of the house, and the car shuddered a little at the harder gusts. I began to get cold. The night was hard and unfriendly. I fought a rising wave of panic in my gut, staring desperately at the back door, willing Jack to come back out. The door was shimmering, and I could see strange patterns in everything.

And then something wet and cold touched the back of my neck. I whipped around to see a big German shepherd looking at me with dark, soulful eyes. I hadn't realized we had a dog for company. More to reassure myself than anything else, I reached back and patted its muzzle and scratched its ears. After a while, the dog gave a comfortable sigh and lay back down on the back seat, watching me in a friendly, sleepy way.

Only years later did it occur to me that Jack's dog had sensed my panic and come to my rescue in the only way it could. It had cared for a frightened stranger.

It worked. My crisis passed, and soon Jack appeared and we drove back to Calgary. I let myself into the house as quietly as I could at two a.m. and went to bed. But not to sleep. That isn't really an option with LSD. I lay wide-eyed in the dark watching patterns on the ceiling, feeling the stoned state gradually ebb, and waiting for my wakeup call. Because Dad and I were going camping first thing in the morning. We were to drive up to the Raven Brood Trout Station where Gordon had a summer job, pick him up, and then continue up into the Clearwater valley to fish some favourite streams.

Dad was up before six, and to his surprise so was I. He was used to having to roust crabby and reluctant kids out of bed, not have them show up wide awake and full of bonhomie. We loaded up the car together in the crisp early morning air. Being wide awake anyway, I offered to drive. Dad handed me the keys and we were off.

I was still a bit stoned. That didn't seem to be a problem until somewhere north of Airdrie when I got distracted by something and looked back at the road only to find that the car was heading for the ditch. I jerked us back into the driving lane and looked at Dad's startled and concerned face. "I think I shouldn't be driving," I said. "I guess I'm more tired than I thought."

Dad was glad to take over the wheel. The moon was still high in the morning sky and, after watching it a while, I asked Dad, "When you look at the moon, do you see a red rim on one side?"

He glanced at it and then, with a bemused look, at me. "No."

There was a question hanging there.

"Huh."

I closed my eyes and pretended to sleep, swearing quietly to myself that I would never use LSD again. I never did.

***

While I and most of my generation were exploring our possibilities, challenging convention, and turning our parents' hair prematurely grey with our drugs and other indulgences, Alberta was undergoing no less radical a conversion. But it was a more addictive drug influencing the province's behaviour: oil. Constant improvements in the technologies for finding black gold and squeezing it out of the ground and into the pipelines that deliver it to market meant that the province was going from one rich discovery to the next. Demand for oil in the US had far surpassed that country's ability to fuel itself, so exporting countries like ours had an eager, and profligate, customer. Alberta was already raking in money hand over fist when Middle East oil producers, furious about how US duplicity had helped determine the outcome of a war with Israel, turned off the taps in 1973 to punish the West. Oil prices went through the roof and so, consequently, did Alberta's oil revenues.

The royalty revenues flowing in from oil and gas had shifted economic power from agriculture to the energy industry. Inevitably, political power shifted too – from rural ridings to fast-growing cities. As the winds shifted, a mood of brash impatience and material entitlement took root, displacing the Christian conservatism of the more frugal era now receding in the province's rear-view mirror. The ruling Social Credit dynasty had taken an electoral jolt in 1967 when Peter Lougheed's Progressive Conservative party came out of nowhere to win six seats in the provincial legislature. Then, in 1971, they won 49 of the 75 seats available and formed a majority government just as oil prices began to rise. They had energy, vision, and, increasingly, more money than they knew what to do with.

Among the things the new "blue-eyed sheikhs" chose to do with the province's resource revenues was to find ways to diversify the economy. Many millions of dollars went into planning and developing a new Kananaskis Country west of Calgary, with paved roads, a well-designed trail system, and new visitor infrastructure, from campgrounds, interpretation trails, and roadside viewpoints to information centres and youth camps.

Many more millions of dollars went to building dams and upgrading irrigation infrastructure to help build the agri-foods industry. Yet more went as grants and loans to national park tourism operators – creating a construction boom that forced Parks Canada to react, belatedly, by bringing in new policies and regulations aimed at limiting commercial growth. Millions more went to forest companies to help underwrite the construction or expansion of seven pulp mills and an oriented-strand-board manufacturing centre in the boreal forests of central and northern Alberta. Those operations needed a secure wood supply, so the government also assigned control over the surrounding forests to the companies running the mills, by way of "forest management agreements" that de facto privatized almost half of Alberta virtually overnight. Those deals got signed with no consideration of treaty or Indigenous Rights and no prior assessment of the land's ecological capabilities and competing values.

It was a heady time for governments, businesses, and unions: money was no object and Alberta appeared destined to become a neoliberal Eden. For Indigenous Peoples, traditional hunters and anglers, and the fast-growing environmental movement, on the other hand, the late 1970s and early 1980s were a series of panics and disasters. The place was being radically changed by wealthy newcomers; opposition was tolerated but ignored. We were going to be rich forever, after all; and rich people can do what they like.

All of which was background noise for those of us caught up in the day-to-day angst and adventure of our late teens and young adulthood. When I enrolled in university at the end of 1970, I had no real ambitions or interests other than to find a niche in some part of the counterculture. Everything about the superficial, entitled society that surrounded me felt strange; it felt not unlike the repressed tension around my aunt's dining table each Sunday. I signed up for art, English, and history courses not because they interested me but because they seemed to offer gateways into other possibilities.

Two years later I received a letter from the office of the registrar advising me that, because of the number of F grades I had accumulated, I was now on probation. One more failing grade and I would be expelled. I had spent more time playing bridge and chess in the student union building than in classes. I had also blown all the money my parents and aunt had saved towards my education and, given my grades, had no prospects of finding more. I had no idea what I was really doing.

The following year, rather than return to school, I went job hunting. For all Alberta's oil wealth, jobs were hard to find. The same high oil prices that were filling the province's treasury had put Canada into an economic recession. I perused the papers and pounded the pavements, filled in forms and waited for phone calls that never came. Finally, one September day, I went through the door of a place on 10th Avenue sw with a sign on its old brick wall reading "Northwestern Fishing and Hunting" and approached the long desk at the back where three men were lined up. The one at the end had a kindly sparkle in his eye so I chose him to pose my hopeless question: Were any jobs available?

Blake Huff took pity on the discouraged-looking teenager facing him across the orders desk. He told me to wait, and vanished into the back offices. A few minutes later he emerged with a job application form and promised to deliver it to his manager as soon as I filled it out. A week later I started work in the shipping department. I loved that job. I saved less money than I had planned because staff were allowed to purchase inventory at the wholesale price, and I had a lot of wants. I gradually acquired most of the outdoors gear that I relied on for many years.

But I was still immature and intemperate. Following a devastating breakup with a young woman, I blew up at the warehouse supervisor one day over a relatively minor issue and found myself unemployed again in the dark of February. I took my depression and failure to bed with me and slept half of each day away, while, I'm sure, my parents had quiet worried talks about this aging child still occupying a room in the basement and seemingly going nowhere.

***

One evening a friend invited me out to the bar. As we sat amid the hubbub nursing our watery draft beer, someone punched me on the shoulder and said, "Kevin!" It was an old birding buddy,

Cleve Wershler. He was at a nearby table with another former field companion, Wayne Smith, and a couple of their university friends. Unlike me, they were flying high; they were due to graduate in the spring, and both had summer jobs already lined up with the provincial parks division of the Alberta government. Although we had been constant field companions a few years previously, we had drifted apart in high school. As we talked and visited, it occurred to me at last that I had taken a wrong turn. These old friends seemed every bit as cool and confident as the aimless souls to whom I had tried to shift my allegiance during my brief foray into hippiedom, but they also shared a common love for wild Alberta.

Now that we were back in touch, we stayed that way. Cleve introduced me to a more recent friend, Cliff Wallis, and with Wayne they told me about their plan to celebrate university graduation with a natural history adventure. The three of them were going to spend a month in the Sonoran desert of southern Arizona, birding, botanizing, and exploring. Cliff had a car. It ran well but would need four new tires for the trip. The deal was that each of them would buy one tire.

If I wanted to join them, that would take care of the as-yet-unfinanced fourth tire.

I was broke but excited about this new prospect. It seemed like ages since I'd been excited about much of anything. I found a job at a fast-food outlet selling fried chicken and spent several weeks watching fragmented birds sizzle in fat while diligently tucking every paycheque away in the bank. When I quit in late March I had saved just barely enough to buy my tire and leave some pocket money for the trip.

The others had been planning this trip for months, reading the work of authors like Joseph Wood Krutch and Edward Abbey, and studying up on field guides and botany manuals. They knew what to expect. I got to play the role of wide-eyed tourist. We arrived in Flagstaff to find the highway south closed due to snow, but a secondary highway enabled us to sneak around the closure in the dark of night. As daybreak lightened strange-looking hills, I saw my first saguaro cactuses, draped with new snow. We were arriving in a desert the likes of which I had never imagined.

Four and a half memorable weeks later, we returned north. The others had to start their summer jobs with Alberta Provincial Parks. As if the trip itself hadn't been enough of a gift to a lost soul, much to my amazement Cleve and Cliff were able to prevail upon their bosses to hire me too. I spent that summer helping Cliff conduct ecological surveys at Young's Point and Saskatoon Island provincial parks. I might be comfortable in the wild, and competent at identifying birds, but beyond that I wasn't really qualified for the work. Fortunately, Cliff was already one of Alberta's most talented naturalists. He did most of the heavy lifting; I did the clerical work. That summer in the field with Cliff was easily worth two years in university lecture halls and laboratories.

The following summer I worked with Cleve. We travelled to every provincial park in the province, conducting preliminary assessments of their natural diversity and ecological health. At that time, like many land and resource agencies in Canada, the Alberta Provincial Parks division was building its professional and planning capacity after decades of treating its holdings essentially as glorified picnic and camping grounds for locals. The senior managers in Edmonton had no idea what they were actually responsible for. Our job was to give them enough information to set management priorities. It was the chance of a lifetime: we were being paid to explore some of the best remaining examples of Alberta's exceptional natural diversity. I'd never imagined an Alberta that wasn't foothills and prairie. Cleve taught me nearly as much that summer as Cliff had the year before.

The university registrars had no further worries about my commitment to study. The Arizona spring and summer parks jobs had brought me to life. Back on campus I discovered and fell in love with the library stacks with their bound sets of scientific journals and esoteric books on every imaginable ecosystem and idea. Here was a different kind of treasure trove of knowledge about nature, ecology, and place. I joined the Palliser Club, a group for students who shared my fascination with landscape. At home my leisure reading became textbooks and photocopied journal articles. I was thoroughly hooked, to the point where, four years after that serendipitous excursion to the Sonoran desert, the one-time probationary truant graduated with distinction.

I'd survived adolescence in spite of myself. It just took a while.

6. Mountains

The Canadian Wildlife Service (cws) was not on the radar screen when I graduated from university in September 1977 with a degree in botany. I had spent almost seven years as an undergraduate, trying to grow up. The university had pretty much become my world.

A decision about what to do next wasn't immediately urgent, because I had a seasonal summer job as a park naturalist at Kootenay National Park. In the Calgary regional office of Parks Canada, there was talk of an ambitious program for inventorying the biophysical resources – soils, vegetation, and wildlife – of all the western national parks. It was part of the movement towards science-based management that swept through most park and resource management agencies in the 1970s. When I talked to Ian Jack, the chief park naturalist and my boss, about future plans, Ian mentioned Kootenay's upcoming biophysical assessment. It sounded like something I'd like to be involved with. Surely my birding knowledge, backcountry skills, and education in plant ecology would be of some value to such an undertaking.

Unfortunately, however, that project was still a few years away. My work in the park entailed the same guided hikes, evening slide talks, and other public education efforts it always had. I liked the challenge of finding creative ways to interpret the nature of the place to visitors, but by this third summer it felt a bit like treading water. I wanted biology fieldwork. So I talked to Larry Halverson, my supervisor, and he agreed to let me devote some of my time that summer to a preliminary bird survey of the park. Even if it didn't become part of the upcoming biophysical study, it might still be a useful resource for seasonal naturalists after I'd moved on.

My idea was to create an annotated list of all the birds breeding in the park, and to supplement that with descriptions of the park's main vegetation types and lists of the birds found there. Like most biologists of the day, and especially after having immersed myself in plant ecology during the last two years at university, I defined wildlife habitat primarily on the basis of vegetation types. It would be a few more years before I learned to see the underlying landscape patterns and ecological processes that gave rise to that vegetation and are, ultimately, more fundamental to the nature of a place.

That was a good summer. Especially in June and early July, when breeding birds are most vocal, I'd be up in the cool dawn and off to another corner of the park to see what lived there. Some mornings the woods would seem nearly empty; other days the places I visited were alive with so many singing birds that it took serious concentration not to overlook some. After hiking hard to get into an open forest of larch and fir up near timberline, or slogging through sodden, mosquito-laden muskeg at the foot of Mount Wardle, I'd jump into the car and race off to the campground or trailhead from which that day's guided hike was to depart. The happy campers waiting there to learn some of the mountains' secrets had no idea I'd been adventuring since daybreak.

By the end of the summer, I'd amassed a copious amount of data but hadn't found the time to summarize and write it up. Larry consulted with Ian, Ian did a bit of arithmetic, and they agreed that they could extend my work term by a few days. I worked feverishly through the allocated time and finally presented a handwritten report to Ingrid Music, the park superintendent's secretary, for her to type up. She made three copies: one for me, one for the regional office, and one for the park library. I hope the latter two proved useful to someone.

And then I was unemployed, still without a plan.

Fortunately, Banff National Park needed some writing done, and one of my co-workers was a well-known poet with a couple of books to his credit. David Zieroth was brilliant with words and ideas, but his training had been in history. I was getting to be a competent prose writer, but I was also an unknown, not having had anything published outside of local natural history newsletters. But I also knew ecology. The texts Banff needed were meant to deal with ecology. David and I were both in need of income, so we teamed up and submitted a contract proposal to the project manager, Liz Holroyd.

Liz was the assistant chief park interpreter for Banff. A fairly recent graduate herself, she had moved, along with her husband, to the west after they finished their university studies in Ontario. She called up David early in September and told him we had the contracts for two projects: sign texts for Johnston Canyon, and sign texts and a brochure for Bow Summit. They were small contracts, but I calculated they would keep me in rent and groceries at least until Christmas. That would buy me time to chase down longer-term employment.

Meanwhile, it was time to go hunting. I was free: no scheduled classes to keep me tied to the city, no scheduled walks and talks to keep me tied to campgrounds and campers. I had a car that worked and, now, a job I could work at on my own time, which, where writing was concerned, tended to be at night. I found a place to live just east of the Banff park gates, at Harvey Heights, and started to plan some hunts.

It was just after five in the morning when I got out of my car beside the quiet chatter of Jumpingpound Creek one Friday morning in late September. The woods smelled of leaf mould and pine sap as I waded the creek and headed up a cutline in the dim pre-dawn shadows. I'd earlier found a good place to watch for game at daybreak. The sunrise was just a faint rumour in the east as I settled against my chosen pine tree, poured out a cup of coffee from my thermos, and waited. A saw-whet owl called for a while. As the world began to take shape around me, a squirrel chattered nearby, and then another one farther off. Juncos chittered somewhere down the cutline. A chickadee visited; and then it was daylight. No deer or moose had appeared.

Never having been good at sitting still for long, I finally stood up, stretched, and started to still-hunt my way through the woods. A couple of unproductive hours later I had worked my way in a broad loop back to the cutline where I'd started, and there I discovered fresh moose tracks. They led right past the place where I had been sitting at daybreak.

Discouraged by that discovery, I decided to leave the cutline and work my way through the woods instead, since by now most animals would likely be bedded down for the day rather than wandering about. I had only gone about 30 metres when something crunched, then grunted, in the woods ahead of me. As I eased forward, my heart nearly stopped at the sight of two huge antlers protruding above the alder understory, not 20 metres away. It was a moose.

Crouched, I could see the white legs and black sides of the animal. At my shot, he bolted. I ran a few steps, unable to see him through the dense understory, and suddenly spotted him again, standing and looking back at me. Another shot and again he plunged out of sight. This time, however, when I had pushed my way out to where I could see better, there was a big antler protruding from behind a downed aspen where the moose lay on his side.

Once I was sure he was dead I began to shake; I'd never really imagined I would ever get a moose and especially not so immense an animal as this. And at that thought the grim reality of the situation became suddenly clear to me: I was alone, two kilometres from the nearest road, with an animal weighing half a ton.

I realized now that I wasn't prepared for this. My day pack wouldn't hold much meat, and I didn't have any better gear back at the car. Even my knife was inadequate; all I'd brought was a cheap plastic-handled belt knife that I'd used mostly for digging up botanical specimens. Its blade was chipped and dull. Standing there as the day's first warmth began to penetrate down through the tree canopy beside this huge animal whose life I had just taken, I felt a growing sense of shame, combined with trepidation. Only now did I realize how disrespectful and irresponsible I'd been to head out hunting with so little preparation. It was a dishonour to the animal that now lay before me.

Grimly, I tried to lift a hind leg so I could begin the task of gutting the animal. That leg weighed more by itself than most of the deer I'd handled in the past. The animal barely budged. Moving to the head, I tugged and pulled until both antlers were flat on the ground, returned to the hind leg and pulled with all my might, straining until I could get a hoof propped behind an aspen trunk. The front leg resisted all my efforts to turn the animal on its back, so I straddled it and began the first incision at the breast bone, sideways.

My knife was too blunt. It wouldn't penetrate the hide, even when I punched against the ribs. Repositioning, I pinched a bit of hide in my fingers to pull it taut, pressed the knife against it, and pushed as hard as I could. The knife slipped, skidded down the hide, and jammed my leg. At first I thought it had been stopped by the pant leg, but when I pulled up my cuff to check, there was a deep puncture in my calf from which blood was gushing. Evidently my hide wasn't as tough as the moose's.

It was nine in the morning, and I was alone, an hour from the road. Nobody knew where I was. I was losing blood fast. I would have to survive this on my own.

I fished a long scarf from my pack, tied it around my leg and made a knot above the wound, cinching it down tight. It was a long, painful hike out to the road. Each time I had to go even the least bit uphill I could feel my body go weak and my head get light.

Eventually, zombie-like, I reached the car, unlocked it, threw my gun and gear in the back, and drove myself to the Foothills Hospital emergency entrance, praying I wouldn't faint at 100 kilometres per hour. The people sitting around the waiting room, each locked into their own private miseries, all looked up briefly and then glanced away as if not wanting to be caught peeking. All except the policeman in one corner who, seeing me start to tilt, jumped up and steadied me until I was seated.

It was a relief to be told by the doctor that there was no lasting damage. I wasn't going to lose my leg after all. He washed the wound, stitched it up, gave me a tetanus shot, and sent me off with a crutch.

The following day being a Saturday, Dad and two of my brothers hiked in and finished cleaning and quartering the moose. It took them all day to get it back to the road. When they arrived at the processing facility in Calgary, the butcher took one look at it and told them to get it out of there. The meat had spoiled. The moose went to a rendering plant. All I ended up with was the antlers, which was really the only part I didn't want. Well, those and an important lesson.

Hunting is hunting, but when one makes a kill it becomes, in essence, a sacrificial event. The animal is an unwilling participant in that sacrifice; it wants to keep on living the only life it will ever have. To end another's existence is a profound and sombre act, one that can be very hard to reconcile with respect for life and love of nature. Some people go so far as to eschew meat altogether. I honour that choice but have never made it myself; I still eat the meat of animals I have hunted.

But losing that first moose was deeply disturbing, because I hadn't just wasted the meat; I had wasted a life that wasn't mine to take. I had done it by failing fully to respect the sacrificial – I would say today, after a lifetime of reflection, the sacramental – nature of the hunt. The least of my responsibilities was to have been fully prepared so I could ensure its death would not be in vain. In the years that followed, the preparations for each hunt took on an elevated importance because I was preparing to accept, as humbly and honourably as possible, a sacrifice given unwillingly by another living creature.

Of course, I could just buy meat for the family at a supermarket. Sometimes we do, but it always feels like a failure to take full responsibility; to be fully present to the animals whose deaths feed us. The anonymity of supermarket food hides its origin in the often miserable lives and anonymous deaths of other creatures, and the exploitation of ecosystems to produce them. Hunting one's own food is a form of taking responsibility, but even so, choosing to end another being's life is virtually impossible to justify. It's a moral conundrum I expect I will take with me, still unresolved, to my own death. I would like to hope that when that death happens, my body will feed other creatures too.

That is, after all, how it's meant to be.

***

In the immediate aftermath, however, my hunting was finished for the year, and I was largely confined to the tiny cabin I'd rented at the old Stockade Motel in Harvey Heights. One day, probably feeling a bit sorry for the young guy with the limp, Liz asked if I'd like to come over for dinner. She thought I might like to meet her husband, Geoff, who was working for the Canadian Wildlife Service. They lived in a former warden residence near Bankhead, at the entrance to the Cascade fire road; I'd often passed their home on solitary sojourns into the upper Cascade valley.

Socializing had never been my strong suit, but I thought it would be churlish to turn down the invitation. Still, I felt a bit like a fish out of water. Liz and Geoff were in their late twenties, intelligent and assertive; more like the graduate students I had sometimes seen around the student union building than the woodsy biologists and naturalists I'd rubbed shoulders with during my summers afield. But they were interesting people and good at visiting. Very soon they had me at ease. Their baby boy helped break up the tension too; if there was one thing my upbringing had prepared me for, it was sharing a dinner table with babies.

Geoff was a very keen birder. He had recently been promoted to the position of project biologist in charge of ecosystem-based wildlife assessments in Banff and Jasper national parks. He was actually working in the biophysical inventory program that Ian Jack had mentioned. I listened to Geoff describe the early morning songbird transects, ungulate pellet group counts, and small mammal trapping that he and his team were doing and shook my head in amazement.

"It sounds like heaven," I said. "I never even dreamed there were jobs like that."

"We're going to be hiring for a position in Jasper," he replied. "What's your background?"

When I told him I'd just graduated with a botany degree, I could see his interest flag. So I added that my interest in botany had been driven by a lifetime obsession with birds.

"You know your birds?" he asked, perking up again. "You can identify them by song?"

By dessert, the conversation had started to feel like a job interview. When it became clear I planned to apply for that Jasper job, Geoff felt the need to caution me.

"If you apply for the job, you need to understand that this work can get pretty intense," he said. "You'd have to spend days on end all by yourself in remote country, no means of communication if you get in trouble, there's bears…It can be pretty lonely and dangerous out there. Are you sure you could handle that?"

I felt like jumping across the table, grabbing his collar, and shouting, "Hire me! Now!" The more he cautioned me, the more I wanted that job. Being a park naturalist had been about dealing more with people than nature. I wanted to be far away from people, surrounded by wild things. Jasper, to my Calgary mind, was the wilderness north: better than Banff!

Later that winter, having gone through the mandated selection process, I got the phone call I'd been hoping for. I would be starting work that spring as Geoff's right-hand man in Jasper – lead hand for a small crew of wildlife contractors. Because the work would take us to remote areas where we would sometimes be based out of Parks Canada's backcountry patrol cabins, it also involved liaising with the warden service. There could be no escape from dealing with people, but at least now there would be some long intermissions in wild, beautiful country.

The Jasper wardens were, for the most part, the kind of people I felt comfortable with. Theirs was what Jane Jacobs, in her book *Systems of Survival*, would have described as a guardian culture: one of strong internal loyalties, pride in technical competence, and fierce dedication to the places they were hired to care for. They were a clique bonded by shared ordeals, mutual support, and an inherent conservatism. Tradition mattered to them, especially their own traditions.

Most wardens in the 1970s were rural farm boys – there were no women – who had grown up around horses and equipment. They were hired for their practical skills and then, once in the job, trained in the more specialized realms of mountain climbing, law enforcement, and firefighting that comprised some of their core responsibilities. It was practical, hands-on outdoors work. Warden recruiters looked to technical schools, not universities, for their intake.

But things were starting to change. Jasper had hired its first female warden. Although she too came from a rural background, she was a university graduate with a strong grounding in ecosystem science. Those very strengths made it harder for her to fit in. She lasted through a couple of years of sexist indignities, scorn from her superiors, and the constant need to prove herself. When a specialist position opened up in a new environmental management unit in the Calgary regional office, she moved on to a post where her skills were more welcome and had wider utility.

The warden service was being challenged not only by the beginnings of a shift away from male fraternity but also by increasing demands for specialized science skills. The regional office was now hiring environmental assessment practitioners and resource specialists. My presence in Jasper was an expression of the same trend, because anecdotal accounts of the park's natural resources were no longer good enough; planners and managers wanted hard data. Within the warden service the changing corporate culture was reflected in a shift from an area-based organization with district wardens to a more function-based one, with senior specialists skilled in public safety, law enforcement, wildlife-human conflict management, and fire management.

In the midst of all this change, I was a naive idealist with high hopes. I just naturally assumed another outdoorsman would be welcomed as family. What I didn't know was that our project was controversial. Lacking its own science capacity, Parks Canada had a standing contractual arrangement with the Canadian Wildlife Service to provide scientists and science advice. There were about 80 of us across the country. Since the project reports we produced were considered capital assets, the money for our salaries and operating costs came from Parks Canada's capital budget. That meant it wasn't available for things more important to practical-minded park managers – trail upgrades, campgrounds, roads, horses, and so on.

At another level, some wardens felt threatened by, and envious of, outsiders like me operating on their turf. They felt – rightly so, in some cases – that they could do the same work we were doing. Instead, we got to go out into the backcountry among their wildlife, using their cabins, while they were stuck patrolling campgrounds and responding to emergencies.

I knew nothing of this when I reported to the warden office to meet Don Dumpleton, Jasper's chief warden, and discuss what kind of collaboration my team could count on, and what rules and constraints we should be aware of. Don was cold and unwelcoming, but he was stuck with us. He quickly shunted me off to Jim Boissoneault, the backcountry coordinator, and Wes Bradford, who had a lead role in managing wildlife. Jim was collegial enough, and Wes and I hit it off pretty quickly. Wes was sufficiently confident and competent not to feel threatened by this eager young stranger. We also shared a passion for bighorn sheep hunting.

Once the CWS team was established, Wes and the other permanent wardens proved generous at sharing travel tips, wildlife insights, and theories about what was happening out in the wild. The wild world was in flux, in part because of climatic changes that nobody was yet, at that time, convinced were real, and in part because of changes in wildlife management practices and the landscape itself – both inside and outside the park. We were aiming at a moving target with a lot of different pieces.

Jasper is a huge park, so it would take several years to describe and evaluate the park's ecosystems. The first year's work, in the most accessible part of the park, had been focused on honing the sampling protocols and fieldwork planning. That work was finished when I arrived to take over. The focus for 1978 was to be the upper headwaters of the Athabasca River, along the Continental Divide.

Scientists from the Alberta Institute of Pedology (soils science) and Canadian Forestry Service (vegetation) made up one team. They mapped and classified the park's ecological landscape units on the basis of soil types and climate zones. Soil is the product of long interactions between what lies beneath the earth's surface and what happens on top of it. It tells a long-term story, while vegetation often changes in response to fires, grazing, and other ephemeral events.

The resulting maps at first frustrated but soon came to fascinate me. I was used to thinking of wildlife habitat in terms of vegetation types: aspen forest, willow thickets, alpine meadows, or grasslands. The maps I was given to work with showed ecosites that often held several vegetation types. It didn't make sense at first. Ultimately, though, the classification of the mountain landscape based on its most enduring features helped me to see landscape and wildlife habitat in a much more nuanced and holistic way. It just took me a while to recognize the gift those earth scientists were giving me.

At the beginning of each field season, we received the maps they had completed the year before, and we used those to plan our sampling season. We had to collect enough wildlife data from each ecosite (the term we used for each distinct combination of soils/climate and vegetation pattern) to be able to compare wildlife use of that ecosite type to each of the 70 or 80 others that comprised the park's landscape mosaic.

Since we needed data on almost the whole range of animals occupying the park, we had to employ a wide variety of sampling types. In June and early July we counted birds on their breeding ranges by walking half-kilometre transects early in the morning, when birds do most of their singing. During spring and fall we tracked migration trends along roadside survey routes. Through the summer and fall we counted how many piles of droppings different ungulates deposited in different ecosites, using that as a proxy for how important each was for those species. We also set traplines for small mammals and, through the winter, skied snow transects looking for the tracks of carnivores that were hard to count any other way.

Meanwhile, a third team was at work evaluating the park's lakes. In the late 1970s, Parks Canada still stocked lakes with non-native trout for anglers. Limnologist David Donald's task was to help them devise the most effective stocking strategy based on the inherent productivity of each lake.

All three teams worked out of a set of work trailers in the parking lot adjacent to the park warden office. David was unquestionably the most popular among us among the wardens, partly because his net-sampling resulted in large hauls of rainbow and brook trout. Once he had finished collecting biological measurements, the fish went into an old refrigerator he had converted into a smoker. Informal feeds of smoked trout became a popular feature of those summers as the ecology crews and wardens mixed and mingled, sharing stories and jokes.

Rich as those social occasions were, my recollections of those Jasper years are mostly of the solitude of the wild. It was often lonely, but always good.

***

At −20°C the high mountain valleys seemed frozen into a stillness colder than death. Nothing stirred. Trees stood rigid beneath a pale sky; the cliffs were hard and aloof. Not a bird called. When a frozen tree cracked back in the blue shadows of the forest it was like a gunshot that seemed not so much to disturb the icy silence as to deepen it.

The helicopter had dropped John Kansas on a white meadow near the boundary cutline, not far from Fortress Lake. From there it lifted and wheeled in a broad arc over the mountain shoulder that separates the Chaba and upper Athabasca Rivers before descending in a sudden flurry and rush of fine snow amid the burned spars at the top of the ridge. Gary Foreman rocked the helicopter back and forth a couple times to make sure it was solid and then gave me the high sign. Cracking the door open, I stepped out onto the strut and then off it into the snow, sinking to my waist. I struggled around to the cargo bay, extracted my pack and skis, made sure the door was properly latched, and then pushed my way through the snow until I was well out of reach of the helicopter blades. Gary waved and the engine roared as he slowly lifted off, tilted, and roared away down the valley. I watched the machine vanish around a mountain shoulder and then I was alone with the cold and the stillness.

Climbing up onto the skis was tricky, but once I had them strapped on I was mobile again. John and I were to rendezvous at the Chaba patrol cabin, ten kilometres away, after a day of counting wildlife tracks along transects we had previously planned out for each of our areas. Descending gradually through the weathered spikes of long-dead trees, I listened to the hiss of my skis and the utter silence of the frozen world. If I were to hurt myself out here, death was a good possibility in spite of all the emergency gear in my pack. At 30 below, there isn't much of a safety margin. That, and the paucity of animal tracks in the burn, had me questioning, again, the wisdom of some of the work we were doing. But the skiing was good and the scenery spectacular. As layers of ice built up on my beard, moustache, and eyebrows, I worked my way down the long slope to the frozen floodplain of the Athabasca River.

The day was getting late by the time I emerged onto windswept gravel flats. Long blue plumes showed where the river had temporarily escaped from its prison of river ice, only to refreeze on top. Two last half-kilometre transects along the edge of the floodplain completed the day's fieldwork, and now it was time to race the fading light down to the cabin.

I was making good progress on the hard-packed snow when I saw movement ahead of me, at the edge of the timber. Another flicker, and two wolves emerged into the open a few hundred metres away, trotting effortlessly up the river. Two more appeared. I hunkered down against a pile of driftwood to watch as they travelled closer and closer. It looked like they might pass right beside me.

Maybe 50 metres away the lead wolves stopped. Soon they were all bunched together, tails wagging, noses touching. Something was being communicated. Then the whole group turned and crossed the flats to the other side of the river. The two smaller wolves sat down and watched as the lead wolves vanished into the timber. After a long, cold wait, one appeared at the edge of a narrow avalanche slope, well above the valley floor. When the other emerged a ways below, both began to forge their way across the opening. The two waiting wolves resumed their travel. One stopped again 100 metres upstream and the other kept going. A while later, the first two appeared again on the edge of the flats and then they all vanished around a bend, travelling again.

I was nearly frozen after watching them execute their fruitless little hunt, but I was thrilled. Only three years earlier I had known wolves only as creatures in the wilderness of my imagination, but I had seen them fairly regularly since moving to Jasper. Still, this was the first time I'd witnessed their hunting behaviour, and they'd never even known I was there. The winter silence beneath the icy peaks of the Continental Divide no longer seemed lifeless and alien; it felt like I'd been admitted into a kind of secret intimacy.

But a cold one. I skied fast for the last few kilometres to the cabin. John had arrived a half hour ahead of me. He had the wood stove blazing and a propane lamp near the window, a welcoming sight as I emerged from the dark forest. Skis standing in the snow outside and winter things hung by the stove, we sat around the little table by the window and compared notes on the day's findings. John had seen more wildlife sign than I had. He was excited to hear about the wolf sighting. He announced that he would follow my back-trail in the morning and see if he could figure out where they went, rather than start for the highway right away as we had planned.

That plan didn't pan out; when John started up-valley in the morning he rounded a bend and my tracks vanished into an open channel of dark, icy river water. Almost a kilometre of ice had collapsed overnight, and he would have had to break a new trail through dense spruce forest to get around the open water. I was just locking up the cabin when he returned to tell me how close I'd come to vanishing into the grim depths of the Athabasca River. We made the trip back to the pavement together after all.

***

We had many encounters with wolves during the Jasper years. Jim Armstrong, an enthusiastic young volunteer from England, watched one hunting mice in the Blue Creek meadows one afternoon. John and I watched a pack of 12 for several days as they cleaned up the remains where a CN train had killed eight elk near Snaring Lake. One moonlit night, canoeing into Jasper Lake from the braided channels of the Athabasca River, I was serenaded from far down the lake with the mournful wail of a solitary wolf. As much as the caribou that ranged through the high timberline meadows, wolves came to define the place for us: big valleys, far mountains, wilderness animals.

The bulk of our fieldwork was between May and September. Our crew ranged from five to ten, depending on how many volunteers joined us each year. At the end of the season the summer contractors said goodbye and headed off for other adventures, leaving just me and John to work up the season's data, conduct twice-weekly roadside surveys for large ungulates, and plan our winter fieldwork. John, like me, was a loner, so we were compatible; we would study the maps together, choose our destinations, and then head off alone in different directions. We had only our skinny trail skis and no training in how to use them. We had no radios or other means of communication. We knew nothing about avalanche hazard. As much as we loved the freedom and independence, our whole approach to fieldwork was often amateurish and sometimes dangerous.

On one occasion I arranged for a helicopter drop at the head of an unnamed tributary of the Rocky River, while John was deposited several kilometres away at an unnamed pass into the upper Restless. We planned to meet and camp together that night and then travel out over Alpland Pass the following day, conducting track-count transects while we travelled. The helicopter left most of our camping supplies and food in a meadow near the foot of the pass. But neither of us had bargained for the kind of terrain we were going to encounter. I ended up sidestepping up the edge of a seemingly endless avalanche slope and then postholing my way down a canyon. I never made it to our cache; well after dark I found a wind-thrown spruce, and built a fire against its root ball. I spent the long night alternately dozing and feeding the fire. At the first hint of dawn I was on my skis again, and an hour later I emerged from the trees to find our supplies stacked where we had left them, but no John. He had had his own unplanned bivouac far up the valley.

I slept a few hours, then packed up my equipment, wrote John a note, and headed downstream to the Rocky River, where I knew there was a Parks Canada patrol cabin. After a night in Grizzly Cabin I broke trail down-valley and up to Jacques Lake cabin. Fortunately, John was there already, having stuck with our original plan to traverse Alpland Pass. We were both exhausted.

On another occasion, Gary, the helicopter pilot, called to suggest we postpone a planned trip because the temperature was stuck at about −30°C. It was early January and the days were short, but the cold snap meant we had perfect track-counting conditions: light, fluffy snow that had sat undisturbed by wind or thaw for almost four days. I persuaded him to fly anyway, and an hour and a half later he deposited me in a frozen muskeg high up the Minaga Creek valley before lifting off to deliver John to another destination a few kilometres away.

This time our afternoon rendezvous worked out, but that was when our problems began. We couldn't find the trail. It wasn't much of a trail at the best of times, but in the deep snow of mid-winter there was no sign of tree blazes or the trail cut. As darkness descended, we decided our best bet would be simply to follow the frozen creek downstream.

That proved not to be the smartest idea. The creek was bumpy, with occasional hidden pockets of dark, open water bulging between snow pillows. Frozen alders, hard and unforgiving, leaned into all the openings and snagged our pack straps or whipped back on us. The darkness and cold and stillness were absolute. The creek seemed to go on forever.

At one point I fell and slid head first into a hole, stopping just before I hit the water. I fought my way back and got up, swearing, only to be swatted a brutal whack by an alder. It was the last straw; furious, I hacked at the branch with my ski poles. Being bamboo, they both shattered. My hands and the electrician's tape in my emergency gear were too cold for a temporary repair. We ended up discarding the broken poles and John let me use one of his. Fortunately, a few hundred metres farther downstream we spotted a narrow gap in the timber: the trail, at last.

It was midnight when we reached the highway. Dee Allison, a friend who had offered to meet us at the trailhead and drive us back to town, had been cruising up and down the road for hours, growing increasingly concerned. She was heading back to call the wardens when we emerged from the shadows, beards and eyebrows caked with frozen rime, grinning with sheepish relief.

Dee never offered to pick us up again; if we wanted to be stupid, she was quite content to leave us to it.

***

Our compulsive natures and obsessive love for wilderness meant that John and I had a few adventures that didn't really need to be adventures. But for the most part, our fieldwork was more rewarding than risky. In the summer, John was happy to work with another team member, whereas I preferred my solitude. I would hand out the field assignments and, just conveniently, save the last one for myself as the odd man out by design. While the more sociable team members camped together in some prime location, I'd be one mountain valley over from them, alone and contented.

It was always a strange and disorienting kind of experience to climb out of a helicopter in some remote alpine basin, haul my gear out of the storage locker underneath the helicopter, and then watch as the engine roared and the machine lifted back into the sky, tilted, turned, and vanished around the shoulder of a nearby mountain, leaving me suddenly alone.

One moment I would be shopping for last-minute supplies in the hubbub of a busy store on a busy street full of tourists; an hour later I would be far into the wilderness, utterly alone, with very little prospect of seeing another human being for the next week.

It was too abrupt an arrival. I would find myself standing in the midst of a timberline meadow under looming cliffs, looking down an isolated valley to some far mountain range where I knew my travel would eventually take me, but my mind wasn't there yet. It was still back in that human world.

Some classic alpine mountaineers disdain motorized access and shortcuts to get them to their base camps. They argue that one must earn one's mountain by way of an arduous, slow approach. The approach serves as a transition whereby one sheds the thoughts, feelings, and images of the contrived world from which one is departing. It's a gradual baptism, back into the silence and slow time of the original world. Those mountains, after all, have stood for millennia. They exist in time so vast and so deep as to be virtually incomprehensible by humans. They are derived from antiquity, from the real time of the real world. The classic alpinist would argue that to earn one's time among the giants, one must show them the respect of arriving slowly, deliberately, and humbly.

The violence and racket of a turbo jet engine and whirling rotor blades is not part of that, and so the price one pays when arriving by that means is in some ways like diving into cold water. For me, as one who had lived most of his life in loneliness, a loneliness I had usually chosen, it deepened my sense of isolation and disconnectedness both from the world I was leaving, and the world into which I had arrived so suddenly.

And so my only solution, usually, was to find the nearest un-sampled ecosite and go to work. With my gear piled nearby, I would lose myself in the task of setting out lines of rodent traps or measuring out plots in which to count the little piles of droppings left there by wild ungulates who, unlike me, belonged here. At the end of that first hour or two, when I would finally straighten up, dust the dryas leaves and shale bits from my hands, and scan my data sheet to make sure I had recorded all the salient information, time would have slowed down. I could begin to feel like maybe my presence here was not an abrupt intrusion but something closer to belonging.

The great beauty of working on an ecological land classification was that it required constant study and consideration of the lay of the land, its vegetation patterns, slope aspect, and elevation, and from those things determining how each piece of that ecological mosaic had been formed, and what that might mean to the animals whose lives we were trying to decipher.

Learning to see landscape through the ecological processes that shape it and the patterns that result was a gift I valued all my life. Unlike so much science that deals with bits of the natural world in isolation from one another, this work was about integrating them. It brought me into a much more intimate relationship to places I had always thought I knew well, but hadn't.

But it wasn't really enough.

The late Narcisse Blood, a respected Kainai Elder and teacher, used to say, "It's not enough to recognize the landscape; does the landscape recognize you?"

My years of off-trail travel and landscape study came to feel as much like a spiritual as a scientific endeavour. I was seeking a deeper way of belonging. And, certainly, by the time our fieldwork ended, not in Jasper but in Mount Revelstoke and Glacier national parks, I'd come a long ways closer to that goal than I might have ever once imagined as a young birdwatcher.

But I still wonder if those landscapes recognize me. I suspect not. Like so many others who interact with these ancient landscapes we so recently colonized with the smug certainties of Western science, I can't help feeling I took much of my knowledge. It was not given. My gratitude, although deep, is seasoned with chagrin.

7. Lines and Limits

With the end of our Banff-Jasper wildlife inventory fieldwork in 1981, I moved to Banff to help Geoff with the data analysis and report writing. Geoff and Liz had split up, and he had bought a small bungalow in Canmore. I decided to rent a room from him; that way I had a place to live, he could pay down his mortgage a bit, and we could commute to work together. The privacy and solitude to which I'd become accustomed weren't on offer in this new arrangement.

As compensation, I went for frequent hikes on the forested benches along the north side of the valley. It was wild, undeveloped countryside of the sort I'd now learned to recognize as critical wildlife habitat, similar to the south-facing slopes along Jasper's Athabasca River valley. Elk, deer, and bighorn sheep droppings were everywhere, evidence they congregated on those sun-exposed slopes in winter when the rest of the mountain landscape was deep in snow. Narrow ridges separated narrow gullies that had evidently been cut by runoff when the big valley glaciers were melting back a few centuries earlier. Dense, tangled spruce woods crowded the shaded bottoms of the draws, aspen thickets covered some of the slopes, and ancient Douglas firs were arrayed along the ridge tops. Some of the slopes were covered with bearberry and juniper, and others had carpets of native grassland. It was a rich, living mosaic, 12,000 years in the making. Only a few Rocky Mountain valleys hold such wealth because it's only in the lowest-elevation gaps out into the foothills that the combination of summer heat, winter wind, and complex landforms can generate the kind of habitat complexity I found here.

Home life might have become a bit claustrophobic, but the wild lower slopes of the Fairholme Range north of the highway were the consolation prize. This was good country.

But much to my consternation, I had barely begun to explore this new paradise when I started finding survey stakes marking out future roads and lots. Developers had persuaded the town to let them develop and sell view lots outside the town core. The fact that some viewed such a pristine part of the landscape simply as undeveloped real estate shocked my conscience, as did the fact that others gave themselves authority to allow it. There was something fundamentally wrong here. I needed to figure it out.

***

The problem seemed to lie with our collective understanding of the land itself, and our relationship to it. The decision to develop so vital a part of the mountain landscape seemed to suggest that governments and communities were either incapable of seeing the intrinsic values of the land they occupied, or incapable of caring.

Sitting among the windflowers and grasses up above the valley, I could see patterns that nature had etched into the landscape, overlaid with newer patterns imposed by human decisions. The natural patterns had organic lines and sinuousities: cirques carved out by long-gone alpine glaciers between the limestone ramparts of Mount Rundle; forest-clad terraces and slopes along the mountain bases; the winding path of the Bow River amid a floodplain of curving oxbows full of balsam poplar and narrow, willow-filled wetlands. The human patterns were more linear: the railway line and highway; the gridwork of roads where the original town had been carved into the river floodplain; a cemetery with lines of headstones marking the resting places of miners whose spoil piles and adits were still visible across the way.

I recognized those natural patterns because we had just spent several years mapping and classifying them in Banff and Jasper. We had created static maps to portray ecological complexity, based on what I was already beginning to see as a set of flawed concepts about the workings of the world.

Our ecological land classification divided the landscape into discrete ecotypes that were derived from its most enduring elements: landform and climate. The climate divisions by which that classification delineated the landscape were the montane, subalpine, and alpine. Each of those climatic zones was separated by elevation; the montane ended at a certain elevation above which all was subalpine, and the subalpine ended at the last trees, where the alpine began. It was a given, in our understanding at the time, that those elevation boundaries were static.

Climate, however, is not static. That should have been obvious, given that we knew the whole Rocky Mountain region had been awash in glacier ice barely 12,000 years previously, and that a smaller glacial episode called the Little Ice Age had reached its peak only a few hundred years ago. The patterns we were seeing had all emerged in recent millennia from processes of climate change that were still underway. Any classification based on climate was going to have a limited shelf life.

The other flaw in our approach was based on a deliberate discounting of the natural ecological processes that continually shape and reshape natural communities in the real world. Our ecosites were described in terms of their "normal" vegetation cover – not what was actually there. On our working maps we used modifiers like B, for burned, or A, for avalanched, almost apologetically, to account for ecosites where the vegetation refused to follow the rules. But fires, avalanches, wind events, insect outbreaks, and episodes of intense grazing by hoofed animals, hares, or rodents are all part of how the world actually works. The patterns that emerge in the land are as much a product of those ephemeral changes as they are of longer-term interactions between climate and physical geology.

In order to give park planners the kind of maps and land classification they felt they needed, we had dumbed down nature. To some degree, that meant we'd dumbed down ourselves. In so doing, we were travelling a well-worn road in Western science; half a century earlier, pioneer ecologist Aldo Leopold had written:

"Education, I fear, is learning to see one thing by going blind to another."

The ecological land classification was meant to derive from the science of ecology. That science, however, is a product of the kind of structured, rational thought that seeks to understand the world by disintegrating its parts and studying them in isolation from one another. Like other sciences, ecology strives to identify simple rules that discount complexity and render nature predictable. Ecology might be the science of relationships, but it is still part of that bigger body of rational, objective science that demands of its practitioners ways of thought that isolate and simplify. We were doing the best we could with our project, but a shoehorn can only get you so far when the foot doesn't fit the shoe.

***

The gridwork carved into the valley was the product of another approach to landscape classification – one that delineates private property from public land and overlays various land use zones on both. Now that I had learned to see the mountain landscape as a living mosaic of unique but connected ecosites, the geometrical lines and patterns spread out along the floor and lower slopes of the Bow valley seemed jarringly strange. They bore no relationship to the actual nature of the place.

It was in contemplating that disharmony – one in which I and so many others lived our daily lives as if these patterns were the normal way of the world – that I began to think about how our cultural perception of landscape flows from the same structured rationality that imposes order on complexity. In planning for the rational and equitable use of a colonized land, planning authorities arbitrarily fill it with boundaries separating parks and multiple-use lands, towns and commons, urban and rural. The boundaries and the resulting pattern have nothing to do with the intrinsic nature of place and everything to do with competing economic interests. Those with the most economic power (and hence the best ability to hire lawyers and lobbyists, and to hog

headlines) get the biggest share of the pie. Those with the least –
for instance, Indigenous Peoples who have occupied the land
longest – get the least. And the rest of nature is an afterthought.
Environmental groups might negotiate for nature, but they do so
at a disadvantage in that the debate is always framed as an economic argument. Not only is emotional connection discounted;
it's often mocked.

I was beginning to suspect that we who feel consoled by the
existence of protected parks like Banff were tacitly conceding the
flawed underlying assumption: that landscape can legitimately
be subdivided and classified around a subset of human interests
without anything of intrinsic value being lost. Another underlying
assumption, never seriously questioned, is that humans need only
negotiate with other humans when deciding the future of land that
sustains countless other species – because we are the only species
that really matters.

***

Geoff's little bungalow was beside the old Banff highway at the
edge of Canmore, a town teetering on the cusp of change. The last
coal mine in the Bow valley had closed in 1979, leaving 120 miners
unemployed and their town hollowed out. South of the highway,
Canmore was a mosaic of vacant lots, old coalminers' homes, and
new condominiums. The population was a mixture of unemployed
and retired coal miners, national park employees, and real estate
speculators.

In 1981, following an aggressive lobbying effort led by the
Calgary Olympic Development Association (CODA), Canada had
won approval to host the 1988 winter games. Partly to assuage
concerns of environmental groups who didn't want new facilities
built inside Banff National Park and partly, no doubt, to address
the economic malaise that had fallen over the Bow valley after the
Canmore mine closed, Canmore was chosen for the site of new
cross-country ski facilities. When I moved in with Geoff, developers were already carving ski runs out of Mount Allan, a few

miles away. Everyone's home had suddenly become an investment. Undeveloped land had become real estate. Prosperity beckoned.

One September day, Gail and I hiked up onto those slopes to watch autumn blaze across the valley. We saw an eagle, seven mule deer, a herd of bighorn sheep, two horseback riders, and large newly bulldozed swaths winding into the woods. More survey markers spread beyond the broken soil into the forest; it was the beginning of a housing subdivision. A sign announced that the new subdivision's name would be Elk Run. That seemed sadly appropriate.

Our pleasure in an otherwise lovely day was dampened by the sight of those fresh bulldozer scars on land that had been undisturbed since the glaciers retreated thousands of years earlier, and of new survey stakes piled next to piles of old deer droppings. We both felt we were witnessing the marks of abuse in the piles of shattered soil burying the crocuses, rose tangles, wildlife winter range, and scenery. Shouldn't such violence be reserved only as a last resort?

When I complained about the destruction to a passionate local conservationist who had fought long and hard to limit development in Banff National Park, however, his response was even more unsettling: "Well, I find it hard to get too upset about it. For one thing, it's not in the park. For another thing, it *is* zoned for municipal development."

The crocuses, bighorn sheep, squirrels, and trees had no say in how that land was zoned; this was simply where they lived. Nobody had consulted the Stoney Nakoda about what part of their culture and memory might be erased in this new race to cash in on Olympics gold. The land was being treated as just dirt and scenic views, not as a living place worthy of respect and restraint.

While reflecting on the underlying meaning of my friend's response, I finally began to realize the degree to which our national parks, wilderness areas, and other protected areas have failed in what should be their fundamental mission: drawing us into a more thoughtful and respectful relationship with nature. For some of us, arguably, they do. But for the most part they fail to teach visitors anything at all. People take photos, enjoy the change of scenery, and then go home unchanged. Those parks rarely persuade anyone that land should be used frugally, with humility and respect. Instead, they offer the false comfort of an approach to conservation that consists mostly of trading a few protected areas in exchange for what we believe is a God-given right to abuse all other land.

For all their value in keeping some land intact, parks are also a symptom of the deeper problem to which well-meaning conservationists have yet to find a solution – our culture's narcissistic compulsion to treat all our relations as inferior and subordinate to us.

***

In 1949 the American conservationist Aldo Leopold published his now-famous argument for the development of a land ethic. He said that we are all members of the biotic community. As such, we should afford to the land the same ethical responsibility and restraint with which we strive to treat our fellow man. He argued that a sense of stewardship, or husbandry, should guide land use decisions – not a self-serving belief in our dominion over all of nature.

In the decades since Leopold's *A Sand County Almanac* was published to earnest acclaim from the conservationists of his day, land use decisions have only become more challenging in a world that has become busier, more urbanized, and more disconnected and distracted from land and the beings with whom we share it. Those decisions may now often be washed with green, but they are rarely informed by a spirit of humility or ethical restraint. Against the complex realities of a shrinking world, growing populations, increasing technology, and spreading urbanization, it's become too easy for those who care about land to taste despair and adopt a kind of siege mentality. This is not the world Aldo Leopold hoped for. It certainly bears increasingly little resemblance to the world the Indigenous signatories to Treaties 6 and 7 agreed to share with newcomer peoples. And by virtually every measure of its ecological vital signs, it's not one that can be sustained.

For most of my lifetime, conservationists have waged a series of staged retreats, trying to establish protected areas in a growing sea of commodification and land exploitation. If we cannot treat all land responsibly, this point of view argues, let's at least settle for protecting some patches from those who would despoil them.

Right from the beginning of Europeans' occupation of North America, concern for the nature of the place took two diverging paths. Both were flawed in that they assumed North American ecosystems to be pristine wilderness, untouched by people. In truth, most of the continent was a mosaic of cultural landscapes shaped by the fire, farming, hunting, and other activities of many dozens of Indigenous cultures. The newcomer people formed their views of the place based on both a Eurocentric, progressivist view of human history and on a kind of breathless sentimentalism that arose from seeing the beauty of unpeopled landscapes. And a lot of the landscape was unpeopled; even before the American government's genocidal slaughters of Indigenous Peoples, novel new diseases like tuberculosis, diphtheria, smallpox, measles, and influenza had swept ahead of the colonists, killing whole villages and tribes of people who had never had the chance to develop immunities.

Those concerned about the rapid pace of landscape conversion pursued either an idealistic approach to preserving representative pieces of the landscape before they could be lost, or a more pragmatic approach of trying to conserve native plants and animals while still exploiting them as resources.

There was merit in both approaches. But conservation is a moving target, too often compromised as corporations identify new resources to exploit, land changes hands, or the latest panic – be it drought, flooding, economic collapse, or pandemic – resets social priorities. As the decades passed, the arguments of the preservationists became more compelling and more urgent. Whole landscapes were changing and whole ecosystems degrading. At least the preserved bits might survive, as long as there were laws protecting them. And since those places drew growing numbers of visitors hoping to connect with wild nature, they also had clearly defined constituencies of support. They didn't require as much thought and negotiation as more hands-on approaches to conservation did, and consequently were less dependent on the complicated task of building and sustaining ecological literacy in surrounding communities.

By the end of the 20th century, however, it had become clear that there was a dark side to the whole approach of preserving pockets of nature rather than learning to cherish and conserve it everywhere. Those protected places became sanctified in the minds of their promoters or visitors. They were seen as fragile, vulnerable to the vulgar and inevitably destructive hand of man. As such, nature in protected areas came to be valued more highly than nature outside of them.

But it's all the same nature. We are the ones drawing the lines, and we do so without consultation with or consent from all the other beings who have to live with the consequences.

In a national park one is not allowed to pick a flower. One is discouraged from – and could be fined for – eating a berry. One must stay on the trail. The many shalt-nots are understandable because of the popularity of parks and protected areas. Parks staff speak of the danger of loving a park to death. Five hundred people a day can trample a mountain meadow to mud in a week.

But the unfortunate corollary of these restrictions is that they perpetuate the myth that humans and nature are not the same thing. In that sense, national parks do not bring people into a deeper relationship with nature; on the contrary, their experiences there too often reinforce the idea that they are outsiders. By extension, park visitors are encouraged to believe that outside the parks, in those unfortunate places that do not enjoy protection from the inevitably destructive choices of us outsiders, nature must be – at least to some degree – written off. Destructive development? Irresponsible land use? Thank God at least we have our national parks.

***

112   Lines and Limits

The irony of this paradox was revealed in the tradeoffs park advocates proved willing to accept to save Banff National Park from the Olympics.

The Calgary Olympic Development Association campaigned aggressively, and successfully, to have the International Olympic Commission (IOC) designate Calgary as the site of the 1988 Winter Olympics. A keystone of CODA's bid was Mount Sparrowhawk, south of Canmore. The Olympic promoters touted the windswept mountain as the ideal race site for the Men's Downhill skiing event, but no sooner had the IOC approved Calgary's bid than disturbing rumours began to appear in the press. Nancy Greene Raine stated that Sparrowhawk was the wrong choice. Others said it would not hold snow. The mutter of rumours swelled. Lobbyists suggested other choices. Two years later, the Alberta government announced its final site selection: Mount Allan, a few miles east, would be the Olympic ski area.

Mount Allan differs from Mount Sparrowhawk in having less snow-holding ability, little suitable racing terrain, and serving as the core winter range for what was, at the time, one of the world's largest and healthiest herds of bighorn sheep.

Sixty kilometres west, in Banff National Park, the sprawling downhill ski complex of Lake Louise had been the subject of repeated controversy and a stormy series of public hearings in 1972 when Parks Canada and Imperial Oil Ltd. jointly proposed a major expansion. Ever since public opinion saved the Lake Louise area from Imperial Oil (but not from Parks Canada, which incrementally developed much of the area anyway), environmental organizations had kept a watchful eye on the area.

With the first suggestion that Mount Sparrowhawk might be unacceptable, the watchdog organizations pricked up their ears. Might this actually be part of a conspiracy to expand Lake Louise? Perhaps CODA intended to use Lake Louise all along and had merely used the Sparrowhawk option, outside the national park, to win the IOC's approval. The government's subsequent selection of Mount Allan, an obviously unsuitable mountain, only served to deepen suspicions that some sort of bait-and-switch was in play.

CODA denied the rumours but, just in case, the environmental groups doubled down on their advocacy efforts to keep those ski races out of their national park.

The Lake Louise ski hill had been in existence for many years already, and had almost doubled in size since 1972. In spite of the National Parks Act, the area was far from unspoiled. The deep snow country of the central Rockies, where it's located, is too far west to sustain wintering populations of elk or bighorn sheep. It already had parking facilities and other infrastructure.

It might have been argued that holding the Men's Downhill at Lake Louise would be unlikely to further degrade so heavily developed an area. It might also have been argued that the undisturbed slopes of Mount Allan had higher and better uses than ski development. It certainly should have been argued that an ethical attitude to all land would favour the concentration of facilities, as much as possible, in areas already developed.

Those points might have been argued, but they were not. Lake Louise was in a national park. Mount Allan was not. National parks are sacrosanct. We could sacrifice Mount Allan.

The fate that befell Mount Allan was the final straw in convincing me that parks advocates – of whom I was, and remain, one – betray ourselves when we default to easy either/or decisions and are willing to look away from damage so long as it lies on the right side of those arbitrary boundaries. In doing so, we choose a simple, rational approach to conservation that too often ends up working against itself. It's too easy to delude ourselves by drawing lines on maps – zoning one area for preservation, another for development, another for exploitation – in the increasingly futile hope of sustaining a living world that has no boundaries, and whose values are not solely ours to determine.

**

There is no easy solution to the conservation conundrum. The problem with most solutions is that they are rooted in the same Western rational world view that sets humanity apart from the rest of nature, that sees land as property, and that believes economic and social well-being can only be attained by carving nature into bundles of resources, assigning ownership, and trading them in the commercial marketplace. It's not realistic to assume that any institution rooted in the same ways of thinking as the problems it purports to solve can deliver a real solution, because it will always fall short of challenging that system of thought, and will inevitably find itself pulled back to the centre of gravity. George Orwell's *Animal Farm* is just one illustration of how reforms and revolutions fail when they leave basic cultural paradigms intact.

Even so, in spite of being the products of a fundamentally flawed system of thought, parks and protected areas remain vital institutions in a world where almost nine billion people continue to take more than the world can spare, to the point where biodiversity is threatened and even the oceans and atmosphere have become unhinged.

In our best blundering way, we continue to refine and improve our management of those spaces – renewing natural processes like fire and flood, protecting at-risk species and restoring those that have been lost, and providing spaces for study, contemplation, and spiritual renewal. For all my personal ambivalence about national and provincial parks, after all, I spent an entire career working in and learning from them. If I am ambivalent about the conservation value of protected spaces, that's in large part because during my years in those places I learned to see more clearly and care more deeply than might have been the case otherwise. So it's not that protected areas don't have social and ecological value; it's that they haven't stopped us from making a mess of everything else.

If this were a perfect world, and most humans viewed ourselves as one with the living world, we would not need national parks. The very notion of national parks would seem absurd.

However, this is not a perfect world. In too many cases we have chosen to make it a world where setting aside national parks and protected areas substitutes for ethical restraint, right relations, and hard choices. We have traded our responsibility towards our fellow creatures and the lands and waters we share for a few small museum pieces that must always remain more a symptom of our affliction than a cure for our ills.

But what an awful world it would be without them.

***

So it became an exercise in applied cognitive dissonance when, two decades later in 2005, I became a park superintendent, charged with managing pieces of lands whose boundaries made no sense either to the other beings that occupy them or to the Indigenous Peoples whose cultures continue to be rooted there. It was a job that made me responsible for protecting nature but also for maintaining the economic argument for the existence of those parks, most of which hangs on recreation and tourism. In order to function effectively, I was required constantly to suppress the knowledge that I didn't fully believe in the basic paradigm that made my job possible and framed my duties.

I saw parks, on the one hand, as pragmatic compromises that at least offer nature an insurance policy of sorts against the grievous errors our culture continues to make everywhere. But on the other hand, I saw them as a symptom of the problem, almost a sort of cultural greenwashing that enables and excuses the destruction of nature. Sometimes I felt like a stranger in my own home, or some kind of double agent determined to find ways for parks to do what they really need to do, rather than what the status quo would have them do. I spent more than a few nights lying on my back, staring at a darkened ceiling, trying to reconcile the conflicts that confounded me each day upon awakening into a flawed and failing world.

It was a dilemma compounded by the fact that, having been formed inside the same cultural ways of knowing, I could not help but be part of the problem too.

8. Rivers

The quiet eddy where we had pulled out at the end of our first day floating the Oldman River was grey and glassy in the fading light of a July evening. It was the summer of 1982. There had been rain while Gail and I cooked dinner over our little pack stove, huddled in the shelter of a blue nylon fly we'd rigged to the wolf willow bushes beside our little backpacking tent, but now the clouds were breaking up and the evening had a sweet, clean smell to it. The sun had emerged into a thin gap of clear sky just above the Livingstone Range to the west, and its last light bathed the nearby flanks of the Porcupine Hills in a brilliant green-gold glow. Robin song and stillness; time felt suspended.

Just where the eddy line began at the point of a cobbly river bar, a fish was rising. Given the inevitable midday heat of a summer float trip in my aluminum canoe, we hadn't packed anything that would spoil, so protein didn't figure prominently in the menu for our four-day float trip. Trout would taste good. I rigged up my fly rod, tied on a muddler minnow that looked, at least to my eyes, like one of the many grasshoppers we'd been seeing during our stops to explore the foothills fescue grasslands that surrounded the river. I cast it gently into the current line where the fish was rising.

On my second cast the fly vanished into an oily swirl. I lifted the rod to set the hook. The fish on the other end felt unexpectedly powerful as it surged into the main current and ran downstream into heavy water, pulling line off the reel. In the ensuing tug of war it never broke the surface once, but when I finally managed to draw it into the shallows my hands began to shake. Shimmering beneath the water-glisten, tired but still resisting stubbornly, it seemed impossibly big for so small a river. When it turned towards the shore briefly, I backed up, sliding it swiftly up onto the wet grass before dropping my rod and pouncing on it before it could flop its way back into the water.

Later, when we knocked on the door of our hosts for the evening, Joe Thibert declared that it was the biggest fish he'd ever seen caught along their stretch of river. A rainbow trout 53 centimetres long was too much fish for Gail and me to consume, so we offered it to Joe and Rosella. They were happy to accept it.

***

Rosella had been raised on a lonely cattle ranch farther upstream in what they called the North Fork country. Joe was born in 1904 on a homestead on Todd Creek, northwest of Cowley. Joe and Rosella still spoke French with each other and English to most everyone else. Joe's parents, like other families who had settled French Flats early in the 20th century, had come west from Quebec to try their fortunes in what to them was an empty frontier full of possibilities. Now, in 1982, Joe was well into his seventies. Although he and Rosella were still ranching their lonely little corner of the North Fork country, they had help from a young Québecoise who boarded on the place with them.

The trout safely stashed in their icebox, we sat at the kitchen table and drank coffee with our kindly hosts as fly-specked windows dimmed and the world outside went secret. Rosella told us childhood memories from when the range was still largely unfenced and travel was still by horse. There was lots of work and few people to help with it. The Blackfoot and Stoney Peoples still travelled the old trails and were often hired out to build fences or do other work. She recollected how the door would sometimes open and three or four tall Indigenous men would step in, make themselves comfortable around the table, and help themselves to whatever food was on hand. When we commented on how disconcerting that must have been, she said, no, it was just the way things were.

***

Joe's city-raised mom had been less sanguine about her neighbours; one day when she was home alone at their Todd Creek homestead with her infant son, a Piikani man had arrived with an axe over his shoulder. He hoped to sharpen it on her husband's grindstone, being well acquainted with him from work they had done together. Unlike her husband, she had been raised in a small Quebec city where Indigenous Peoples were usually portrayed as savages in the stories she heard. She saw the axe and, assuming the worst, barricaded the door with table and chairs and hid with little Joe until the uninvited visitor gave up and left. A dull axe can be a dangerous thing; if he had hurt himself with it later, her fears would have been partly to blame.

Rosella remembered that country, and the Indigenous Peoples who still traversed it freely then, in a different way. "It was hard sometimes. You never locked your door and you always shared what you had. Everybody had to help each other. That's how people lived."

The stories Joe and Rosella told us went back nearly a century, to a time before good roads. We listened half in gratitude and half in envy, wistful for the places and ways of being we imagined through their words. For me, it felt a bit like when I'd sat at my parents' kitchen table a decade and a half earlier, lost in the mystery and adventure that my truculent grandfather's Irish voice inspired, as he reminisced about hunting and fishing in what I felt then must have been the good old days – days I had missed through having been born too late.

Later, in the dark, we picked our stumbling way back by flashlight to our tent and curled up together while the river whispered past.

The morning dawned cool, everything wet to the touch in the silver light. The world smelled of wet grass and, when the roar of our pack stove finally went silent, fresh coffee. And the sweet exhalations of an ancient stream: Napi's river, the Old Man. In

Siksikaitsitapi stories, Napi is the first man, a troublemaker whose judgment often can't be trusted; he has his own ways of doing things and when he involves himself in the affairs of people the outcomes aren't always what they might have hoped for. I try to imagine him, and what I see is my grandfather: that twinkle in his eyes, the pain behind them, the impatient humour; the easily awakened need to take himself somewhere else, away from pesky people.

***

Farewells said, we slid the canoe out into the current and were adrift again, slipping past cottonwood groves and under banded cliffs of eroding sandstone. We didn't know where to look or how to see, but if we had we might have seen dinosaur bones embedded in those sandstone cliffs, and would certainly have seen the skulls and femurs of bison in the rubble at their bases, remnants of long-forgotten hunts. There were stories here much older than those we'd heard the evening before, but we had no way of hearing them.

And we, of course, were creating new stories of our own.

The river carried us around one mysterious curve to another. Sometimes the bend might reveal a barn, a house, some sheds, and machinery. The next stretch would offer views of a long, flat field of green alfalfa and golden grass behind the trees, waiting for the haying equipment to arrive. Mostly, we saw groves of black cottonwood, cobble bars covered with sandbar willow, and pale sandstone cliffs topped with Douglas fir and limber pine. Once or twice we saw dust plumes above the valley rim, hinting of roads and traffic in that other world up there, but the river bluffs, for the most part, kept the river valley a place where wildness and isolation lingered on beneath that settled and well-used landscape.

People should help each other, Rosella had said. We were there because we wanted to help the river and the people who loved it in its natural state. When I had told my friend Cliff Wallis that I intended to do this trip in order to write a story about a dam that was proposed for the valley, I said I had no idea how to start. Cliff gave me Mike Cooper's contact information. The interviews I had lined up came about because Mike Cooper had helped me.

Mike Cooper and some of his neighbours had formed a small, and largely ineffective, lobby group called the Committee for the Preservation of the Three Rivers. Mike had political experience – he had run as a candidate in the previous provincial election, motivated largely by the dam proposal – but the insistence by its members that his committee be comprised only of local landowners wasn't smart politics. Then, as now, conservative politicians took rural votes and rural voters for granted. For a government based in faraway Edmonton, a few disenchanted locals in a thinly populated rural corner of the province were easy to ignore. Those dam opponents needed more friends; I hoped to gain them a few.

***

Almost all of prairie Canada's water comes from the Rocky Mountains and is carried down to farms and communities by rivers that originate in groundwater springs up where the elk, bighorn sheep, and grizzly bears live. Each year's winter snowpack and spring rain generates that groundwater; from April through June the melting snow and spring showers soak into forest soils and fill the hidden aquifers beneath them. There it seeps through buried gravels and cracks in bedrock until it emerges, sometimes weeks or even months later, in springs and seeps or as base flow that emerges right into the beds of creeks.

I didn't fully understand this concept when Gail and I did that first float of the Oldman, but I had often been bemused, while following streams down out of the mountains, by the way they seemed to get bigger even when there were apparently no tributary streams to add water. They were, indeed, getting bigger – because of that unseen base flow emerging from the earth into the stream bed. Filtered and cooled in the subterranean stillness of that hidden world beneath the trees, groundwater doesn't just keep those streams filled with fresh filtered water during the dry season; it keeps them cold enough for trout and other aquatic life.

North of the Oldman watershed, Alberta rivers get a summer subsidy in the form of meltwater from glaciers. There may be little snow left to melt by late July and August, and less frequent rains, but the same hot weather that drives our need for summer water has the benefit of melting the ancient ice that lingers in shaded mountain valleys at the head of the Bow, Red Deer, North Saskatchewan, and Athabasca Rivers. The silt ground out of rock from those slow-moving masses of ice might cloud the water there, making it less appealing than the crystal-clear streams farther south, but it's still a fortuitous arrangement that supplements the river base flows and keeps them flowing strong even during dry spells.

That's not, however, the case with the Oldman. The Oldman depends completely on groundwater recharge from contemporary precipitation. Its headwater glaciers melted away centuries ago because of the relatively low elevation of the mountains and the generally warmer climate of the river's southern location. All the water on which we floated came from last winter's snows and the early spring rains.

Precipitation varies a lot from year to year; sometimes the river is richly served and other times it shrinks and dwindles because of drought. The flow that swept Gail and me along through the foothills landscape was strong, but if we'd tried the float five years earlier, we'd probably have had to wade and pull the canoe for much of the distance. The Oldman's 1977 flow had been the lowest ever documented, a consequence of thin winter snow cover and thirsty soils that soaked up what little rain fell that year. It was just a one-year drought, but its regional impact was big: over $100 million in lost hydroelectric power, another $20 million in unanticipated firefighting costs, $10 million in drought relief programs and to address depleted irrigation water storage reservoirs. The panic resulting from that 1977 drought had inspired downstream farmers to demand that the government build a water storage dam and end their water insecurity. The clock was ticking on a final decision on the river's fate.

There were three dam sites under consideration. Each had pros and cons, supporters and opponents. In 1978, recognizing that any final decision would prove controversial, the government had commissioned the arms-length Environment Council of Alberta (ECA) to objectively evaluate the sites, consult the public, and report back with a recommendation as to where to build a dam that would bring the Oldman River's flows under control. The government wasn't interested in hearing about the option preferred by local ranchers, the Piikani, and most Alberta environmentalists and biologists: no dam at all.

The final 1979 ECA report didn't help the government avoid controversy – just the opposite. After reviewing the engineering studies already completed and consulting intensively with the public, the ECA concluded that "an on-stream dam is not required at this time nor in the foreseeable future." Acknowledging that the government might choose to proceed with a dam in spite of this advice, the authors advised that the least worst sites would be near Fort Macleod or on the Piikani Reserve near Brocket. The worst would be the Three Rivers site, just downstream from where the Crowsnest and the Castle Rivers joined the Oldman. A dam there, they concluded, would have the greatest environmental and social impact while offering no appreciable cost or engineering advantage over the site near Brocket.

Unfortunately, the old-boy water engineers in the provincial bureaucracy saw things differently. In their confident world of Christian dominion and cold science, water not put to work was wasted. They saw northern Canada as having an excess of water flowing in the wrong direction: to the Arctic, where there were no crops to irrigate. That's why Edmonton's water establishment were true believers in the North American Water and Power Alliance (NAWAPA) and its Canadian mini-me: the Prairie Rivers Improvement, Management, and Evaluation (PRIME) scheme. Both plans called for building a network of dams and canals to divert the wasted flows of the Peace and Athabasca Rivers south to the dry plains of prairie Canada and the western US. The plan was all mapped out on their office walls. One of the key links was a dam at the Three Rivers site.

To say that the water engineers were unhappy with the ECA recommendations would be putting it mildly. But with memories of the 1977 drought still fresh, and serving a government that needed to solidify its political support in irrigation country, those water engineers knew they could win this one. They just needed another drought.

In August 1980 the Alberta government announced it would be proceeding with the construction of a dam across the Oldman River. The final location would depend on whether the Piikani offered an acceptable deal for a dam on their reserve near Brocket. Failing that, regardless of anything the ECA might have said, it would be built at the Three Rivers site.

In retrospect, it should have been pretty clear to an idealistic young writer that an eleventh-hour magazine article intended to mobilize public opposition to a river-choking dam was doomed to failure. Given that Alberta's last major free-flowing river was at stake, however, there really seemed no option but to try.

A few hours after launching into the river current at the Thiberts' lonely ranch, Gail and I found ourselves floating around a bend into a steep-walled foothills canyon. Eroded boulders from the canyon walls turned the river's flow into a series of rapids, eddies, and occasional big holes. We were kept too busy manoeuvring through the boulder gardens to take much note of our surroundings, until we finally swung around a long bend and the canyon walls grew lower. Cattle watched us sombrely from the shade of a sun-dappled cottonwood forest as we drifted the long sweep around that final entrenched oxbow and bobbed past the last big rapid beside the Brockwell ranch buildings. We had no way of imagining that the land inside that curve, a decade later, would become our home place.

A short way downstream we entered the reach that would be flooded if the Three Rivers dam actually got built. It seemed impossible that anyone who had ever seen this valley could contemplate such an act of terminal violence. Maybe the water engineers hadn't. Maybe they didn't have hearts, or souls. There had to be some explanation.

A house, barn, and outbuildings appeared on the right bank, sheltered by big Douglas firs and groves of black cottonwood. Just past the yard we could see the dancing water of another river coursing out of a shallow valley that receded back into the foothills to the west. This was the Crowsnest River, a fabled trout stream sparkling in the late afternoon sun as it raced to merge its waters with those of the river upon which we'd spent the day floating. We eddied out behind a rock spur and pulled the canoe up, stretching the stiffness out of our legs, ready for another interview.

This was the home of Reno and Corine Welsch, another multi-generational ranching family for whom fortune and fate had ordained that they would get to live out their lives in one of the windiest and most beautiful corners of foothills Alberta. They were friendly, soft-spoken people who welcomed us into their kitchen and besieged us with baking as they talked about the shock of learning their whole valley was likely to be flooded, and the disruption it was causing to their life there. Like many rural Albertans, they were live-and-let-live folks; they didn't feel comfortable expressing strong emotions, especially about political matters. Instead, they talked about their memories of the place, their neighbours, the way they felt about working hard and taking pride in that work. Corine's voice, however, betrayed the depth of her concern when she said, "I don't know. It's really time we painted that barn, but maybe it's not worth the bother. You just don't really know what to do. It's just waiting."

I said, "It's got to be hard. I imagine this government won't be getting your votes anymore."

Reno looked startled, as if I'd just suggested the sky was actually orange. "Oh," he said, "I wouldn't say that. We've always voted conservative. I don't see that changing."

The year after our float, the Piikani government announced it was willing to have the dam built on its reserve near Brocket, while also making it clear it would have to be co-owners of the dam and share in its benefits. The government water managers, however, were in the business of taking from First Nations, not giving back. The Brocket dam wasn't going to happen if those were the terms.

The following year, 1984, brought another deep drought. This one was, by some measures, the worst since 1916. The absence of soil moisture was devastating for Porcupine Hills ranchers who had no forage crops that year. Some had no choice but to sell off their cattle herds for lack of feed. But it was the golden moment the water czars had been waiting for. On August 9, after having toured the dried-up farming country near Lethbridge, handing out relief money, Premier Peter Lougheed put an end to uncertainty. Construction of a dam at the Three Rivers site would begin in 1986.

The Welsches didn't paint that barn.

***

The article I wrote after our Oldman River float was printed in *Western Sportsman*, an outdoor magazine published out of Saskatchewan with a wide readership in Alberta's fishing and hunting community. I don't know if reading it influenced many people, but writing it persuaded me that there were matters I simply could not turn my back on if I cared about the places and people who had come to define me. The wrong people kept making the wrong decisions for what they seemed truly to believe were the right reasons. That wouldn't change, in my view, until more grassroots citizens learned about these threatened places and developed the ecological literacy and self-confidence to challenge powerful elites like Alberta's water establishment.

The decision to proceed with damming the Oldman River took most of the wind out of the sails of the Committee for the Preservation of the Three Rivers, but like a phoenix arising out of the ashes a new organizations replaced it. Friends of the Oldman River (FOR) had much wider membership than just the locally affected landowners. Its leaders were two experienced environmental leaders: Martha Kostuch and my old friend Cliff Wallis.

They were able to marshal scientific evidence and legal arguments against the dam decision, and to assemble the financial and human resources to fight it. Two legal challenges by the FOR made it all the way to the Supreme Court of Canada. The courts ruled in its favour both times. The Alberta government shrugged and carried on.

**

Gail and I married soon after that canoe trip. I was working on a wildlife inventory of BC's Mount Revelstoke and Glacier national parks. One day she met me on the driveway of the small A-frame we rented at the eastern entrance to Glacier and announced that our suspicions were correct; she was pregnant. Shortly after, we moved to Edmonton and bought our first home. Corey, the first of three children, was born. I worked 12 to 14 hours a day, racing deadlines for the data analysis and report writing for the wildlife inventories Geoff and I had completed in the mountain national parks over the previous eight years. There wasn't much time or energy left for writing and advocacy work.

The federal election of 1984 brought in a new conservative government impatient to make changes, one of which was to shrink the size and power of the federal government. The entire national parks research unit was disbanded. Gail and I loaded our new baby into the back of our old car and headed back into the mountains where my next job and our next home awaited.

The pace of life became more manageable in Jasper. There was time for family, fishing, and writing again. We had another baby, Katie. In 1987 Gail became pregnant with Brian, our third child. By now the Three Rivers dam was under construction. It felt like just another loss in a world determined to devour itself. With a house filling up with babies there seemed little point in dwelling on a planned disaster taking place so far to the south.

Then one September day I opened the newspaper and read of an organization I'd never heard of before – Friends of the Oldman River – that was taking the government to court for violating its own Water Resource Act in issuing itself a licence to build the dam. I felt a wave of shame; I had given up, but others were fighting on. Not only that but Martha and Cliff were leading this fight while running small businesses, raising families, and coping with bigger personal challenges than I now had to worry about.

Still, my ability to contribute was limited both by our remote location and by my own family responsibilities and introverted nature. It occurred to me that my best way to support those closer to the action might be to use my writing skills to increase public awareness and promote grassroots action. With the consent of *Western Sportsman*'s editor, I made hundreds of photocopies of my Oldman article and began stuffing envelopes, ultimately sending the article and a covering letter to every sporting goods store, outdoors shop, and weekly newspaper in Alberta. I wrote letters to the editors of daily papers, drafted up news articles for other publications, and joined the executives of the Alberta Wilderness Association and the Federation of Alberta Naturalists, where I helped with those organizations' outreach efforts too.

***

Gail describes the autumn of 1987: "I went into the hospital to have a baby and came home to find my husband had gone crazy."

Not totally crazy. There was still time for fishing. With the new addition to our family we needed more space in our rental unit, so I asked the park carpenters to frame in another room in the basement. The space they enclosed initially contained my office and fly-tying bench. One day I got home from work to find a large yellow fly in the vise, with a note beside it: "Pyramid Lake after sunset."

I examined the fly. It was very simple: no hackle, a dubbed yellow body, tail and wings of deer hair. Kind of like a giant mayfly without legs. Curious, I tied another four or five copies of the fly and went upstairs. The kids were in bed and Gail was in the rocking chair that stood across from the crib, nursing the baby with a sleepy, stoned-looking smile. The room smelled of baby powder and love.

I told her I was going out fishing for a while. She nodded contentedly.

Pyramid Lake was glassy-smooth and dark along the shoreline as darkness spilled out from the shadowed forest across the water. It was after 11 when I arrived. There was nobody else in the parking lot, but I could see lights on at the lodge across the lake. A single barn swallow skimmed silently above the lake. The sky was low; cloud continents darkening against that long, lingering glow that follows a northern sunset. Standing by the edge of the beach, I could see a few desultory-looking rises from anonymous fish, but they were well out from the lakeshore. Feeling my way carefully in case of a sudden drop-off, I waded out until the water was nearly to the tops of my chest waders. Out here there was lots of space for casting, so I got a lot of line out and dropped the new fly as far out as I could. It looked like a pom-pom out there; what self-respecting fish would be fooled by something that big and hairy?

An oily bulge, and the fly vanished into the spreading ring of a rise form. I set the hook into something strong. The reel screeched and a moment later a big silver form erupted far out in the lake, slashing back into the water. Then the rod went soft and I started reeling for all I was worth. The fish was almost past me before I got the slack out and felt the pull of its struggle again. Backing carefully to shore as the fish repeatedly ran the line out, I finally managed to slide it out onto the beach. It was a heavy rainbow trout, almost 50 centimetres in length.

As I rinsed the sand off the fish, something brushed my face and then lit for a quivering moment on my wet hand: a pale brown mayfly half the length of my little finger. Crouched there, I could see more of them against the sky. Not many, but enough. Later I learned these were brown drake mayflies, not common in the Rockies, but evidently quite happy to live, reproduce, and feed the trout of Pyramid and other silty-bottomed lakes along the Athabasca valley.

I arrived at work tired a lot that month, because I often fished until well after midnight, reluctant to leave until the last bit of light was gone from the sky. It was spotty fishing – most of the fish fed beyond my reach – but each trout I caught made it worthwhile all over again.

It turned out that the fly I had found in my vise had been tied by one of the carpenters, Ray Magnan, during his lunch break. Ray was a legendary Jasper fly angler; I hadn't realized he worked for the same outfit as I did. As a dedicated devotee of catch-and-release angling, I imagine he might have regretted his generosity if he knew I was one of the old guard who still considered some trout to be food.

The brown drake hatch tailed off after a few more evenings, but the fish still sometimes rose along the lake edge. I would open the stomachs of those I kept and poke through the contents to see what they were eating now that the big flies were done. One morning in late July I got home well after midnight and found that the stomach of the fish I'd caught that night was hard and swollen. I cut it open and a solid mass of carpenter ants spilled out. The fish had gorged itself on the winged ants blundering down out of the sky during their annual mating flight.

The house was silent, everyone asleep. But this was too fascinating not to share. I scooped all the ants into a saucer and left it on the counter for Gail to see in the morning.

I woke up in an empty bed. Gail was already up. Suddenly remembering the ants, it occurred to me that I'd better get downstairs and explain to Gail what they were all about. Gail's a naturalist too; I knew she'd be fascinated.

She met me at the foot of the stairs, eyes blazing. Pointing behind her with a quivering finger, she said, "You get in there, and you clean up that mess!"

Okay, I felt a bit hurt. It wasn't really a mess, after all; I'd left them all neatly piled in a saucer.

Apparently, however, when a trout eats an ant it takes a while before that ant actually dies. The whole kitchen was crawling with half-stunned carpenter ants: curtains, stove, under the fridge, ceiling…There was no leisurely breakfast option for me that day. The kids watched, bemused, as their dad chased ants around the house. There was so much about the grown-up world that didn't make sense to them yet, but this must be normal if Daddy was doing it.

To my relief, Gail was back on speaking terms with me again when I got home from work that afternoon.

In a rare moment of good judgment, I decided not to go fishing that evening.

Anyway, there was a river to save.

***

More than just one river, unfortunately.

By the late 1980s, Alberta was spending oil money like crazy to diversify its economy. One thing the government did was to underwrite the expansion or construction of seven pulp mills and a lumber mill in northern Alberta, all of which were forecast to dump huge amounts of pollution into northern rivers. Meanwhile, in the south we were coming up on ten years of fighting to stop the Three Rivers dam on the Oldman, which was now nearing completion.

By 1986 I was tired of the frustration of watching friends and colleagues forced to fight endlessly for healthy rivers, and unhappy with my own behaviour as the struggles became more desperate. In the face of widespread public disinterest, I was coming increasingly to the view that a big part of the problem was that nobody actually thought about rivers at all – people just took them for granted as conduits to supply water to us and take our pollution away. Those who saw rivers as living beings couldn't get government to listen to them. Our rivers were dying of our society's mindlessness.

It seemed to me that we needed to find some positive energy and a space to hear each other and learn. We needed to move from a reactive stance, after bad decisions had already been taken, to a more proactive one of identifying what we valued about our home rivers, what needed to be fixed, and how we might get there.

I approached Dr. Timothy Pyrch at the University of Calgary Faculty of Continuing Education with a concept and two thousand

132   Rivers

dollars in seed money the Mountain Equipment Co-op (MEC) had generously granted based on a project proposal I had sent it. My idea was to have a conference on Alberta rivers that would put the voices of ordinary people on an equal footing with those of the experts and bureaucrats, who would also be invited – last.

We'd call it "Flowing to the Future." It would be built from the grassroots up, not the bureaucracy down. It took a while to overcome his initial caution at being cold-called by a stranger looking for his institution's support, but once we got past that hurdle Tim proved to be the perfect colleague. He saw the planned rivers conference as a practical application of something he had long advocated: "People's Knowledge."

Once Tim brought the university on board, that institutional support and the MEC money gave the project the wheels it needed. Tim and I began chasing down more partners. Eventually, only the most critical one still evaded us: Alberta Environment. The department responsible for dam building, water management, pollution control, and environmental protection was an old boys' club of smug and cynical senior water bureaucrats led by Deputy Minister Peter Melnychuk.

Melnychuk was a devoted missionary of water engineering. Based on discussions with fish and wildlife people, who almost universally despised him, I knew he was going to be a hard nut to crack. Melnychuk's department viewed any suggestion of grassroots river democracy as a threat to their water engineering kingdom. In fairness, I suppose they were also feeling pretty twitchy after several years of public abuse over the Oldman and the northern pulp mills.

At length, however, Tim and our University of Alberta partner, Dr. Bert Einsiedel, talked the new Minister of Environment Ralph Klein into directing his staff to join the team and help make the conference happen.

The minister is the boss, but that doesn't mean the old boys have to like it. Senior water management staff made it very clear that they were reluctant partners at best and would withdraw their support at the first sign of uppityness from the proletariat. So it came as no surprise when, at the eleventh hour, after the steering committee asked me to present the closing address, Peter Melnychuk insisted through his minions that he see and approve my draft speech. That clearly unethical request was an awkward moment for all of us. The sheer arrogance of a public servant assuming he could limit a Canadian citizen's freedom of speech shows just how unassailable the water establishment felt it was.

Still, we needed Alberta Environment both for its financial commitment and for its participation. Those old boys needed to be there to listen to the people who actually employed them – and to be accountable to those same people.

So I handed over my draft speech. Sure enough, on the very eve of the conference I got a worried call from Tim. Alberta Environment staff were in the parking lot with a big display that they had planned to install, but they weren't allowed to unload it until I made three changes to my speech – deleting references to the Three Rivers dam. Melnychuk would withdraw all support and cancel staff attendance otherwise. Months of planning, speakers already in transit, all the hard work – I said that if three changes were needed, I'd make three changes.

Crisis averted, the conference went on. Piikani Elder Joe Crowshoe travelled up from the Peigan Reserve to open it with a prayer. People came from all over the province to report, from the grassroots, on the condition of their home rivers. Experts gave us background and insights into how land use, dams, and industry affect rivers. Others talked fisheries, Indigenous Rights, etc., etc. Everyone had to listen to each other – often for the first time ever.

A highlight for me was overhearing two Alberta Environment suits in the hallway commenting to one another about what a great idea this kind of conference was. "We should do all our consultation like this," one said to the other as I hurried past.

Yeah, I thought, you should. Then we wouldn't have had to do all the work for you, and in spite of you.

Final day: my closing speech. I was still furious at Melnychuk.

In my day job I, too, was a public servant. His bullying tactic had violated public servant principles that I considered inviolable. I was also frustrated and bruised from the fruitless years so many of us had spent trying to get powerful bureaucrats and hostile government ministers to put the health of rivers and the concerns of ordinary, powerless Albertans at least on par with the powerful vested interests to whom they preferred to pander.

So I made three changes. I deleted three adjectives. Those weren't the changes Melnychuk had prescribed, but I had kept my promise. And then I gave the speech pretty much as originally written. It garnered a standing ovation...mostly. One row of well-fed white men in dark blue suits remained seated, glowering.

We had a second Flowing to the Future conference two years later, this one at the University of Alberta. Ralph Klein (by then the premier) used it to announce Alberta's entry into the Canadian Heritage Rivers Program and nomination of the Clearwater River near Fort McMurray as the province's first heritage river. Alberta Environment was a full participant. There wasn't a whiff of bureaucratic power-mongering.

The conferences might have helped improve official attitudes towards living rivers and the values they bring to the lives of those who live near them. I'd like to hope so. They are pretty much forgotten now.

By then, in any case, the Three Rivers (Oldman) dam was up and operating, all those northern pulp mills were spewing out dioxins and other pollutants into the livers and kidneys of fish and the drinking water of small Cree communities, and coal mines near Hinton were being expanded into the McLeod River headwaters.

At least we had tried and, in doing so, had spoken words that made those rivers more explicitly a part of how both Indigenous Albertans and the more recently arrived people define ourselves. The slogan for both conferences was: "A river is more than just water."

Maybe the fact that ordinary Albertans continue to defend our streams against the powerful, the panderers, and the perverse means that we are finding our collective soul. It was grassroots Albertans who mobilized successfully to save Eastern Slopes creeks and rivers from coal mines in 2021. That win, fragile and incomplete though it might have been, suggests that Albertans have made some progress towards recognizing, and standing up for, that part of our identity that resides in the land, and that lives in the rivers that drain from it. And we did it together. Maybe this is what it means to be Treaty people.

We'll have to save those rivers again. Even with such brief flashes of hope, we remain part of a culture that feels entitled to destroy and devour the best things about itself while remaining blithely confident there will be no consequences.

9. Grey Ghosts

One day in 1983 I walked down the hall at the Northern Forest Research Centre in Edmonton and popped into the coffee room. The coffee room was actually just a small lab with a couple of tables and a coffee maker, but it was a popular spot for my Canadian Wildlife Service colleagues and me to exchange the latest fishing and hunting tales or to discuss our fieldwork.

John Stelfox, a tall, gentlemanly ungulate biologist, was at one table leafing through a book with a couple of other biologists. The book looked like one of the bound theses I'd seen in the library at the University of Alberta, where I went regularly to review scientific literature. As it turned out, that was because it had been produced at the same bindery that did the theses. It was not the product of some keen university student, however; it was the work of a frontier lifetime. John had assembled a collection of essays and memoirs by his father, and paid for a limited-edition printing to distribute to family. He was selling the leftover copies to interested friends.

I bought one and stayed up late that night reading it, fascinated by those older stories of places I had come to think of as my own.

***

I felt like a bit of an imposter when I moved to Edmonton and met the cws old guard. I was the youngest biologist there and painfully aware of having only a bachelor's degree – in botany. Fortunately, hunting offered a comfortable source for coffee conversations that wouldn't completely betray my lack of depth in wildlife biology. I needn't have worried anyway, because John Stelfox, Ed Telfer, and most of the other biologists with whom I now rubbed shoulders were generous, kind souls who went out of their way to welcome me.

Before meeting him, I'd already formed a good impression of John from the reports he had produced in the previous decade when he'd been tasked with helping figure out why caribou numbers were decreasing in Jasper National Park. Park wardens suspected they might be losing out to competition with elk because at the same time as caribou counts were dropping, elk numbers were increasing rapidly. John was tasked with testing out that hypothesis.

He established that there was little or no competition between the two species. Elk and caribou eat different foods and use different parts of the landscape. In winter, elk concentrate in areas where the snow remains shallow – mostly the windswept montane grasslands of the Athabasca River valley and a few isolated backcountry areas in the Front Ranges. Caribou do the opposite: they retreat to subalpine deep-snow country where their large feet and relatively light bodies enable them to travel through drifts that stymie their main winter predator, the wolf. In summer the two species sometimes grazed the same alpine and subalpine meadows, but their diets barely overlapped, and the forage supply was far greater than either species could exhaust.

John wondered if elk were bringing parasites into the caribou ranges, but his analysis of caribou droppings showed no evidence of that, and the few dead caribou he was able to necropsy were in good condition.

Although it wasn't a term that had much mileage on it yet in the 1970s, John offered up another possibility: climate change. He noted that caribou spend a lot of their time in summer bedded on perennial snowfields at high elevations, likely for the cooling effect of the snow and also to escape biting flies. Long-time park wardens told him that those year-round snowdrifts were growing fewer and smaller. In reviewing his paper, I recall being impressed with his willingness to think outside the box, based both on detailed, thoughtful field observations and on listening to others. Unlike ivory tower experts, John had an easy affinity with the park wardens, sharing with them, as he did, a farming background and practical horse sense. He took their experiences and ideas seriously.

Reading the book I'd gotten from John, it soon became clear that his dad, pioneer Alberta conservationist Henry Stelfox, had been a remarkably good soul too.

Henry Stelfox had arrived in Alberta during one of the worst winters in our history – the endless cold and snow of 1906/07 that, by some estimates, killed more than half the cattle in the province. He and his wife eventually settled their family near Rocky Mountain House. He ranched cattle, cut wood, dabbled in real estate, and bought furs.

Henry also believed in public service, but as a civic duty, not as a sinecure. He signed on as the region's game warden and travelled the upper Clearwater River country keeping an eye on wildlife conditions and making sure hunters and anglers stuck to the rules. His work brought him into contact with Cree, Chippewa, and Stoney Peoples who lived in those remote foothills, and he soon became their advocate to Edmonton and Ottawa.

I was startled to read that Henry Stelfox had seen his first caribou near Peppers Creek, a tributary of the Clearwater River. I'd fished there as a kid. It wasn't my idea of caribou country at all. We had driven there on good gravel roads, but back in June 1938, when Stelfox saw his caribou, the only access had been by horse outfit.

"I approached to within sixty yards of them," he wrote. "They were not afraid, they stood facing me, as if to enquire, 'Well, what do you want?' Two of these caribou were magnificent specimens."[5]

By the time his son John began studying caribou decline in Jasper, the species had vanished from that high foothills country. The Forestry Trunk Road (now Highway 40), built in the 1950s to improve fire protection, had made it easier for resource companies to exploit the timber, gas, and other resources of Alberta's foothills region and for hunters to penetrate once-remote game ranges. The newly accessible caribou soon succumbed to overhunting and habitat loss.

Henry Stelfox wrote that caribou also ranged the Bighorn Mountains north of the Blackstone River, the headwaters of Brown and Chungo Creeks, and the Coalspur area. New roads and hunters' guns brought an end to those herds too.

***

It was late June 1978 when I had my first close encounter with a caribou, not far from where John Stelfox had studied them only a few years previously. I had been deposited by helicopter in the headwaters of Simon Creek, a silty glacial stream that drops steeply from its headwater meadows against the Continental Divide to merge with the glacier-fed Whirlpool River. It was my second summer working on Jasper's wildlife inventory.

Stepping around a clump of old fir trees near timberline, I ran right into a yearling caribou. It seemed a goofy-looking animal, homelier than the deer and elk I was more familiar with, and evidently as curious about me as I was about it. It stampeded away with a strange double-jointed trot, then stopped and stared back, its stubbly little tail sticking up in the air. It tested the breeze and, getting no answers there about the identity of this strange two-legged creature, trotted back to about five metres from me and tried again. It walked towards me, walked away, worked its way around as far as it could on either side, ate a couple of mouthfuls of globeflower as if to show it wasn't really worried, and then – having finally caught my scent – headed up the slope and out of sight behind some trees.

A few days later I met another caribou in an isolated valley above the headwaters of the Maligne River. I was camped out alone in a site that gave access to several alpine and timberline habitats that I needed to sample for wildlife use. From my journal:

> I followed the edge of my sedge meadow down to the end, glassing it and the alpine slopes opposite, but seeing nothing. I turned to head back – and there was a caribou moving along the dead centre of the sedge meadow, a couple of hundred yards away, oblivious to me. I'll never know where she came from so suddenly.

She ambled along, eating on the walk except now and then when she'd stop for a second or two to work some little patch of something over more thoroughly. I hurried along behind her, freezing every so often when a ground squirrel would peep at me, and she would stop to look around and listen. With the help of a couple of low rises I got to within about seventy yards of her before she caught sight of me and froze. Her stubby little tail popped up to three-quarters mast like it was pulled by a string.

Like the one I saw last week, she couldn't make up her mind whether to be scared or curious, so she alternated one with the other. She'd trot off a ways, then trot back. Finally, I started on again, diagonally up to my camp and she watched me a bit, then trotted away with that strange, springy floating run that caribou have. Her tail came down pretty soon, though, and when I last saw her, she was eating on the run again.

The following day I hiked out of that emerald-green valley on a deeply worn caribou trail.

By the time our Jasper wildlife inventory ended in 1981, wild caribou and big alpine country had come to define the place for me. Doing my field surveys in remote basins, I would look up and see those grey forms scattered across the meadow flats or up on an open mountainside like remnants of older, wilder times. They were the place personified: the big mountain wilds where memories of the Pleistocene persisted.

But it was ending. After peaking in the late 1950s, caribou numbers had been dropping, to one degree or another, ever since. John Stelfox found no answers to their decline, only hypotheses. My team's work was framed more around counting what was there than interpreting the whys and wherefores, so we did no better. Wes Bradford, the park's wildlife warden, suggested to me during one of our many conversations that the high numbers in the 1950s might have been an artifact – an unnaturally high peak triggered by the province-wide war against rabies in the middle of that decade. By the time that campaign of poisoning, shooting, and targeted trapping wound down, wolves and other carnivores had been virtually eliminated from the Rockies and their foothills. Wes wondered if those predators, as they recovered, were whittling the caribou herds back to their normal status.

It was as good a theory as any, but wrong. Caribou were actually heading towards oblivion.

***

During my spare time, I had begun writing articles for outdoor magazines. Having devoured so many articles by others as part of my own obsession with the outdoors, I was originally motivated simply to tell my own stories from hunting and fishing trips. It wasn't long before spinning memories into tales to offer others a vicarious experience began to lose its appeal. There had to be a better reason for spending time behind a typewriter. I decided to try using my personal anecdotes as the base for more serious expositions about conservation issues, fleshed out with research and subject-expert interviews. I hoped that kind of work might help motivate more readers towards conservation action.

The plight of the caribou seemed like an issue more people should know about. To avoid any potential conflict of interest, I chose to write about the small woodland caribou bands ranging the boreal forests east and north of the national park. Half a century after the herds Henry Stelfox had documented were gone, those other small herds still survived north of the Athabasca River.

One herd – the À la Pêche band – was migratory, summering in the north end of Jasper National Park and the southern Willmore Wilderness Park and then hoofing it east to spend the winter in black spruce bogs and pine forests around the upper Berland and Wildhay Rivers. Other herds were more sedentary and lived year-round in that forested mosaic. One little-known herd occupied the untouched wilderness of the Little Smoky River, a bit farther north.

The provincial biologist responsible for advising government and industry on the management needs of those caribou herds was Jan Edmonds. It felt a bit awkward asking a colleague and friend for an interview, but she was happy to talk. Jan was a small, slightly built woman, and in the 1970s both her stature and her gender put her at a disadvantage in dealing with the forestry old boys' club and the male-dominated bureaucratic culture of the provincial government.

In fact, regardless of stature, gender, or personality, anyone working as a provincial biologist faced (and still faces) frequent frustration in a province where resource exploitation is virtually a government religion. Nobody wants to hear from those biologists because their advice rarely supports full-speed-ahead development of forests, oil, gas, water, and gravel. When biologists speak up, resource company heads roll their eyes and make phone calls to their buddies in government. Cabinet ministers frequently pounce on department heads, too many of whom seem quite willing to silence, or reassign, their staff in order to protect their own careers. Jan's predecessor had been hounded out of his job in just this way.

Habitat damage was, and remains, the biggest problem facing caribou and other sensitive boreal species, but provincial biologists have no power to protect wildlife habitat. The agencies that actually manage forests, streams, and land use are, for the most part, fully invested in promoting economic activities that degrade habitat. Mid-career burnout is not uncommon among Alberta's provincial biologists. Cynicism is a job hazard for those who survive.

All of which may be why Jan came across as passionate and informed, but also a bit resigned. Although she saw little hope for those caribou herds, she was doggedly determined to influence the decisions that would determine their fate. I had a great deal of respect for her.

Jan had co-authored a draft caribou recovery plan for the Alberta government. Based on several years study and analysis, it identified habitat loss to resource industry activities as the biggest long-term threat to the caribou. Predators, poaching, and road kills were problems, too, but mostly as secondary effects of the same industrial exploitation, which was riddling the landscape with roads and cutlines while chopping up the habitat into patches of second growth where once there had been extensive intact forests.

***

Alberta Fish and Wildlife released the draft plan for public comment in 1986. The plan called for no-hunting zones along several key roads; public education to reduce road kills and accidental hunter kills; long-term protection of key habitat areas from logging and motor vehicles; and a three-year program to reduce the number of wolves in key caribou areas.

The proposal for wolf control torpedoed the plan. The proposed wolf kill turned the debate away from habitat protection and towards wolves, a species many people considered more charismatic than caribou. Forest industry lobbyists were delighted by the public uproar.

"I guess I was a bit naive," Jan said. "But if you look at the data, there was no other conclusion you could make. Predators are taking up to 19 per cent of the adults each year. Calf recruitment is only 15 per cent. If we are going to buy time for those caribou, there has to be wolf control."

Some environmental groups were willing to consider a one-time wolf kill as long as it came with meaningful habitat restoration and protection. But the public outcry gave jaded Alberta politicians an excuse to put the recovery plan into the pending file, where good ideas go to die.

Instead, Alberta's conservative government turned the region's critical caribou winter ranges over to logging companies. In 1988 and 1989, Alberta launched a veritable blitz of new forestry projects across northern Alberta. Within one year, the government de facto privatized almost a quarter of the province by awarding "forest management agreements" to private companies. The land was still notionally public, but the FMAs delegated control over wildlife habitat to private companies so as to supply wood to seven new or expanded pulp mills and some smaller lumber and particle-board plants.

A subsequent environmental review of one of these projects – the Alberta-Pacific bleached kraft pulp mill north of Edmonton – showed that the government had no baseline data on forest ecology and had consulted neither with the general public nor the Indigenous communities whose cultural identities and sustenance rely on those lands. In fact, most of the area so suddenly dedicated to wood fibre production was virtually unknown to government planners.

**

Shortly after my caribou article appeared in *Nature Canada* magazine, John Stelfox retired from the Canadian Wildlife Service and accepted a seat on a panel appointed by Alberta's minister of forestry, lands, and wildlife. The minister had struck the panel in the wake of public uproar over the forest giveaways. He tasked them with looking into forest management concerns. Maybe, I hoped, the publicity I and others were creating for caribou would put wind in the sails of the hard, frustrating work biologists like Jan Edmonds and John Stelfox were doing behind the scenes.

John's panel, in its final report, proposed that the government establish at least one large boreal wilderness area, echoing recommendations of public advisory panels, government biologists, and many Alberta conservationists over the previous decade and a half.

The government sent that recommendation to the pending file too.

**

When faced with environmental issues demanding unpalatable solutions, like saving woodland caribou from habitat loss, government and industry have three go-to responses that offer the illusion of action while continuing with business as usual.

One is "monitoring." Monitoring is almost always a key recommendation in environmental assessments of potentially destructive industrial projects. Monitoring solves nothing; it simply tracks change. It's like asking a medical team to monitor heart rate and respiration – while the patient dies. An earnest promise of careful monitoring gives proponents an easy out when they can't deny that their project will harm the environment. The public, too often, is reassured; "monitoring" sounds so scientific, after all. And the project goes ahead.

The other solution is "more study." More study offers a vague hope of finding future solutions but is never accompanied by a delay in the actual project. During our interview, Jan Edmonds had lots of tales of the "more study" that government had already done and that it had prescribed for the future. And as we spoke, the road building and logging continued, all through Alberta's dwindling caribou ranges.

The most recent solution is the most offensive because it delivers the least while appearing to offer the most: "adaptive management." Adaptive management is actually a thing: it involves applying the scientific method to management by identifying hypotheses and then testing them with management actions, then sharpening the focus and trying again. But for Alberta's resource industries it means, "Trust us. We'll figure stuff out on the go." They usually don't. They rarely even try, once they have the go-ahead they were after.

If the 1970s was an era of increased professionalization and science capacity in conservation, the 1980s and 1990s were the era of collaboration and planning. In both cases the assumption was that positive change would result. Surely if we have better expertise, we can make better decisions? Surely if people work together across boundaries, we'll get collaborative solutions? Isn't planning a rational way to balance competing interests?

And all through the 1970s, 1980s, and 1990s, while biologists studied, and environmentalists marked up flip chart sheets in endless planning meetings, the industrial and recreational assault on western Canada's ecosystems continued to ramp up.

Canada's Model Forest Program was an attempt to bring experts together across the industrial and organizational divides that separate them in hopes of better outcomes in the woods. Canada's forests and other natural resources fall under the jurisdiction of the provinces, not the federal government. Lacking any direct control, the Canadian Forestry Service hoped that the program would influence provincial forest management practices for the better by offering federal money for collaborative research and planning that pulled together provincial agencies, private forest companies, Indigenous communities, and universities. Given that forests, and the issues facing them, vary across the country, each of Canada's ten model forests had its own unique structure and priorities.

Alberta's version – the Foothills Model Forest, centred in Hinton – encompassed a lot of caribou habitat both in Jasper National Park and in the operating area of Weldwood Forest Products (now West Fraser) east of the park. The key funding partners were the Canadian Forest Service, Parks Canada, Weldwood, and the Alberta Forest Service.

Ron Hooper, the superintendent of Jasper National Park, hired me on as a member of his management team in 2000. I was put in charge of what was called the Ecosystem Secretariat, a small work unit that coordinated science, environmental assessments, and strategic planning for the park. It was no surprise when Ron told me I would be joining him on the board of the Foothills Model Forest.

I was not, however, excited by the prospect. During earlier postings in Jasper I had spent a lot of my spare time helping the Jasper Environmental Association and Alberta Wilderness Association to try and protect caribou and other threatened species like grizzly bears and the unique little Athabasca rainbow trout from industrialization of their forest habitats. It was hard to reconcile the hostility I had faced from Weldwood then with the idea that I would now be expected to collaborate with people I had come to perceive as timber beasts.

First impressions didn't improve my disposition. The board was solidly male, white, and invested in the idea that forestry was the highest and best use of the foothills landscape. The chair of the model forest was then-mayor of Hinton, Ross Risvold. Ross was a hyper-partisan fan of Premier Ralph Klein's hard-right conservative government; he rarely missed an opportunity to demean environmental groups to which I still belonged. Weldwood's representative was Bob Udell, one of the firm's vice-presidents and a man with whom I had crossed swords before during the public controversy over the late-1980s forest management area expansions. A seasoned public relations man, he turned out to be a generous colleague and a man who clearly loved those foothills landscapes. I think the fact that I never quite got past my initial distrust was more a failure on my part than his.

Alberta's main guy was Cliff Henderson, a seasoned veteran of the provincial public service who served as the assistant deputy minister for forestry in the Alberta Department of Sustainable Resource Development. He had the confidence and bluster of an alpha male with access to big budgets. He knew all the right people and had no doubts about his power, and right, to control agendas.

I not only didn't trust the model forest board, I wasn't sure what to make of my own boss at first. Ron seemed to get along too well with this bunch of forestry old boys. I was reassured, however, when after a board meeting that had consisted largely of listening to Ross hold forth about the many ways in which environmentalists and socialists got in the way of the forest industry, we stepped out into the sour pulp mill tang of a grey Hinton evening and Ron paused, looked around with a bemused, almost lost, expression on his face, and finally muttered, "Sometimes I wonder what on earth we're even doing here."

It got better, but it never got good.

***

A condition of CFS funding was that each model forest have Indigenous representation on its board. In the Jasper-Hinton region there were communities that should have been represented – from the traditionalist Smallboy Mountain Cree Camp south of

Hinton to the Mountain Métis People who had been evicted from Jasper National Park decades earlier and now lived in the foothills north of Hinton and around Grande Cache. But nobody on the board seemed to believe that anybody in those groups would be a productive member – which meant, essentially, that they were impatient with Indigenous perspectives. It was pretty clear they felt their own world view to be superior to those whom they saw as social inferiors.

When I reminded the board of our need to find Indigenous members, the response made it clear that, as the new kid on the block, I was simply being naive.

No less discouraging was a jolly conversation I walked in on one day in 2002 when I arrived early for a board meeting at the Hinton Training Centre. Cliff, Bob, and a couple of others were discussing yet another draft caribou recovery strategy then under development, and the effects it might have on forest planning. Cliff Henderson reassured them it would have no impact at all. It was clear that, as far as he and others at senior levels in the Klein government were concerned, caribou were already finished. They just had to go through the motions of planning for them to placate the environmentalists and keep caribou out of the headlines.

I lay awake that night reflecting on that dark revelation. Ron had assured me that Cliff's personal opinion was just that, and that our board's guidelines for caribou and other key species would be binding on land managers, including Weldwood, in the region. But I couldn't help feeling that, from the Alberta government's point of view, our role was more about greenwashing the forest industry than about changing it. Cliff, after all, was the big wheel where provincial forest policy was concerned, and it was clear he wasn't looking to the board or anyone else for advice on how to protect any species – even endangered ones – that couldn't survive in logged-over forests.

***

I had other reasons for lying awake at night agonizing over caribou, however. Monitoring by our own park staff was showing a continuing, alarming decrease in caribou herds that lived entirely, or most of the time, within Jasper National Park. Provincial bureaucrats wielded no influence in the park; saving the park's caribou was our responsibility. Ron assigned me to make sure we got it right.

We didn't.

It wasn't for lack of effort. If anything, it was for trying too hard to do it right.

Park biologists had dug deep to understand the caribou decline. While they acknowledged that changing climate was a problem, especially the more frequent mild winter spells that harden the snow and make it easier for predators to get around, they also pointed out that the park's approach to recreation management was causing major problems. Sustained by an excessively high elk population, wolf numbers were near an all-time high. That normally wouldn't be a big problem because caribou stay in high-elevation forests in winter where the snow is too deep and the rewards too sparse for wolves to make the effort to hunt them. But in 1969 Parks Canada had built a road to Maligne Lake that we now kept plowed in winter for skier access. The plowed road enabled wolves to penetrate deep into caribou country. So too did the snowmobile trails that backcountry lodge operators in the Tonquin Valley used for freighting supplies and gear to their lodges beside Amethyst Lake.

Caribou are remarkably accepting of human beings, but our dogs look like wolves to them and trigger instant stress, even when the dog is on a leash. What's a leash to a caribou? So another problem was the steady increase in hikers taking dogs with them into the alpine meadows where caribou raise their calves. Every minute spent staring, heartbeat elevated, at a distant dog is a minute taken away from feeding during the one brief season when good forage is available and essential. Already living at the limits of their natural range, Jasper's caribou didn't need that kind of added stress.

George Mercer, the park's main wildlife biologist in the 1990s, recommended that Parks Canada stop plowing the Maligne Road in winter and require lodge operators in the Tonquin to bring in their supplies by helicopter rather than snowmobile. Both those changes would discourage wolves from hunting in the high country. In addition, he suggested, dogs should be prohibited on trails traversing caribou summer range.

His advice was solid. We should have taken it.

The challenge, as often, was political. Making those changes would upset a lot of people and significantly cut into the already-thin profit margins for the Tonquin lodge owners. Ron Hooper needed convincing, especially because he knew that if controversy blew up, he was the one who was going to have to explain to the minister's office why we hadn't been able to bring local stakeholders along with us.

It's often said that politics is the art of the possible. By the time I took over Jasper's ecosystem secretariat I had come to understand that, given that it's often joined at the hip to politics, conservation is too. As Jack Ward Thomas, former head of the US Forest Service and a seasoned veteran of conservation battles south of the 49th parallel, told me once during an interview, "Conservation is only about 10 per cent biology and 90 per cent people. But we train our wildlife professionals 90 per cent biology and 10 per cent people, and then we wonder why things go wrong."

When I told George we weren't going to get support for his recommendations without doing some front-end work with the local stakeholders, he became frustrated and annoyed. He and his colleagues had done the biology. The caribou weren't going to wait forever for us to sweet-talk a few locals. Parks Canada's one overriding legal directive is to protect or restore ecological integrity – not to dither.

In the view of the park's biological staff, it didn't need to be this complicated. Managers should just act on their advice.

I had spent a good part of my career as a biologist, however, and I knew that there is sometimes a big difference between *science* advice, and *scientists'* advice. Scientists aren't infallible. In fact, the same Jasper biologists insisting that we simply impose their caribou solutions on the locals had been just as annoyed by my refusal to support an earlier recommendation they'd brought forward – one that would have worked against caribou protection.

***

Even as caribou numbers declined, elk numbers were approaching record highs. Those elk were eating the front country habitats down to stubble, partly because those areas were full of roads, trails, and people that deterred their warier predators from hanging around. Wolf predation keeps elk on the move and reduces their numbers, but wolves rarely den close to people. Consequently, when park staff had found a wolf den in the montane not far from Jasper Park Lodge, we had used the superintendent's authority under park legislation to close the area to all human activity. We wanted those wolves to stay. They had important work to do.

But when local climbers reported another wolf den where Watchtower Creek drains into Medicine Lake, the biological staff came to me with a request for another area closure. This den, however, was in an area lightly used by humans, well away from the montane elk habitats we were most concerned about, and close to an important caribou calving area in the upper Watchtower basin. I refused to take their recommendation forward to the superintendent – if the protections in the Canada National Parks Act weren't enough for those wolves, they were out of luck. That pack, after all, was bound to end up feeding caribou calves to its pups. And it was caribou, not wolves, that were most in need of special protections.

My refusal to protect that subalpine wolf den, I suspect, made me a bit suspect in the eyes of my biologist colleagues. Clearly, to them, I had become one of those wishy-washy managers more concerned about politics than about listening to scientist staff.

***

Nonetheless, I set to work designing a caribou recovery team that would include a full range of stakeholders. Having seen other collaborative planning exercises go off the rails, I went into this one with pretty strongly held views. For one thing, this was to be about caribou, not about stakeholders. We used a stakeholders approach to determine who needed to be on the committee – lodge operators, hikers, backcountry skiers, environmentalists, biologists, and so on – but once they were around the table the rule was that they were to stop thinking of themselves as people with a stake in the outcome and, instead, to participate as experts in their particular realms. No biologist, after all, knows as much about backcountry lodge operations as a lodge owner. But no lodge owner or skier knows as much about caribou ecology as a biologist. Mutual respect was a rule of the game.

It was a challenging task. In the course of several meetings, participants educated one another about caribou population trends, ecology, and behaviour; about wolves and other predators; about what skiers and hikers wanted and what the trends were for those activities; and finally we got to the point of listing management changes that might benefit the caribou. No idea was dismissed, no matter how strange, except those that would be inconsistent with the Canada National Parks Act or other laws.

This was where my hopeful idealism ran into cold reality. A few key participants proved unwilling to accept constraints they felt might inconvenience them, regardless of benefit to the caribou. The pivotal meeting involved voting on each of the suggested options based not on personal preference but on what the participants had learned about caribou, their predators, and other factors affecting them. Participants scored each option on two aspects: likelihood, based on what we had all learned, that it would reduce conservation risk to caribou; and practical feasibility of implementing it. It was clear to everyone by this stage of the process that George's original suggestions were right on.

When the votes were tallied, however, the group's priority was to ban dogs from summer caribou ranges and a couple of other experimental approaches that might prove useful. But there weren't enough votes to keep the Maligne Road unplowed or to shut down the snowmobile trail into the Tonquin. George was understandably furious. I was profoundly disappointed.

At the end of the meeting, as we all stepped out into the winter dark of a Jasper evening, two of the participants – co-owners of one of the lodges in the Tonquin Valley, a last critical refuge for Jasper's caribou – laughed and bumped fists in triumph. They had won – not for the caribou but for their bank accounts. Until that evening, I had considered one of those individuals a principled community leader. I was profoundly disappointed in him.

***

Within a year both George Mercer and I had left Jasper for other jobs. The intended follow-up meeting to review progress and elevate the next set of management options never happened. The Maligne Road remained open. And the caribou that had ranged the alpine meadows and timberline forests along the Maligne Valley died, one by one, until there was not a single one left. Not one.

In subsequent years, in fairness, Parks Canada took some harder decisions. Largely to the credit of George's replacements, wildlife biologists Layla Neufeld, John Wilmshurst, and Mark Bradley, and superintendent Alan Fehr, the backcountry lodges in the Tonquin had their winter seasons shortened to deter wolf travel. In 2022, with those measures having failed, both lodges closed for good. Winter recreational use is now prohibited in known caribou areas. It helps too that elk numbers have dropped dramatically and, in response to the depleted food supply, wolves are fewer too.

But it was all too little, too late. Caribou are gone now from the Maligne Range, nearly gone from the upper Brazeau, and teetering on the brink of disaster even in the Tonquin Valley, where they were abundant in the 1980s. Those green alpine meadows still gleam with glory when the sun shines on them, but their spirit is diminished; for the most part only grey ghosts graze there now.

In a last gesture of desperation, Parks Canada has chosen to try pen-raising caribou for release back into the wild, fencing off a portion of that once-wild park to turn it into a predator-free nursery. Too little, too late, too desperate – at a time of rapid climate and landscape change.

In failing the caribou, we failed ourselves. Their ghosts haunt me every single day.

***

Outside the national park, caribou populations continued to crater. By the end of the 20th century, partly because of greater public awareness and concern, the Alberta government had run out of excuses for inaction. The Little Smoky watershed – virtually roadless when I first saw it in the 1980s – had become the poster child for Alberta's disastrous failures. By the turn of the century the Little Smoky was classified as over 95 per cent disturbed by oil and gas development and logging. Its caribou herd was on the brink of extirpation.

Whereas public opposition to predator control had been the government's excuse for inaction in the mid-1980s, in the early 2000s such control now became the go-to solution, wolf-huggers be damned. Starting in 2005, government wildlife staff contracted professional trappers to launch total war on the area's wolf population.

There were unquestionably a lot of wolves in the area, along with other caribou predators like black bears. But they were only there because they'd been invited. The massive logging, roading, and pipeline construction activity in the area had replaced much of the old conifer forests with openings that soon filled with willows, poplars, and other food plants favoured by moose, deer, and elk. Those big ungulates previously had been scarce in the area, but abundant second-growth vegetation created a population boom. Inevitably, as prey populations increased, so too did the numbers of predators.

Caribou numbers, however, shrank. Caribou rely for food not on leafy shrubs but on arboreal lichens in the older spruce and pine forests that were being hewed down as fodder for pulp and lumber mills. Even as they struggled harder than ever to find food in the increasingly industrialized landscape, they found themselves facing heavier predation by wolves and bears whose populations were propped up by all those moose and deer. It was the same problem Jan Edmonds and her colleagues had flagged two decades earlier, only worse.

While the government continued to permit and actively promote the industrial habitat destruction driving the whole problem, it needed to show it was doing something to save the caribou. The response: go to war on predators. Alberta increased the allocation of big game hunting licences to reduce prey populations, paid trappers bounties so they would snare more wolves, hired gunners to shoot wolves from the air, and even brought back strychnine – a cruel and indiscriminate poison that had previously been banned.

The poisoning campaign turned an ecological problem into an utter disaster.

In boreal Canada, winter is largely a scavenging economy for those birds and mammals that don't migrate or hibernate. Predators and bad weather provide a steady supply of carrion that other species – from chickadees and deer mice to martens, fishers, wolverines, wolves, eagles, and jays – rely upon for food. When Alberta Fish and Wildlife staff killed dozens of moose across the Little Smoky watershed and salted the carcasses with strychnine, everything died – not just wolves. Among the nontarget species found dead at strychnine baits during the first seven years of the poison blitz were a grizzly bear, six lynx, 31 foxes, 91 ravens, 36 coyotes, four fishers, eight martens, and four weasels. Bald and golden eagles, grey jays, and chickadees died too; other victims were never found, having died under the snow or after wandering off into the woods.

When wildlife photographer John Marriott visited the area in 2012, he said it was like a frozen graveyard. Nothing stirred; everything was dead.

In addition to the poisoning deaths, during the same period of time trappers using snares choked almost 700 wolves to death while at the same time accidentally killing 676 other animals – including cougars, deer, bears, and even two caribou.

Politics – and conservation – might be the art of the possible, but that means those possibilities are subject to the whims of the electorate. Caribou and other forest animals don't vote. Loggers, rig workers, road contractors, and others whose families rely on paycheques from the industrial corporations that exploit the land, on the other hand, do. The deck is fatally stacked against the grey ghosts of Alberta's boreal forests. Their fate rests in the hands of a government that knows from experience that there are no real political consequences for simply not trying.

Getting it right for caribou and other wildlife species now facing the risk of extirpation demands more than just a deeper understanding of their nature and needs. The only real hope for conserving such vulnerable creatures is that we humans come to better understand, and address, our own cultural weaknesses, especially the sense of entitlement so deeply entrenched in Western society that most of us don't even recognize it in ourselves or question its validity. We too readily see other animals as mere objects or resources, and feel entitled to dismiss them when their needs don't align with ours. It's always all about us – an "us" we invented when we allowed Western science and old religions to delude us into believing that humankind is somehow separate from, and above, the rest of Creation.

The decisions being made in caribou country are cold, pragmatic ones. Pragmatism is the repression of the spirit.

***

Those caribou I saw in upper Simon Creek and headwaters of the Maligne River may have both summered in different parts of Jasper, but I suspect they sometimes encountered one another along the braided channels of the Sunwapta River. Small bands of caribou showed up there regularly in the last decades of the 20th century, usually in early spring. Motorists on the Icefields Parkway would stop to watch them grazing along the forest edges or ease slowly past as the animals quietly licked salt from the highway surface. By late May the caribou would be gone, following the snowmelt back into their high country retreats.

One day I crested a rise south of the Jonas Slide and saw a brownish-grey form on the highway right-of-way. It was a yearling caribou, all by itself, grazing in a patch of river dryas that carpeted the gravel verge. I had some time to kill, so I eased to a stop several metres past the animal. It barely glanced up as I got out of the car and dug my camera out of my day pack.

When I stepped into the ditch and up onto the terrace where it was feeding, however, the caribou raised its head and stared at me. It was watchful but not yet concerned. I turned away and leaned down, plucking loose leaves from the ground until it relaxed and began to graze again. Slowly, indirectly, I wandered towards it. Every time it raised its head I pretended to be doing my own human version of what it was doing.

Eventually, I was barely three metres from that beautiful creature, astonished at how close the caribou had allowed me to approach. I lowered myself to the ground and stared in the other direction for a while, listening to the peaceful crop-crop sound of its incisors snipping off vegetation next to me. Then I turned, focused my camera, and photographed its hooves, its face, and even a close-up of its nose. We were that close. The caribou was probably used to the companionship of other herd members, and my slow, meandering approach had persuaded it that I was more like a part of the herd than a predator.

We were no longer separate, but together. I felt like this quiet animal had granted me a gift of belonging.

Another car appeared, also southbound. I thought it was going to pass, but then it slowed abruptly and stopped beside us. A man got out, slammed the door, and hurried towards us, lifting a small camera to his face. Before he could snap a photo, the caribou's head came up, eyes bulging with sudden alarm. It pivoted and, tail raised, fled down through the willows. It vanished into the spruce trees.

The man stopped, staring at me, evidently wondering how I had gotten so close. Then he gave a comical shrug of resignation and said, "Oh well, next time."

He went back to his car and drove away.

He hadn't really seen that caribou; he'd only seen the picture he hoped to snap and the attention it might get him. He had been there only long enough to shatter the magic, then he was gone.

The caribou was gone too.

And there won't be a next time.

10. Transitions

Glenn Webber called me up in the spring of 1980 and asked if I would like to join him and some friends for a camping and canoeing trip to the Pincher Creek area. Glenn and I were old friends dating back to our university years, but I half-suspected it might be my shiny new Grumman canoe he was inviting more than me. Regardless, I accepted with alacrity, and that May long weekend found me heading south with the canoe bouncing on top of my Land Cruiser.

Glenn's friends, like him, worked in the Western Regional Office of Parks Canada, in Calgary. Rob Ward, an artist whose day job was exhibit design for Parks Canada, had driven down in a little two-seater MG sports car. It was shiny and red, clearly a source of pride, but it looked very much out of place in rural southwestern Alberta.

At the end of a two-day rain, the Oldman River was in full spate: brown, muddy, and laden with driftwood and other flotsam. It would have been suicide for paddlers of our limited skill to try launching into that torrent. We decided instead to try the Castle, a few miles south. It, too, was swollen with runoff and chewing at its banks. Determined not to waste the weekend, however, we convinced ourselves to give it a try. Thirty seconds in that hungry torrent was all it took to persuade us we were well out of our depth; we'd have to wait and see if the river might drop a bit overnight.

So we set up camp at an idyllic-looking little provincial campground in a poplar grove beside the Castle River.

As the evening progressed, trucks and cars began to arrive. Soon a couple of dozen vehicles were crammed in among the cottonwoods at the far end of the campground. We could hear music playing and the happy sound of cheerful voices over there. All was well. As the light faded from the sky and the river hissed its sullen way through the streamside willows, our little group visited around our fire, discussing the prospects for the morrow. At length we went to bed.

The partiers, unfortunately, didn't. Vehicles came and went, the cheery voices down the lane became louder and more boisterous, and the music did too.

The night went on and on. As did the party. Lying in my tent, I found myself increasingly frustrated and annoyed; it was bad enough worrying about the prospects of paddling in water that was well beyond my skill level, but now I faced the prospect of having to get through the coming day without having gotten any sleep. What remained of the night got shorter and shorter until finally it was over and the first light was coming through the wall of my tent. Surely the party would wind down now? But, just as things seemed to be fading to a lull, somebody cranked up Willie Nelson to full volume.

I like Willie Nelson, in measured doses, at appropriate times. This wasn't that. Furious, desperate to get at least an hour's sleep, I scrambled out of my tent, stuffed my sleeping bag into the Land Cruiser, and followed it in. I figured I would drive a few miles away and park in a field or something. Anything.

But as I got into the vehicle I noticed two things: all that noise was coming from a large stereo speaker on the roof of somebody's vehicle, and I had left my axe crammed beside my driver's seat. In a fit of spontaneous inspiration, I fired up my machine, roared over to the offending vehicle, jumped out, and yelled at the five or six drunks still sitting around their monster fire to turn the goddam music down. Predictably, they yelled worse profanities back.

I reached for my axe, wound up a mighty swing, and silenced Willie Nelson mid-warble. As the shattered speaker flew into a nearby rain puddle, I could suddenly hear robins singing.

It was a golden moment of peace, that perfect dawn beauty you get in late May with the sweet balsam scent of newly opened cottonwood leaves and the steady rush of the nearby river and the birds – but forget all that. The idyll lasted maybe a second, and then I was swamped in a tangle of swinging fists, kicking boots, and beery breath. My springer spaniel Penny jumped out of the Land Cruiser to join the melee – but not to heroically save her master. Assuming this was all good fun, she started bringing sticks and dropping them hopefully in front of us as the fists flew and I went down to the ground.

The second time a boot connected with my head it suddenly occurred to me that this was real and the people surrounding me were not in a condition to exercise good judgment or restraint. I extricated myself from the pile – easy enough to do as they were all drunk – jumped back in my vehicle, and staged a hasty retreat to our campsite to figure out my next move. Penny followed, carrying yet another a stick, still hoping to get in on the fun.

Having armed themselves with tire irons, my axe, and other sundry implements, the angry mob followed me too. We all arrived together, just as my companions, who had miraculously slept through most of the earlier chaos, emerged blinking into a version of hell they had never imagined. Rob's shiny MG stood in the dripping dawn as a symbol of all that these gentlemen hated about city people who ruin perfectly good bush parties. They began pounding on that poor little beauty with their armament.

Which, though certainly better than the alternative, was an awful sight to behold.

Rob saved the day by telling me to leave and persuading them I was their only real problem. Abandoning his badly marred car, the little band of drunken warriors started to follow me as I backed my vehicle gradually out to the road. Once I had decoyed the worst of them well away from our campsite, I drove myself into Pincher Creek and delivered myself to the emergency ward at the hospital to be patched up. My head was a mess from all the hits I'd taken.

Having been poked, prodded, and dosed with painkillers by the nurses in attendance, I was tucked in for the night to await the arrival of a doctor in the morning. An old rancher, clearly in a lot of pain, lay grimly in the bed next to mine. Like inmates everywhere, we got to talking, and soon asked about each other's reasons for being in the hospital. The old guy got a grim chuckle out of my story. When I asked him his, he lifted the sheet covering his right leg and showed me: from hip to foot it was black, blue, green, yellow, and various other unnatural colours.

"Wow," I said reverently. "How did that happen?"

He explained that his grazing land butted up against the Forest Reserve, not too far north of Waterton Lakes National Park, and that he always carried an old six-gun pistol in a hip holster when working alone back there, in case of bears. He'd been lifting a bale of barbed wire when a strand caught the hammer of his gun and it had discharged. The bullet went right down the length of his leg. He was not a happy man, in spite of the painkillers.

The irony was immediately evident to me: it hadn't been a bear that put him in the hospital; it was his fear of bears. Somehow, in spite of my proven lack of judgment, I managed not to say that out loud. A few years later, however, I heard about that six-gun again; this time it had been used by one of his sons to shoot a trespassing bull between the eyes. Good judgment and firearms, it seems, are sometimes strangers to one another.

Clearly, I had been lucky my assailants had only had access to tire irons and axes.

The saga continued in the morning. Even before the doctor arrived, I had a visit from two Mounties. They advised me they would be filing charges against me for destruction of property and that, once they'd tracked down the partiers, there would be some assault charges laid too. Glenn told me later that, after interviewing my companions at the campground, one officer had said to him, "Next time you take your buddy camping, maybe just tie him to a tree or something."

The police finally tracked down four of the offenders (one of whom they caught up with in jail, where he was serving time for some subsequent offence) and charged them with assault. Many weeks later, when our trials came up, they had suits and haircuts.

None of us could make a positive identification. The Crown prosecutor had to drop the charges. He took me aside and said, "If we can't charge those guys, I'm dropping the charge against you too."

That came as a relief. A Criminal Code conviction would not have improved my resumé.

I did, however, pay a further price for my bad judgment. A few weeks later I met a very nice young woman during an evening out in Banff. We exchanged phone numbers and agreed to meet in Calgary the following week for dinner. Dinner went well. She was a nursing student at the university and had recently graduated from high school in Pincher Creek.

Pincher Creek? That reminded me of a tale I thought she'd enjoy. I wasn't halfway through it, however, when I felt an icy chill spilling across the table and it occurred to me that I was maybe missing something. "You've heard about this before?" I asked.

"That was my birthday party," she replied. By now she was looking at me like I'd suddenly been revealed as some kind of space alien. She and her friends had been long gone by the time the axe-and-speaker event transpired, and clearly she'd heard a different version than the one I remembered.

There was no second date.

The following year I was camping in Arizona with another young woman, Gail Baker, who would eventually become my wife. We had just gotten into the tent for the night when vehicles began to arrive, music began to play, and voices began to rise.

At my suggestion, we broke camp and drove 50 kilometres to a different campground.

See? It's called learning. Even young males can do it. And since there are always lots of learning experiences to be had, for several years the western region of Parks Canada had an award it gave out to whoever had done the flat-out-stupidest thing of the year. Rob Ward designed it.

It was a papier-mâché sculpture of an axe embedded in a speaker.

Geoff Holroyd's first marriage having ended, his life took an ironic twist; he was now dating his first wife's former roommate, Elisabeth Beaubien. I was renting a spare room from Geoff in Canmore, but Elisabeth was increasingly a part of our household. Elisabeth was a vivacious soul noted for her spontaneous enthusiasm that sometimes landed her in awkward spots.

One such awkward spot was the situation she found herself in after volunteering to teach a birding course for the Bow Valley Naturalists club in the spring of 1981. It would have been a great idea – if she had been more confident of her ability to identify birds in the field. She collared me one day after work, looking a bit stressed out, and asked if I would be willing to lead the field trip portion. That was why, on the May long weekend following that disastrous one on the Castle River, I found myself leading a dozen of her students around the Cave and Basin loop trail in Banff National Park.

It was an exceptional day for birding. A major spring snowstorm had dumped 20 centimetres of wet snow just as a major wave of spring migrants was passing through the valley. The snow lay heavy on the tree canopy and ground, except where the hot springs emerged along the wooded slope below Sulphur Mountain. There the mosses and emerging spring understory plants glowed a brilliant green. Dozens of warblers, sparrows, and other birds were foraging on the ground instead of in the snow-coated canopy, seemingly unconcerned by fascinated watchers arrayed along the trail.

At one point a group of us watched a short-tailed weasel emerge from the underbrush and begin a strange, almost hypnotic, bouncing dance amid a mixed flock of warblers, chipping sparrows, juncos, and other birds. All of a sudden, he made a quick sideways dive and just missed snapping up a male Wilson's warbler. Apparently unfazed by failure, the skinny little creature bounded off into the underbrush again before the two young women at the back of the line had a chance to see him. They had missed the excitement because they were having such a good time visiting with one another.

One of the laggards was a small, soft-spoken woman with dark bangs and big eyes. Her quiet, self-contained aura appealed to me as much as her appearance. She stayed on my mind and, later, after seeing her again at a meeting of the Bow Valley Naturalists, I asked Geoff and Elisabeth, in what I hoped was a casual, disinterested sort of way, who that little quiet person was. Elisabeth pounced on the question with her usual zeal, and took it upon herself to ensure we connected. It didn't take her long to track down the young woman's name and phone number, and pass them on.

When I called Gail Baker and asked her if she'd like to join me for dinner, she sounded quite startled. She evidently hadn't noticed me noticing her. After some initial hesitation, she agreed.

It turned out we were kindred spirits. Gail had moved to Banff a year previously, and when she wasn't working at the Banff Centre music library, she was out hiking the various park trails, bicycling along the Bow River in the evenings, or watching birds with other members of the Bow Valley Naturalists. She preferred to do most things alone, as did I. We agreed to meet again and do some things alone, together. One of our first dates, in fact, was to rent bicycles in town and ride up the Cascade fire road to camp beside Wigmore Lake, miles from anywhere.

That winter, she was rash enough to agree that a winter camping trip might be a nice idea. It dropped to −25°C that night, and I, being chivalrous, offered Gail my four-season down sleeping bag. She vanished into its depths and slept like a log, toasty and warm. It hadn't occurred to me that her sleeping bag, besides being designed for milder temperatures, might also be too short for me. As on so many other previous winter adventures, I ended up spending half the night feeding the fire in between short, chilly catnaps.

That spring, Gail and I spent four weeks exploring the desert southwest of the US border. We were completely smitten with one another. In Tucson I surprised myself one evening by asking her

168   Transitions

to marry me. She surprised both of us by agreeing. Holding her in my arms, stunned, I said to her, "Do you realize what we just did?"

She nodded silently against my chest. Neither of us could imagine what the road forward was going to look like after so momentous a decision. We married in the fall.

***

With the completion of the wildlife work in Mount Revelstoke and Glacier national parks in 1984, as well as the Kootenay inventory, which had been led by Dave Poll, word came down from senior management that Geoff and I were expected to move to Edmonton. There were offices waiting for us on the second floor of the Northern Forest Research Centre, where the rest of the cws team was already housed. It wasn't considered normal for the cws staff in our region not to live in Edmonton. George Scotter, our division head, felt it was past time for Geoff and me to be integrated into the team.

So Gail and I moved to Edmonton, something neither of us had ever planned. Nor had we planned that she would be pregnant so soon with our first child. In fact, nothing was going as planned, but everything, it turned out, was going very well.

We bought our first home. It was a daunting investment – we had to cash in all our retirement savings, sell her car, and borrow a bit from family in order to scrape together a minimal down payment, and then the mortgage rate came in at 14.5 per cent – but we loved the house and its wooded backyard. I applied for and won a promotion to a full biologist position. Our section head assigned me the first project I would lead on my own – a backcountry range inventory in Jasper National Park. On the strength of that assignment, I proposed that I turn the study into a Master of Science project. To my surprise, the powers that be said yes and offered funding support. I enrolled in Range Management at the University of Alberta. Gail gave birth to our first child, Corey, and a few months later was pregnant with our second.

Life had never seemed so great.

Then, one Friday in November 1984, Geoff stuck his head in my office door and said we had all been summoned to an unscheduled meeting in the basement seminar room. Mystified, I joined a small crowd of sombre-looking colleagues and waited. George Scotter arrived last and sat down at the front table, facing us. He rustled some papers, reluctant to begin, then finally looked up and announced that there were going to be some changes.

Most of the people in the room, he said, could expect to be affected.

Two months earlier, on September 17, a new government led by Brian Mulroney had been sworn into office after winning the second-largest electoral victory in Canada's history. The Progressive Conservatives had won their mandate with promises to cut government spending and get the economy – at that time in recession – back on its feet again. He had appointed a rookie MP from Quebec to the post of environment minister and instructed her to find savings.

Suzanne Blais-Grenier had taken less than a month to decide that the CWS was largely useless and certainly had no role to play in Canada's national parks. The entire national park research unit, George said, would be disbanded effective March 31, 1985. He then read out a list of names of those who would have to find new jobs. The list included me. The last name he read was his own.

George assured us that the federal government, in announcing cuts to all departments, had committed to giving laid-off employees first dibs on any surviving job vacancies, so long as we qualified. The human resources department would make our soft landings their priority. Then he stood and left the room. We filed out behind him. Not a word was spoken as people walked down halls and office doors closed. I could hear people talking on phones as I walked past. I closed my office door and picked up my phone too.

Gail and I were floored. The bottom had fallen out of everything. With mortgage rates as high as they were, house prices had dropped. We would have to sell our new home at a loss, and paying off the mortgage loan would cost more than we could actually hope to recover from the sale. I withdrew from university. I waited for a call from Human Resources, who had a list of all the vacant jobs in Canada but insisted on doing the matchmaking. As the weeks passed, hope faded. I applied for private sector jobs, but the recession had made them scarce.

Finally, in late January, I appealed to George Scotter to intercede with Human Resources. Just let me look at that list, I said; maybe there's something they've overlooked.

There was. Jasper National Park had an unfilled vacancy for a park interpretation supervisor. Its pay scale was well below my biologist salary, but it was a job, and I was qualified for it. The human resources staff hadn't matched me to it because it was classified as a technical job, and my existing job was a professional one. As if that mattered to Gail and me!

Jim Todgham, a friend who had previously given us office space during the wildlife inventory work, was the manager of Jasper's interpretation unit. I called and asked if there would be any problem from his end if I were to ask for that job. He reassured me that in his view it would a perfect fit; they couldn't do any better than to get someone with my depth of knowledge about the park and its ecology. I went home and hugged Gail.

The next day, Jim called me back.

"There's a...bit of a snag at our end," he said.

My mind was racing. What could be the problem?

"I told Rory we were planning to bring you on, and he said that over his dead body would that goddam Van Tighem ever work in his park."

Rory Flanagan was a tall, wiry Scot, former military engineer, who now served as superintendent of Jasper National Park. He was a man of stern mien, colourful language, and firmly held views. I'd always admired him, even if I found him more than a little bit daunting.

"What...why did he say that?"

Jim said, "He says you wrote a letter to the editor one time? About something at the Palisades?"

My heart stopped. I remembered that.

One of my responsibilities when I had been stationed in Jasper National Park previously had been to serve as the federal lead for environmental assessments under what was then called the Environmental Assessment Review Process Government Order, or EARP-GO. There weren't a lot of them, because environmental assessment was still a new policy area for most governments, but there were rules. If government money or land was involved, there had to be at least a cursory assessment of potential environmental issues so that those issues could be properly mitigated. For those simple environmental screenings, the park's warden service took the lead. For major project reviews, I was expected to coordinate things.

Northeast of the town of Jasper there was an old bungalow camp that had previously been owned by the Lewis Swift family. The government bought them out in the 1920s as part of the process of extinguishing previous claims to land in the national park, and later turned the buildings into a training centre for national parks staff. The approach to the Palisades, as it was known, was by way of a gravel road that crossed the CN Rail main line by an unmarked level crossing. CN didn't like the liability, and Parks Canada didn't like the risks. Rory had taken the decision to have his highways staff build a new road access that would avoid the railway by coming in off a different park road. It was less than a kilometre long.

Park wardens had pointed out that road projects were subject to the need for environmental assessment. Rory figured that was nonsense; it was a simple project, it was necessary, and they were going to get it done.

One of the wardens collared me one day and shared his discontent. There wasn't much I could do. This was clearly Parks Canada's responsibility. But I was in full world-saving mode at that stage, working in my evenings on a campaign to save the Oldman River from the Three Rivers dam. I wrote a polite, but pointed, letter to Rory offering him my read on the project and why it was wrong to proceed without proper review.

I also copied the letter to the *Edmonton Journal*, and it printed it.

Rory had responded to my letter with an equally polite explanation of why Parks Canada felt the project was exempt, and that had seemed to be the end of that.

It wasn't. I now learned Rory had been furious that I hadn't shown him the respect of talking to him directly but instead had gone straight to what should have been my last resort: the media. It offended his sense of how public servants should comport themselves, and he felt personally insulted. I had been too young, untutored, and inexperienced to think about any of that.

The world had a way of crumbling on me that winter, and it had crumbled again. Desperate, I did the only thing I could think of: I hopped in my car and drove the four and a half hours to Jasper in hopes of bearding the old lion in his den. I didn't really know what I would do there: beg, probably.

But Rory wasn't in the office when I arrived. His administrative assistant said he might be at the post office since he usually picked up his mail after lunch. Weaving my miserable way past throngs of happy tourists, I crossed the Information Centre lawn and spotted Rory standing at the top of the post office stairs, looking at a stack of letters.

At my approach, he looked up and glared at me.

"Mr. Van Tighem," he said.

My heart was pounding, but I tried not to let my emotions show.

"Rory, I think I owe you an apology."

"I think you do too."

"Well...I'm sorry."

Rory waited a few beats before responding. I was thinking of my pregnant wife at home with our toddler, waiting to learn if we had any kind of a future at all. I was thinking how tall Rory was, how stern – and I was thinking about cockiness and consequences.

"You should be," he said, at length. "So when are you going to be able to start work?"

We arrived in Jasper that spring utterly broke but happy. We were back in the mountains, I had a good job, and the fears and uncertainty of the past few months were behind us. Rory and his wife Mildred soon became valued friends. The eager young crew I now supervised might not be able to lead guided walks anymore – Blais-Grenier had banned those too – but we found creative ways to connect with park visitors and deepen their knowledge and appreciation of the natural and cultural history of their park. The golden future Gail and I had seen unfolding for us only a few months earlier would never happen now, but other possibilities had opened their arms to us.

It was good to be back in Jasper – a place to which my career would bring us yet again, a few years later – but the stay was relatively brief. Four years later Gail and I moved our family, which had now grown to three children, to the other side of the Continental Divide where I had been offered the job of chief of heritage interpretation in Yoho National Park.

***

The tiny town of Field is squeezed between the CPR main line and the looming bulk of Mount Stephen. It huddles in the shade all through the long winter months while blue shadows slide across the braided flats of the Kicking Horse River. Across the river, passing traffic on the Trans-Canada Highway flickers in and out of bits of daylight that tease and then retreat, but never quite reach the town.

Coming home from work one day for lunch, I found Gail sitting on the couch in the living room, looking across the valley. It occurred to me that I'd found her in the same position a couple of times previously that week.

"What are you looking at over there?" I asked.

"Sunshine," she said, wistfully. "I miss it."

Others who had lived in Field longer than us had evidently come to terms with the nature of the place better than we had. Two doors down from us, the Brooks brothers shifted their furniture out onto their front porch each March. After work each day they would hang out there with friends, drinking beer and watching the afternoon avalanches spill off the surrounding peaks as the spring sun weakened the snowpack. Our little mountain community might lack amenities that other, larger towns enjoyed, but at least we got that annual avalanche show.

Other towns didn't have resident bears, either. Ours had Field and Sissy, two grizzly bear siblings who often grazed in residents' yards, as well as a huge male black bear who believed he owned the joint. Field and Sissy were two years old when they lost their mother, and their lack of experience in the bigger mountain world might have had something to do with why they found refuge in our little town. When that big black bear was around, however, they vanished. Sissy, in particular, lacked confidence; hence her name.

The kids became accustomed to seeing the bears and would simply ride their bikes down a different street when they met one. One day we had lunch with the big black bear. We sat at the table, and the bear fed outside. It was June and thousands of dandelions were in bloom. After starting to graze his way through the patch, he surrendered to abundance and plopped himself down on his belly, munching the flower tops in an arc around him until there were none left in reach. Rather than stand up, he pulled himself along on his belly a few feet and resumed his feast, gradually belly-ing and humping his way the whole length of the yard. Then he went off into the woods and the kids headed back to school, still giggling.

***

When Gail and I moved our family to Field, we hadn't bargained on the dark winters, nor the claustrophobia of being squeezed into a narrow valley containing a major rail line and a transcontinent-al highway. Our children soon found friends there, and the small community made room for us, but a trip to a doctor, dentist, or grocery store always involved a hairy drive down the twisting Kicking Horse Canyon for Gail and our three preschoolers. She managed to bring them back alive every time, but she was often frazzled – especially the day a semi loaded with metal pipe veered unexpectedly around a sharp corner on her side of the road, forcing her to bail onto the shoulder as it shrieked past her window, leaving the stench of burning brakes and a badly shaken mother behind.

When a posting for a senior interpretation specialist opened up in the Parks Canada head office in Calgary, I applied for it and, after two short years in Field, we moved again.

Calgary was no longer the small city we both remembered. We wanted to raise our children somewhere that might at least be a reasonable facsimile, so we ended up buying a home in Okotoks, a half hour's drive outside the city. This was the town whose bank my grandfather had managed, not far from the farm where my grandmother had grown up. I remembered it, from long-ago fishing trips up into the foothills, as the little town where we would catch our first glimpse of the Sheep River sparkling in spring sunshine as we followed the gravel road across its bridge and on into the hills.

But you can't go back to a time that has passed. Okotoks might still be small, but it had abandoned most of its rural identity and become a bedroom community for the nearby city. Its downtown, spread along the floor of the Sheep River's valley, still had most of the original buildings that gave it its character, but the streets could no longer handle the traffic from new subdivisions spreading into the rolling farmland above the valley slopes. Our house was in one of those subdivisions. A gate in the back fence opened onto a half section of hayfield with a couple of willow-lined wetlands, offering an illusion of pastoral well-being that was belied by large signs showing a developer's plans for that space.

It's all town now. Its roads are paved, and they all lead away from what used to be.

Okotoks derives its name from the Blackfoot name for an immense split rock a few kilometres west of town. The town itself grew up where the old Macleod Trail crossed the Sheep River, which got its name from the herds of bighorn sheep that used to range along its valley breaks and still survive in the shale canyons and mountain slopes a few kilometres to the west.

The Blackfoot story of this sacred place, where bison once rubbed itchy hides against the two huge pieces of rock, is that the big rock arrived there in pursuit of Napi, who had gifted it with a buffalo hide but then taken his gift back when he grew cold. Angered, the rock pursued him down from the mountains, undeterred by animals that threw themselves in its way to try and save Napi. The pursuit only ended when a small bat hit the boulder in just the right spot to split it in two. It is now a sacred place.

Geologists have identified the rock as Gog quartzite, a metamorphic rock that forms the massive cliffs of Mount Edith Cavell and other Main Range peaks in the headwaters of the Athabasca River. Their story is that many thousands of years ago the boulder broke off one of those mountain cliffs and lodged in one of the glaciers that in those days, during the Pleistocene Ice Age, spilled far out from the mountains. As the ice flowed north and east, it ran into much vaster cordilleran ice sheets that were advancing south across the continent from Arctic regions. Deflected southward, the ice continued slowly to flow, bearing its load of rocky debris out into the foothills of what would one day be southern Alberta. A warming climate stalled the advance of the glaciers 15,000 to 12,000 years ago and the ice melted down, depositing the Big Rock and other glacial erratics all along the foothills.

Both stories are true.

Although our travels took a different path, when Gail and I moved to Okotoks in 1991 we were following the Big Rock from Jasper to the heart of Ksahkominoon – Blackfoot country. Unlike the brooding mountain walls and endless conifer forests of the upper Athabasca, here the chinook arch forms regularly above open country: bunchgrass foothills, coulees, and plains shaped by long-gone glaciers, and haunted with memories of people who once travelled the trail of stories that leads past that brooding stone. It was, and remains, a sacred place to those who recognize it. Okotoks felt in many ways like a return home.

But, as Thomas Wolfe said, you can't go home again.

***

Before leaving Jasper two years earlier, Gail had studied to become a Catholic. When my younger brother Tom married a Jasper girl and arranged to have Frank perform the wedding ceremony, we took advantage of everyone being in town for the event by having our own, second, wedding the following day. Our first had been a civil ceremony in Calgary, with only our parents and two favourite aunts in attendance. Frank presided over the Jasper ceremony, and I could tell that, in Dad's eyes at least, we were only now properly wedded to one another. It was that reconciliation with family religious tradition that had motivated both Gail and me to try to find a way to shoehorn our own spiritual beliefs into a religious institution they didn't really fit.

For Gail, the rituals, rules, and rigour of Catholicism were utterly unfamiliar. Not so on my part, but that didn't make coming back to the Catholic faith any easier. I had to reconcile a lot of conflicting thoughts about a religion hard-wired to a species of misogyny that denies women any role as clergy and insists their only true calling is to raise babies. This was a faith that chose to interpret its sacred scripture as giving man dominion over all other creatures and not only the right, but the duty, to "subdue" the earth.

I was determined to make it work, but it demanded an uncomfortable amount of cognitive dissonance. Thomas Berry, a Jesuit eco-theologian whose book *The Dream of the Earth* explores many of the conundrums that confronted me in my return to the Church, was a great help. Even so, I couldn't help feeling a hypocrite. I knew I wasn't reconciling my doubts, just repressing them.

That was, in any case, something I had experience with.

The kids went to a Catholic school, we all attended a Catholic church, but it was nothing like my childhood, when there were few questions or doubts about our faith, and no aspect of family life that it didn't touch. The role of religion in community life was changing all around us, diluted by secularism and materialism as much as it was confounded by multiculturalism: Who would have guessed, decades earlier, that Canada could be home to so many religious traditions?

***

Change was everywhere. Alberta was riding wave after wave of prosperity as the province's buried treasures – oil, gas, coal – were unearthed and sent off to market. Calgary couldn't keep up with the demand for new housing developments, schools, medical facilities, and infrastructure. Every town within a one-hour radius of the city was becoming a bedroom community where instant neighbourhoods seemed to sprout overnight. Farms and ranches were being sold to developers who turned them into clusters of acreage estates, each with its own road, monster home, and undersized pastures overgrazed by pet horses.

Okotoks quickly proved a disappointment. It wasn't a piece of the slow-paced, low-rise almost-rural Alberta we remembered. It was, if anything, in a hurry to become the exact opposite. Most of the town councillors were realtors and developers. Neighbours came and went so fast we barely got to know them before their lawns sprouted "For Sale" signs and the next moving van arrived.

It seemed to me that many of these newcomers were blindly killing the very thing they hoped to embrace. With the best of intentions, many had chosen to move here because of a hope of attaching their family identity to the Alberta foothills mythos: open range, close to nature, cowboy country. Pickup truck sales boomed. Cowboy hat sales boomed. Real estate sales boomed. Yet each instant westerner, in helping to fragment the landscape and urbanize rural culture, was contributing to the erosion of the values to which they meant to attach themselves. Alberta seemed to be devouring itself.

I wrote a nature column for the local paper for a while, hoping to imbue at least a few readers with a more holistic sense of place and understanding of consequence. But each time I saw bulldozers and backhoes at work on another rural property, it fed my deepening disillusionment. Those piles of dirt beside the newly carved roads had only days earlier been living prairie soil, rich with life, built and sustained by a diversity of perfectly adapted plants whose entangled roots sustained hundreds of species of invertebrate life. There had been a sustainable agricultural economy here, founded on the living diversity of a real place whose stories, written in the landscape, were being scribbled over and erased. And all our well-intentioned neighbours, eager to be a part of this foothills landscape, couldn't see the cost of their lifestyle choices because to those who haven't learned to see it for what it is, prairie is simply grass. One can always plant more grass.

It didn't help to know that we were part of the problem. Our entire suburb had been built barely a decade earlier.

***

I started taking the kids out for drives after work, looking for new development sites. If the material in the spoil piles was still green, I would grab a few hunks of sod and stow them in the trunk before returning to add them to what the family was soon calling my "front-yard prairie." It was a space about two metres square, where we'd cut down and removed a hybrid poplar the original developer had planted in the centre of the lawn. I salvaged some large slabs of sandstone from a road cut and built an outcropping in the middle of our suburban prairie and then, bit by bit, replaced the missing tree with fragments assembled from the original prairie being desecrated all around town. When weeds sprouted, as they always do when land is disturbed, I pulled them out.

I suppose the kids considered all this to be normal. The neighbours didn't.

The first shooting stars were an unexpected surprise and, a month later, so was the elegant wood lily that unfurled its orange glory next to the sandstone. By the second summer I had built a list of almost a hundred species of native plants growing in that little plot. Those sods were full of buried treasures. Gradually, that little patch came to look like an outcropping of foothills nature that might have spontaneously erupted from our suburban lawn. It constantly sprouted new reminders of just how much living diversity Alberta's native prairie actually contains. But passersby clearly didn't see the beauty I saw, so I printed out a little interpretive sign, laminated it, and stuck it between the sidewalk and my patch of salvaged nature.

Like so many other labours of love and atonement, it was a futile, quixotic endeavour. Shortly after we moved away, I received a nice letter from the new owner of our house. She explained that she didn't share my aesthetic sense, but reassured me that after digging up the prairie she had turned it into a nice flower garden.

She sounded like a very nice person. And it was only a very small patch of prairie compared to the ruined tracts from which its pieces had been rescued. Still, I was startled by the depth of my grief. That front-yard prairie and I had grown very close.

***

Commuting from Okotoks to the Anderson C-Train station every week day to work in the cubicle farms of the Harry Hays Building in downtown Calgary inspired no joy. Simply getting to and from work took two and a half hours out of each day, and the days were long even without that. Parks Canada was going through an intense period of navel gazing and reorganization. We didn't get much real work done because we were too busy doing business with ourselves. Task forces were formed, discussion papers were drafted, power struggles broke out, and morale deteriorated. A new regional director had been hired from outside the organization, largely on the basis of her shiny new Master of Business Administration degree. Sandi Davis didn't need to respect the organization's history or culture; she had learned how to do strategic planning. So that's what we did. Much to my dismay, I found myself tasked with helping to tear down the park interpretation function and replace it with a corporate communications unit. In the modern new world of managing the nation's great parks, we would no longer pursue a mandate of teaching visitors about the nature of their country but would instead concentrate on public relations and issue management for our corporate leaders.

Park visits would no longer be about connecting to heritage. They would be about having experiences and growing the tourism industry.

It was horrible work, from which Parks Canada has never recovered. Some of the mentors and colleagues I most admired found themselves marginalized or hounded into retirement, while a new generation of eager sycophants fought for favour and sneered at tradition. There was no question in my mind that Parks Canada had to change. But it felt to me like a heartless, soulless exercise of throwing babies out with bathwater – a triumph of method and deconstruction over heart and spirit.

At least one good thing came out of those months of organizational self-abuse, however: Parks Canada finally came to terms with having lost the Canadian Wildlife Service research unit almost a decade earlier. Park managers were expected to account for the ecological health of the parks entrusted to their care, and to implement scientifically sound strategies to restore ecological integrity where it was impaired. They needed expertise. And so the decision was made to hire professional biologists for each park, whose task it would be to run monitoring programs, advise management on ecological issues, and develop restoration projects where those were needed.

Bureaucracies have a lot of similarities to dysfunctional families. There are issues with sibling rivalries, unacknowledged abuses, and competing agendas. In this case, problems soon arose from the fact that the new biologists would be embedded in the warden service. Park wardens, at that time, were rarely university educated. They were hired on the basis of their practical skills with horses, boats, alpine climbing gear, or firefighting equipment, and they were paid technician wages.

In the federal public service, biologists were seen as professional staff and were classified and paid accordingly. They had to have a minimum of a bachelor's degree from a university. In many, if not most, cases, they lacked the technical skills and backcountry experience that park wardens had because most were urban and had gone straight to university out of high school. They were a different species, and an awkward fit. And warden culture was so strong that, even with her MBA and an army of bureaucratic courtesans, the new regional director had not managed to make any headway at reorganizing the warden service.

None of which mattered to me: I just wanted one of those jobs. It was essentially the same job I'd been yanked out of in 1985. In my opinion, there shouldn't be anything even to think about; I should simply be appointed to one of the new slots. But my opinion didn't matter. I had to apply and go through the same selection process as everyone else.

Bill Dolan, the chief park warden in Waterton Lakes National Park, was in charge of the hiring process. He had spent a few years as staff biologist in Winnipeg before joining the warden service and moving with his family to the High Arctic. Bill may have come late to the warden service, but he believed firmly that the new jobs should go to park wardens who had earned their spurs already and would consequently have no problem being accepted by their peers. I wasn't one of those. But I was also a problem, because I had already worked at the level he was hiring for, and my credentials almost exactly matched the job description.

There were six vacancies in the first round. I qualified sixth.

A principled team player, Bill stood aside while other parks scooped up the new hires until there was only one left; I ended up as his employee in Waterton Lakes National Park. In keeping with his view that my biologist position required practical warden experience, however, he insisted that I spend my first year working as a park warden before focusing on my ecosystem science role. That proved to be a wise decision. I was out of my depth as a rookie warden and forced to rely on the support and counsel of the others on the team. That kept me humble and built strong relationships with my warden peers.

Half a decade after what had felt like the end of all our hopes, those Waterton years proved to be some of the most rewarding of my Parks Canada career and the best years for our family too. It had been a lesson lived; a good one.

Something involving faith, albeit not the kind I was raised in.

11. Paahtómahksikimi

Calm winter days are rare in Waterton. They seldom last long. Drifts and dunes of hardened snow lie banked behind buildings in the near-deserted town. The lake is white and still, as if it has forgotten it is even there. Mountains gaze stonily across frozen forests at a steel-blue winter sky that stretches far off to the north.

Gail was often at home alone when the wind came. She got used to looking south across Waterton Lake to see the first hint that the wind was coming back. The change began subtly; a faint, glowing halo would frame the peaks up near Goat Haunt. Then wraiths of snow would begin to dance out of the steep forests closer in. Plumes of spindrift spilled from the nearer mountains – Boswell, then Vimy – and what looked like a wall of mist appeared on the lake, drawing near.

Then it would hit. Houses shuddered. Leafless poplars writhed. A roar of sound enveloped the town, and all was suddenly a chaos of wind and driven snow. Waterton would be back to normal.

John Russell told Gail and me about jumping into that wind with his boyhood friends from the top of the hill where the Prince of Wales Hotel stands. They leaped confidently into space, trusting the tempest to toss them back. It must have worked; he was still there, decades later, sipping coffee at our kitchen table and telling tales while the house shuddered and the eaves rattled.

One of those tales was about his grandparents' first home. The wind blew it into the creek. That was an easy story to believe; we had our own similar tale.

One winter a friend from Calgary, Denis Gourdeau, came down to visit and work on a digital atlas project we were collaborating on. He rented a car for the trip and, since Gail and I were putting him up for the night in our house beside the townsite campground, he parked it in the driveway beside the minivan we owned at the time. The wind, as usual, was howling. It grew in intensity as the night progressed.

In the morning Gail met me in the kitchen with a puzzled look on her face.

"Did you go out again last night?"

"No."

"Then who moved the van?"

I looked out the window. Our van was parked halfway across the back lawn. Denis's rental car had a big gouge along one side. The packed snow on the driveway was sufficiently slippery that the wind had been able to slide the van ten metres into the yard until it stopped against a drift.

Denis reassured me that he had taken out the extra vehicle insurance offered by the rental company, so there wouldn't be any problem. There wasn't, but when he explained what had happened the woman at the rental counter made him wait. She went and got her manager.

"You've got to hear this story," she said. "This guy says he got hit by a parked car – while he was parked!"

***

Gail wasn't sure about moving to Waterton Lakes National Park, even though it had long been an ambition of mine. The first time our family visited there we had camped in the rain and our daughter Katie came down with bronchitis. It hadn't been a positive first impression. Gail felt that the town might be too far away from shopping and services in winter. She'd heard about that wind too.

I knew the park would be hiring its first conservation biologist, and I wanted that job. But any move to Waterton would have to be a mutual decision. I called a friend, Charlie Russell, who owned a ranch just outside the park, to see if he was open to a visit. Charlie had pretty much gotten out of the cattle business in order to pursue his personal passion for grizzly bears. In all my years in bear country, I never met a person who understood bears as deeply as him. His father, Andy Russell, a well-known wildlife videographer, author, and conservationist, lived in an old hunting lodge, the Hawk's Nest, on a knoll not far from the northeast edge of the park. Charlie told me the Hawk's Nest was currently unoccupied, because Andy was living in the Millarville area at the home of his current partner. Charlie suggested I bring the family down and stay at the Hawk's Nest. That way Gail could check things out first-hand.

We arrived in the middle of the June rainy season. But the sun shone for four days straight. The wind didn't blow. Lazuli buntings and black-headed grosbeaks sang us awake each morning, and chipmunks played on the porch. All was green and flower strewn. It was as if nature had pulled out all the stops to help erase Gail's doubts.

When I was finally offered the job in 1993, there was no longer any question about whether to accept it. We sold our house in Okotoks and moved to the place the Blackfoot know as Paahtómahksikimi, and which I soon came to think of as the centre of the living universe.

Waterton Lakes National Park and its larger sister park on the US side of the international border, Glacier National Park, share honours as the world's first International Peace Park. The Peace Park is recognized by the United Nations Environmental, Scientific and Cultural Organization (UNESCO) as a World Heritage Site. It's also the protected core of an International Biosphere Reserve. Those honours reflect its significance as a place of outstanding beauty, exceptional biodiversity, and profound cultural significance.

In the 1990s the Peace Park and its surrounding landscapes also became known as the Crown of the Continent Ecosystem. That name is considerably more apt than "Waterton," a name British explorer Thomas Blakiston arbitrarily assigned to the lakes in honour of his friend Charles Waterton, who never got anywhere near this homeland of the Siksikaitsitapi and Ktunaxa Peoples.

Glacier National Park's Triple Divide Peak is, in fact, the hydrological apex of the North American continent. Rain falling there can flow to the Arctic, Atlantic, or Pacific Ocean, depending on which way it drains from the summit, hence the label "crown of the continent." But as the many international honours bestowed on the area show, the significance of the Crown of the Continent runs far deeper than that. The 400,000 or so hectares of landscape surrounding that peak are one of the continent's centres of biological diversity and cultural significance.

Regardless of all its new titles, Waterton already had a name: Paahtómahksikimi translates to Inner Sacred Lake. And the mountains that enclose it are part of Miistakis, the backbone of the world.

***

The Crown of the Continent region overlies the narrowest part of the Rocky Mountains. Here prairie ecosystems extend right up to mountain summits, Pacific coast plants and animals spill across into the interior of the continent, and species from Canada's northern Rockies intermingle with others from the American high plains. It's a meeting place of continental biomes. Summers are more humid than elsewhere in Alberta's mountains, and in winter the winds can be furious and unrelenting.

The wind is one reason for the Crown's exceptional diversity. Southwest of Waterton the broad Columbia plateau creates a gap in the chains of mountains that stand between the Rockies and the Pacific Ocean. With so little resistance, vast seas of moist air surge inland across that gap, funnelled up against the one barrier that still stands between the ocean and the prairies: the Rocky Mountains. Coincidentally – if one is content with coincidence as an explanation for the world's many marvels – the Lewis Overthrust squeezed the Rockies to their narrowest dimension just here, more than 58 million years ago. And so, in a continental-scale demonstration of the Bernoulli effect, those winds come raging across the Continental Divide again and again, gnarling the timberline larches and whitebark pines, opening lush gaps in the lower forests, piling snowdrifts in gullies and the edges of aspen stands, and scouring the bunchgrass flats clear. In doing so, they open up dozens of unique niches for living things.

I came to think of those winds as God's breath.

There was something about this place I had only rarely sensed before. New Agers talk about vortex places where spiritual energy crosses into or out of the earth's plane of existence. As I spent more time in Waterton and its surroundings, I found myself becoming less skeptical about that idea. The Crown seems almost to hum with life and meaning.

Nearly all of its mountain summits have lichen-splattered Vision Quest sites. Campsites, cairns, weapon fragments, and other artifacts in the valleys below record a continuous history of more than 12,000 years of human presence. Many of the medicine plants that are found here and nowhere else in Alberta – like blue camas lily and biscuitroot – were almost certainly brought here by the Ktunaxa and Siksikaitsitapi Peoples who at various times occupied those valleys and traded back and forth across the mountain passes.

The descendants of those people live nearby on the Blood and Peigan Reserves. A very few still climb to the vision sites. There they fast, pray, and are visited by dreams that give meaning and shape to their lives after they come down out of the rocks and wind. They know the nature of this place, and the place knows them.

Everyone who spends any time in southern Alberta is familiar with the mild chinook winds that periodically come out of the mountains to thaw the snowdrifts and turn the foothills brown, but in the Crown of the Continent the gales are of a whole different order of magnitude. Wind gauges measure gusts over 150 kilometres per hour most winters. The aspen forests are stunted and shattered from endless battering. Snowdrifts are higher than houses. Our kids wore snow goggles for their walks to school. In summer, tents regularly blew through our yard from the adjacent campground.

John Russell said, "People like to complain about the wind, but we like it. If it wasn't so windy, more people would move here."

It didn't discourage us from moving there, but it sometimes kept us indoors for days at a time.

***

On one of those rare winter days when the wind wasn't blowing, 11-year-old Katie announced that I was going to take her out looking for wolves. She knew that Elliot Fox and I had been working to keep track of wolves that had moved into the region a few months previously, and she wanted to see one.

I explained to my daughter that I was pretty sure there were no more wolves. Hunters, ranchers, trappers, and accidents had killed pretty much the entire wolf population. Over the previous ten months an estimated regional population of 60 had dwindled to perhaps ten or so, and those wary survivors inhabited remote country an hour's drive north. There wasn't much point in looking for a wolf anywhere south of Banff.

Katie was insistent, however, so we bundled up for the cold and set off into the winter woods on snowshoes.

We soon cut coyote tracks, and Katie was happy to follow those. It would still be an adventure. We found where the coyotes had hunted mice, frolicked in the snow, and stopped to watch their back-trail. The coyotes knew we were following; as we returned along the half-frozen Waterton River, one yapped at us from the forest.

I yelped back. A moment later, two or three coyotes responded with a maniacal caterwauling. As the echoes faded, I thought I heard a deeper voice in the distance. Katie stood stock-still, listening. She looked up with a question on her face.

I tried a wolf howl. This time, the deep and mournful answer that came resonating through the winter afternoon was unmistakable.

"I told you we'd find one," Katie whispered.

Another howled, closer, somewhere in the tangle of cottonwoods and willows across the river. The two conversed: long-drawn moans interspersed with deep barks. We were just about to go looking for them when a third, deeper howl resonated out of the shadows right across the river.

We stood, surrounded by the hair-lifting chorus, for several minutes. Then, with the sun setting behind Sáíkímao'pii (Mount Crandell), we hurried back to our vehicle and drove to where we could glass the area. In the patchy forest across the river, small bunches of white-tailed deer and two groups of bull elk were feeding in scattered meadows. Katie peered through our window-mounted spotting scope.

"The elk are running," she announced.

A grey wolf appeared at the edge of the aspens, trotting leisurely towards a cluster of elk. The elk ran a few metres and then stopped as the wolf turned away. Now we could see a second grey wolf. Both rushed a group of deer. The deer darted away, then stopped and watched, white flags lifted. Again the wolves abandoned the pursuit.

We watched, enthralled, as the two greys and a large black wolf tested several more bunches in the fading evening light. At length, the wolves vanished into the aspens. When we got home, Katie burst into the house to tell her mom and brothers the news: "Dad said we wouldn't find any wolves, but we did!"

***

A year and a half earlier I'd gotten a phone call at work from a US Fish and Wildlife Service biologist named Joe Fontaine. Joe explained that he had been tasked with monitoring the growing population of wolves in north-central Montana. Those wolves had found their way to the US along the Flathead River, west of the Continental Divide, several years previously. Protected under the US Endangered Species Act, the first colonizers had soon given rise to several packs. Now, in a sort of ecological free trade, some of those Montana wolves had come back north on the Alberta side of the divide. Joe was calling to say that one of their radio-collared wolves had dispersed into Canada and appeared to be part of a pack that spent most of its time in the Belly River valley on the eastern side of Waterton Lakes National Park.

The pack might be in Canada, but it was part of Joe's Northern Continental Divide wolf population. He asked if we'd be willing to invite him across the border to try and radio collar another two wolves in the pack, since their protocol was to have three collars in each pack in case of animals dying or dispersing. He was also kind of hoping we'd be interested in monitoring the wolves once that was done; he already had ten packs to keep track of.

The western US is primarily federal public land, but Canada's federal presence is limited to national parks, First Nations reserves, and military training areas. Ever since the 1930 Natural Resources Transfer Acts transferred jurisdiction over land, resources, and most wildlife to the western provinces, the federal footprint in our west has been small. Ever conscious of local sensitivities, federal agencies like Parks Canada try to keep that footprint as light as possible too.

Waterton, at only 505 square kilometres, is too small to protect so wide-ranging an animal as the wolf. The Belly pack's daily travels took it into the Blood Tribe Timber Limit, which was the jurisdiction of the Kainai First Nation, as well as onto Alberta public land and privately owned ranches. Outside the national park, wolves in our area could be legally shot and killed pretty much anywhere – another big difference from the US.

I told Joe that his best option, under those circumstances, would be to come up and meet the neighbours. He could make his pitch to all of them at once. I offered to work with the Waterton Biosphere Reserve Association to pull a couple of meetings together.

***

Larry Frith, a Twin Butte organic rancher, was chair of the Waterton Biosphere Reserve Association at the time. He and I jointly hosted two public information sessions in June 1994: one in Twin Butte, on the west side of the Waterton River, and the other at Mountain View, on the east side.

Larry introduced the resource people at the head table. Joe Fontaine then explained what the US was doing on the wolf recovery front. He made it clear that its only interest in Canadian wolves was to monitor them, not to interfere in their management. Richard Quinlan, the head wildlife biologist for the Alberta Fish and Wildlife Service's southern Rocky Mountains and foothills region, then gave a presentation on the province's wolf management plan. While noting that the plan set a population target for southwestern Alberta of 50 wolves, he emphasized that there were no plans to change the province's very liberal wolf-killing regulations.

I gave Parks Canada's perspective: wolves would be rigorously protected in Waterton Lakes National Park, but we understood and respected the interests of the neighbours. Then Larry opened the floor to questions. There weren't many.

At both meetings, most of the 50 or so mostly male ranchers in attendance leaned back in their seats, legs fully extended and arms crossed, leaning over occasionally to mutter a few words to their neighbours. The asides were usually met with a short chuckle or a cynical shake of the head. I had a nagging sense that the body language was telling me something I didn't want to know.

I was right. The day after the Mountain View meeting, a rancher, who also worked for Parks Canada to supplement his income, collared me in my office. He hadn't been able to get to the meeting, so he'd asked one of his neighbours for an update.

"What's this I hear about you guys flying a bunch of wolves into the country?" he demanded.

"What?"

"You know. The ones you're stocking near Payne Lake. Where are you going to get 50 wolves, and why on earth would you put them right out where I live? Who is this Fontaine guy, anyway, and who's paying for the helicopter?"

A well-intended effort to create an informed community and get everyone on a level playing field had failed utterly. The muttered asides, evidently by individuals who figured they could read between the lines to get at what must be the real, hidden agendas of those government experts at the head table, had been the only information effectively transmitted at either meeting. It was my first encounter with conspiracy theory; sadly, it was far from the last.

***

Nevertheless, a few weeks later, Joe arrived with Carter Niemeyer, a seasoned trapper who had spent many years with the US Animal Damage Control group but was now a wolf specialist with the US Federal Wildlife Service. The American team would trap and collar the wolves, and then the ongoing monitoring responsibility was going to fall to Parks Canada and Alberta Fish and Wildlife. To that end, Richard and I had pooled our resources to hire a student assistant.

Elliot Fox was a recent graduate of the Lethbridge Community College's renewable resources program, a deeply committed con- servationist, and an idealist who hoped to help grow the Kainai First Nation's leadership in environmental stewardship. Elliot proved to be more than an exceptional hire; he became a valued lifelong friend.

The Belly wolves, however, eluded the team. We would have to hope that the original collared wolf, named Salix by biologist Diane Boyd, who had originally caught her in Montana's Flathead valley, would manage to stay alive. Two more of Diane's radio-collared wolves had emigrated to Canada in the meantime. Conveniently, each became alpha female in a new pack. Richard and I extended Elliot's work contract to cover the whole region so he could keep track of all three packs.

The Belly pack denned in Waterton Lakes National Park and ranged south into Montana and north into the ranchlands around Mountain View, occasionally crossing the Waterton River to the west. The Beauvais pack denned on private land southwest of Pincher Creek, ranging through ranch country and up into the provincial public lands in the Castle River drainage. Their range overlapped with that of the Carbondale pack, which lived mostly on public lands in the upper Carbondale and Castle River drainages, as well as adjoining ranches.

Surprisingly, given the abundance of cattle in that corner of Alberta, the wolves caused no problems. The Belly River wolves, for example, hunted white-tailed deer, elk, and beaver in forested grazing areas full of domestic cattle – but they never succumbed to the temptation to eat beef. By now I knew several ranchers adjacent to the national park whose land the wolves hunted. Although all expected the Belly pack to wreak havoc, none could find any evidence of wolves chasing cattle.

Farther north, however, other wolves confirmed the fears of naysayers. West of Highway 22, in the Whaleback and Breeding Valley areas, one elusive and seldom-seen pack attacked cattle on a regular basis over a period of several months. In some cases, the wolves killed and fed on their prey. Sometimes they left cows badly wounded from unsuccessful attacks. In spite of concerted efforts by problem-wildlife staff of Alberta Fish and Wildlife to find and kill them, by the spring of 1995 those wolves had killed or painfully mauled at least 30 head of cattle.

***

Having learned our lesson about public meetings, Richard, Elliot, and I began, instead, to visit people at their homes to discuss wolves. Elliot had another reason, as he needed permission to access property in his ongoing efforts to locate the radio signals of the highly mobile animals. This, it turned out, was the right way to communicate. Most of the people we met were willing to talk, but they wanted us to listen too. They had good reasons for worrying about predation, given that their family incomes relied on their annual calf crop. Most felt they couldn't afford to simply live and let live.

Alberta's progressive era under Peter Lougheed was long past. Ralph Klein now presided over a conservative caucus determined to undo much of what the Lougheed Tories had built. Klein's priorities were small government and deficit-killing. One of the victims of his government's cost-cutting obsession was a program that had paid farmers and ranchers compensation for predator kills. It was not an expensive program. Total payouts averaged less than $50,000 per year, province wide.

Although cutting that compensation program had little impact on the province's balance sheets, the decision's impact in rural Alberta was huge. Ranchers felt the government had abandoned them just as predator populations were increasing. This was not a good time to ask for tolerance.

Wolf conservation has always been less a biological issue than a sociological one. Richard and I knew we had to find a solution to the loss of the compensation program. There seemed little hope of persuading the provincial government to change its mind. Without government money, funding would have to come from those who most wanted wolves in southwestern Alberta: environmental groups and visitors to the national park.

That would be challenging, but we had no difficulty agreeing that property owners whose good habitat stewardship supported ungulate prey should not have to bear the costs of losing livestock to the predators those herds attracted.

The Waterton Natural History Association, a volunteer-based organization that helps Parks Canada educate park visitors, agreed to solicit donations from park visitors, but only if its funds went to compensate local ranchers suffering losses to "park" wolves. That was a good start, but to be effective the program would have to cover a larger area. Richard, who as a provincial biologist was dealing with other pressures, insisted that compensation needed to be available for losses to grizzly bears too.

Much to our surprise, the Canadian Parks and Wilderness Society stepped up to fill in the gap. It was Mike Going, president of the Calgary chapter of CPAWS, who persuaded his group to solicit donations even though the one thing we could not offer was increased protection for wolves. The compensation program would be strictly a goodwill initiative aimed at building social tolerance and reducing the risk of organized, unofficial eradication campaigns.

The steering committee included Richard Quinlan, representing Alberta Fish and Wildlife; myself for Parks Canada; Mike Going for the environmental community; and a Beaver Mines-area rancher by the name of Keith Everts, representing the Alberta Cattle Commission. Rick Neville, a sheep rancher, rounded the group out.

Mike had grown up on a ranch near Longview. Now, when not representing CPAWS, he ran Good Earth Coffeehouses in Calgary, catering largely to vegetarian and vegan clients.

The pony-tailed and upbeat Keith was a former hippie and vegetarian who, with his wife, Bev, had gotten into ranching through a farm apprenticeship program they signed up for in the 1970s. He raised and marketed organic beef. So we had a former rancher who now ran vegetarian restaurants, and a former vegetarian who now ran a beef ranch. The Alberta Cattle Commission may have been a bit skeptical about the mix, so Keith was soon joined by Kim Hansen, a multi-generational rancher from just outside Waterton Lakes National Park. Kim had no love for wolves, so he was mostly there to keep an eye on us. He was a principled and fair-minded man, but he wasn't so sure about the rest of us.

The steering committee decided to offer full fall-market-value compensation for confirmed kills, a considerably sweeter deal than had been available through the former government program. It didn't help. Conspiracy theorists in the ranching community warned their peers not to apply for compensation for fear there would be strings attached.

At last, however, in early 1995 a rancher from north of Pincher Creek contacted Fish and Wildlife and asked to be compensated for the loss of a yearling cow. A conservation officer investigated and confirmed it as a wolf kill. CPAWS sent a cheque for $1,000 to the rancher. A few days later, Mike Going called to say that the cheque had been returned. Paranoid neighbours had persuaded the rancher that if he cashed an "environmental" cheque, it would be the thin edge of the wedge leading to total protection for wolves.

Conspiracy theories won; the rancher lost.

The Alberta Cattle Commission, under pressure from the same naysayers, warned Klein's government that environmental groups were getting too involved in predator management. It also stressed the unfairness of having compensation available only to south-western livestock producers when other parts of the province had losses too. The government quietly reinstated its province-wide, taxpayer-funded livestock compensation program.

That was a success of sorts, but the wolves were mostly dead by then anyway.

***

Wolves had never played much of a role in Elliot's life until he took on the task of keeping track of them. They soon came to feel like family to him. One day he told me he was curious now about what role the wolf might have in Blackfoot traditions and culture. The fact that he didn't know already was clearly troubling to him. As he got ready to head home for the weekend, he said he was going to ask his uncle, a Kainai Elder.

The following week I asked him what he'd learned. He shook his head.

"He died on the weekend," he said. "I never got a chance to ask."

***

With the demise of all three radio-collared females, and their pack members, there wasn't much left for Elliot to do. Fortunately, the Alberta government, having designated the bull trout a species of special concern, had released a management plan in 1994 that called for more research and monitoring. Richard and I agreed to collaborate again, this time to see what could be done to help the dwindling bull trout populations in the Belly and Waterton Rivers. We'd need a reliable technician, and access to the Blood Tribe Timber Limit. Elliot agreed to take the project on.

Bull trout are predatory char that can grow to a metre or more in length in the productive lower reaches of rivers draining from the Rockies. But they can only spawn in cold, spring-fed headwater streams, so each summer they work their way up into the high country, where they dig large nests, called redds, in the gravelly bottoms of small mountain creeks. Once they've deposited their eggs and buried them, they migrate downstream to the larger, warmer waters full of their prey: whitefish, suckers, dace, and other fish species. When people build dams and irrigation diversion weirs across rivers, as had been done to both the Waterton and Belly Rivers, bull trout lose their ability to make that annual migration. Their predatory nature and large size also make them appealing to anglers. It was no surprise that the big fish were growing scarce.

Locals from the Mountain View area, a few kilometres outside the park, used to ride by horseback up a well-kept trail into the valley of the North Belly River, where they caught huge bull trout by the sackful, or so we were told. None went in there anymore because the old-timers had passed on and an outbreak of mountain pine beetles in the mid-1980s had killed most of the old trees in the valley. Now, a decade later, the old trail had almost entirely vanished under a criss-crossed jungle of fallen dead pine trees. Elliot and I decided to hike in and see if any fish had survived the fish hog era.

It was a gruelling, but gorgeous, hike. Bull trout spawn in late September, so the aspens were gold and the ground cover a paisley carpet of green, red, orange, and yellow. We found the old trail but following it was a challenge. For the most part, we simply kept the river beside us and worked our way upstream along the path of least resistance. Like all the streams in the Crown of the Continent, the North Belly is almost impossibly beautiful. The gravel in its bed is composed of smooth rounded stones – brick-red, blue, brown, and pale grey, like a jumble of precious stones eroded out of ancient mountains. And they are ancient; the Crown has the oldest sedimentary rock in the world.

We were hot and sweaty and pretty much ready to give up when Elliot spotted the first redd. It was a scooped-out hollow in the riverbed, a metre long, where the pebbles were clean of the algae that normally coats the gravel. Just downstream of the hollow the gravel was slightly mounded. A pair of bull trout hung suspended in the current, the big female hugging the bottom and a smaller male hanging close by her side.

We had found the spawning reach. Over the next half kilometre we found several more redds, sometimes by seeing the telltale cleaned-off spot in the gravel and other times by startling the big fish. Elliot waved me over at one point and said, "Look at this one."

It was the biggest redd we'd seen yet, almost three metres long, tucked in against the bank where the current was strong. As I crouched beside it, I saw movement in the water-flicker just downstream, as if part of the stream bed had come loose, and then an immense female bull trout eased up out of the shadows and into the cleaned space beside me. She hung there, close enough that I could almost have touched her. She was as long as my leg, golden and sleek, white-edged fins moving slowly. I could see the red in her gills as she breathed the same sweet mountain water that her ancestors had breathed here for centuries.

For a few moments the world disappeared and all that existed was a trout, a river, and the deep, breathing silence of this remote mountain valley. I remembered my grandfather's tales that had so enthralled me, of hunting, catching, and killing huge bull trout. I remembered all the small bull trout my family had eaten at campsites beside similar streams over the years. I thought about how we were here because a native trout that had survived ice ages, droughts, forest fires, and floods for tens of thousands of years was now, because of choices made by newcomer people to the land, classified as a species at risk. There was a lump in my throat and an ache in my chest. I wanted to scream out loud into the cliffs looming above us.

In this sacred mountain place, I saw this fish now for what it was: a living song thousands of years in the making; a being that was a product of, and one with, the living rhythms and patterns of this one place, this Crown of the Continent; a holder of faith and a promise of meaning and an offer of relationship – and my people had put it all at risk. Because, to us, it was just a fish. And we could do what we liked, because we had granted ourselves dominion.

But the bull trout shifting gently in the current beside us was immersed in its own world, living in its own good way as its kind always had. Its faith was absolute; its sense of belonging unquestioned and complete. We were just passing shadows; it would remain.

Elliot and I hiked out in the long, golden light of a September evening, talking quietly of what we had seen and what we would do next. Whatever that moment had meant to each of us, we kept that to ourselves. But we both knew we had a duty to those golden fish now that we had found them. I've never fished for bull trout since that day, but I visit them often.

The important choices are never the ones we regret, only the ones we have yet to make. Those are the ones we still have a chance to get right. Bull trout are long-forgotten relatives who wait for us to get tomorrow right, in spite of yesterday's missteps.

***

You can run, but you can't hide. Gail and I had been relieved to escape Okotoks, where every day we faced reminders of the rate at which foothills Alberta was being broken up into little parcels of real estate and sold off. Waterton, as a national park, seemed safe from those sorts of pressures. Even on our frequent trips into Pincher Creek for errands, the drive took us through the kind of foothills landscape that used to lap right up against the Calgary city limits but had long since been lost to land development. John Russell was right; those crazy Waterton winds were our friend. But the intactness of the land around the park also derived from the stubborn determination of multi-generational ranch families to keep their land intact and their lifestyle viable.

Nonetheless, the land vultures seemed to have followed us south, and now they were circling over the Crown of the Continent. One day a worried-looking Bill Dolan told me he'd just got wind of a subdivision proposal right on the park boundary. It had been bound to happen; Waterton Lakes National Park, unlike other mountain national parks, is not buffered by public land. Where Waterton ends, private property begins. What better way to acquire wealth than to build and sell nice recreational second homes, right at the edge of a national park?

If so remote a parcel were to be turned into a grid of roads and recreational second homes, we were sure it would turn out to be the first domino. Dollar signs would be flashing in front of some landowners' eyes. A lot of the neighbouring ranchers were aging, and their children weren't interested in taking over. Bill and I worried that, once they saw the first few developments go in, they might well throw in the towel and sell out too. For all that the land around the park seemed intact and secure, it was a fragile situation. And since some of the most productive wildlife habitat in the Crown is not in the national parks but on those lower-elevation private lands adjoining it, the stakes were high.

I called Larry Simpson, a friend who had spent much of his life building the Nature Conservancy of Canada's presence in Alberta. NCC's conservation work is focused primarily on private lands. It seeks out properties with high conservation values and then either buys out the development rights by means of a conservation easement or, if necessary and possible, simply buys the property outright. I explained the situation to Larry. He promised to see if he could find a donor with big enough pockets to buy out the developers' interest. He told me, however, not to get my hopes up.

There were already three small cottage properties subdivided out of the quarter section the developers had their eyes on. The owners accessed their property by way of a gravel access off the Chief Mountain Highway, which runs through the park. It occurred to me that meant the access might not even be legal, since they were driving off-road (albeit, only for a few metres) across national park land.

Any straw seemed worth snatching at, so I called Steve Faulknor, a senior lawyer with the federal justice department who was responsible for litigation involving national park issues. When

I explained the situation, Steve agreed with my interpretation. Nobody had a legal right to access that property from the park road. I knew that if the developer couldn't use that access, he would have to come in from the north and build about five kilometres of road. Prohibiting access from the park wouldn't stop the development, but it might make the project less economically viable.

Steve worked with me to develop legal instruments that would give the current cottage owners access but not grant the right to transfer that instrument without Parks Canada approval. When I met with them, they were startled, then disgruntled. Bureaucracy had found their peaceful little retreats. It was just a formality, however, so they all soon rolled their eyes and accepted the permits we had written up.

Then we went to work designing a sign that would go up on the edge of the highway, putting off-road access clearly out of bounds to anyone without a permit. Steve was a stickler for wording, however, so the process stretched on for several days as he and I emailed various drafts back and forth. The clock was ticking towards the meeting of the Cardston County council, where the subdivision would almost certainly be approved. I knew we might have a solid legal position, but I also knew how politics could render that moot.

Then Larry called. The Weston Family Foundation had bought the property from the developer. There would be no subdivision. The land would remain as it was.

***

The same threat loomed over many more properties adjacent to the park, however. Now that Larry had turned his attention to Waterton, he became increasingly concerned. The Alberta portion of the Crown of the Continent might be one of the province's most biologically important landscapes, but only 505 square kilometres of its mountainous high country was protected in Waterton Lakes National Park. Species like sandhill crane, trumpeter swan, blue camas, and blue flag iris live mostly in the well-watered aspen parkland outside the park. Waterton might be known for its bears, but there are often more grizzlies out on those ranches than in the park; the foraging is better in all that low-elevation greenery and it's often more peaceful there, far from the summer tourist crowds. Losing the ranch landscape would mean losing some of the most productive habitats in the area – habitats that actually contribute to the ecological health of the national park.

Blaine Marr, who ranched a few kilometres north of the park, complained to me one day: "It doesn't matter how many real estate guys I chase off the place, they just wait until I'm not home and stick their business cards in my door."

I had arrived in Waterton thinking my job would involve protecting the park from the ranchers. Now I realized we needed to protect the ranchers from the park, because the park was a big part of what was attracting real estate speculators into the area. Fortunately, Larry saw the same thing. And he knew people who were willing to contribute their money to the cause of keeping natural landscapes intact.

That's how the Nature Conservancy of Canada's Waterton Front Project was born. In the years that followed, what had once been unimaginable became true. Thanks to the Weston Family Foundation, John and Barbara Poole, and other conservation-minded donors, the NCC protected over 120 square kilometres of ranchland adjacent to the park. Had real estate development gained traction in the area, land prices and taxes would have skyrocketed, pricing ranchers out of business. So the Waterton Front Project, in keeping most of that landscape intact, proved vital in protecting both ranching and nature.

Intact, but not completely natural. Most of those ranches were established in the late 1800s and very early 1900s. There were lots of mistakes and learning experiences over the years, from the disastrous winter cattle die-off of 1886/87, to stocking native pastures too heavily in summer when rough fescue and other members of the plant community are particularly vulnerable to grazing, to failing to protect wetlands and riparian areas where cattle like to congregate. Ranchers who couldn't learn and adapt went out of business; the rest became adept at caring for their range and using the domestic cow as a surrogate for the wild bison who used to live there.

But cows are cows, and bison are bison. They evolved in very different environments and behave differently. Fenced pastures aren't open range. It takes a lot of work, creativity, and tolerance of failure for ranchers to manage domestic cattle herds in ways that sustain and renew native vegetation in the way that bison used to do. To their credit, many fourth- and fifth-generation ranchers in Alberta's foothills have it figured out.

Those winter winds that roar out of Waterton's valleys always made the area important to the plains bison. When winter snows grew deep on the open prairies over which bison herds ranged in summer, most of the herds moved into the foothills and lower mountain valleys where wind keeps the grass exposed. Foothills rough fescue grasslands grow more lushly than the drier grasslands out on the dry plains. Rough fescue – the dominant grass – stores protein and starches in its leaves during the winter. Having been only lightly grazed during the summer growing season, that foothills grassland was a rich resource for the returning bison, swept clear of snow by God's breath.

The snow blown off the open grassland collects in deep drifts behind hills and in coulees and draws. Indigenous hunters used to hunt bison there by driving them into the snowdrifts and slaughtering them while the big animals floundered. Traces of those drive lanes and snow pounds survive today, but there are no bison.

That's not completely true. Waterton maintains a fenced paddock with a small herd of plains bison for visitors to see. But they don't roam free. The bison are there, but their ecology is turned upside down: they graze those winter grasses all summer long, and are fed hay in the winter when they should be eating the native stuff.

I thought a lot about the possibilities. Where in North America are there still free-ranging herds of bison fully integrated with the ecology of the landscapes they once shaped so dramatically? Not just display herds, or even conservation herds like the pure-strain plains bison held in Elk Island National Park, east of Edmonton, but wild herds exposed to predation by wolves and grizzly bears? Yellowstone National Park in the US, Prince Albert National Park in Saskatchewan – but nowhere in the core area of their former wild range.

If Parks Canada were to collaborate with the NCC, the Niitsítapi, and area ranchers to bring bison back on a larger scale, not only would that landscape be protected from development but much of its original ecology would be restored. The bison could be held in summer on cultivated fields currently used for growing hay, and then left free to forage for themselves throughout the Waterton Front properties and the park itself in winter. They'd live among grizzly bears and wolves like they used to. Perhaps they'd be hunted again by the Niitsítapi. They'd be real bison, restoring realness to the world. In a world of losses and disconnection, it would be a current flowing in the other direction – towards restoration and reconciliation.

I pitched the idea to Bill Dolan when the park management plan came up for renewal. Couldn't we add a few words to the effect that Parks Canada was willing to entertain such an idea?

The barriers were too many, though. There is an inherent conservatism in the ranching community that, in many ways, is both its biggest strength and its biggest weakness. Where bison are concerned, the social blowback would be huge from a community that sometimes feels under siege from a world that seems always ready to find new ways to threaten what they have. I'd already experienced the reaction to wolves coming back into the country, after all. Senior park bureaucrats are risk-averse by nature; they would want no part of such an adventure. They would worry about fencing challenges, costs, liability issues, and manpower.

Perhaps it was enough that the landscape surrounding the national park was still intact and would stay that way, given that most of those ranchers are careful and thoughtful stewards of the land.

Each spring the sound of sandhill cranes, chorus frogs, and song-birds and the sight of trumpeter swans feeding in quiet wetlands and bear tracks along the creek bottoms reminded me that was probably good enough.

At least for now.

***

Only a couple of kilometres from Waterton's forlorn fenced bison paddock the Waterton River widens and backs into a shallow lake and wetland where swallows dip and dive each evening. Loons wail on summer evenings and for a while each fall the sky above is full of the clamour of migrating waterfowl. Sometimes the wild, ancient sound of sandhill cranes emerges from back in the sedges and rushes.

I watched a grizzly bear hunting elk calves there one June evening, coursing like a spaniel dog at full speed in and out of the fringing willow thickets. Then it was gone as if it had never been there; golden light glimmered sideways across the water and the green world was so still I found myself holding my breath. The air fairly quivered with something that felt like magic.

The newcomers who insisted on imposing new names on places called this the Maskinonge, after a fish that is found nowhere on the western half of the continent. Weird, but that was how we named things: as if names don't really matter.

The real name of the place is Aohkiaahkoinimaan, which means Water Nation Pipe. The sacred beaver bundle came to the Siksikaitsitapi here in ancient times. According to Ninna Piiksii (Dr. Mike Bruised Head), the last ceremonial opening of the bundle was in 1926. During the 20th century, the Siksikaitsitapi lost their ancient connections to the birthplace of the oldest of their sacred bundles and to the mountains surrounding it. First the names by which they knew the places got replaced by new names invented with little thought and no ceremony by strangers. Then, through much of the 20th century, they felt unwelcome. Paahtómahksikimi had become Waterton, a place for holidayers and tourists. That loss was only compounded by the residential school era, during which well-meaning missionaries and government people (and too many who were less than well-meaning) tried to extinguish Indigenous languages and cultures, and turn them into something more like the strangers who had so quickly taken over their territory.

A decade and a half after Gail and I left Waterton Lakes National Park, a lightning strike started a forest fire in BC, west of the park. Pushed by furious winds, the 2017 Kenow Fire spilled over the divide and burned across much of the park. Dense forest fuels and the bellows-like effect of the wind made it one of the most intense fires in Alberta history. In many areas, not only was the vegetation burned away but the soil was scorched down to the underlying rock and till.

Park archaeologists saw the aftermath as a once-in-a-lifetime opportunity to find evidence of previous occupation. With the vegetation and duff burned away, old campsites, structures, and artifacts lay exposed in the ashes. Crews hastened to inventory the park's archaeology before it could be obscured again by vegetation. They found camps and remains everywhere – a startling record of more than 12,000 years of continuous occupation by the Siksikaitsitapi. This was not a place the Blackfoot visited occasionally or travelled through to trade or hunt; it was a centre of their existence. They were not just a prairie people; they were mountain people. But that had almost been forgotten.

The researchers, including two young Blackfoot archaeologists, decided to examine the mountaintops. They found 17 different Vision Quest sites.

Mike Bruised Head was deeply troubled. These Itaksiistsimoo'pi were meant to be places of fasting and visions. But almost nobody visited them anymore. There was little point. The mountains no longer had their original Indigenous names. A Vision Quest begins with an invocation of the mountain's spirits, and that requires that the seeker pray to the mountain by its name. The names seemed to have vanished.

Dr. Bruised Head made it a personal mission to reclaim

Paahtómahksikimi for the Siksikaitsitapi. For him, as he explained in his PhD dissertation, it starts with the names:

> There seems to be sort of an atheist presence when people attain higher learning; and as a Niitsítapi, I come along and express to a certain degree my spirituality. That is why I am talking about getting the names of the mountains back so that the younger generation will have that experience, that pure absolute experience of fasting in the mountains with those mountains that have a name. In the process of being gifted, at some point in time, of that knowledge, through spiritual transfer of knowledge, on survival, on health, on medicine, on songs. Because right now, Waterton does not recognize that. To me I feel it's a sabotage of our Blackfoot spirituality, and I want to erase the feeling of being foreigners to our own sacred mountains. They are sacred. From those Vision Quest sites, of thousands of years, way before Europeans even landed here, before the early explorers, map surveyors and what have you even saw mountains, we were already doing that. And all that changed in the 1850s, 1884 when the Dominion Lands Protection Act was established – which is now the National Parks Act – and it disconnected that relationship with the mountains.[6]

None of this had yet begun when Gail and I loaded up our family to leave Waterton Lakes National Park and move back to Jasper. Maybe some of the work Elliot and I did helped to prepare the ground; maybe not. Things seem to happen when their time comes. The national park has a new visitor centre now only a few metres from where Gail woke up that winter morning to find our van parked sideways in the middle of our snow-covered backyard. The focus of the interpretive centre is the story of Paahtómahksikimi, a story that is slowly being rediscovered. The spirits of the place are returning. I believe the buffalo will come back too, because they are part of that. When that happens, it will be the Niitsítapi who bring them.

One reason we left Waterton was that the school closed down. Now it appears the teachers are returning.

12. The Road to Banff

Earth's memories are stored in its bones. Those long-ago eras when continents had different shapes and unseen oceans shimmered silent under birdless skies would be forgotten were it not for rocks that preserved their stories for a far distant time when evolution would deliver a mammal curious enough to try and decipher them.

Western Canada's geological archives were, however, partly erased during an Ice Age that ended only a few centuries ago. For two million years vast Pleistocene glaciers spread across the land, wearing down exposed rock and burying the rest beneath rubble. Like giant, slow-motion grinding machines, the immense masses of ice plucked at and scoured the earth's surface, even while the annual cycle of freezing and thawing chipped more rock loose from the ridges and mountains between which the ice flowed. Inside all that moving ice, stone fragments ground together, breaking into smaller pieces. During warm weather and longer intervals when the climate briefly warmed, meltwaters ground the cobbles smooth, turned boulders into sand and silt, and then washed it away.

Twenty thousand centuries of moving ice can grind up an awful lot of rock.

That's why the rolling landscape between Prince Albert and Elk Island national parks no longer tells the story of the earth's deep history; now it records a more recent story of ice, rubble, and floods. When the big glaciers melted away – about 12,000–15,000 years ago – they left their accumulated load of ground-up earth memories behind in newly deposited heaps and mounds of cobbles, stones, sand, and silt.

Today's coulees are the channels where meltwater trapped behind stagnant ice drained suddenly away in massive floods. Esker ridges that snake across the landscape mark the paths of gravel-laden streams that once flowed inside or beside the glaciers. Rolling hills are piles of glacial till. Hollows are often the remains of isolated ice chunks that, melting, left holes amid the rubble.

Centuries later, fescue grassland, aspen woods, farm fields, and towns overlay the earth's jumbled memories of the late Pleistocene. Deep beneath, layers of sandstone, shale, limestone, and conglomerate still bear silent witness to earlier, stranger times, but the surface of the plains now tell only the story of the Ice Age, and of that which came after – including us.

I was driving through that landscape one day in 2007, thinking about whooping cranes, when my cellphone rang.

I'd been promoted, two years earlier, to superintendent of Parks Canada's Northern Prairies field unit. The field unit was basically two national parks – Elk Island in Alberta and Prince Albert in Saskatchewan – and some smaller national historic sites. Most of my time was spent in Prince Albert National Park because the care of Elk Island was delegated to a site superintendent whom I supervised. On the rare occasions when I had to meet with her or help troubleshoot thorny issues, like today, I could look forward to another long drive though the rolling aspen parkland landscape between the two parks.

This was, and remains, the land of Nêhiyawak, the Plains Cree. The highway I was on followed a route that Mistahi-maskwa, the great Cree Chief whom history remembers as Big Bear, would have known well. This was the heart of the unrest that accompanied Louis Riel and Gabriel Dumont's short-lived Métis rebellion in 1885, and that led to Big Bear's tragic and unjust imprisonment. Many of the area's historic sites commemorate aspects of that conflict.

Even now, after a century of settlement and agricultural development, the landscape's ecological wealth was still apparent. Watching the land roll past, it was easy to see why the Cree were so reluctant to surrender their freedom to live here as they always had. Before Europeans arrived, the land through which I was driving would have teemed with herds of bison, elk, and moose. Even in the short bitter days of mid-winter there was food to be found. At other seasons the skies were noisy with the gabble of migrating waterfowl, and the woods and prairies a bedlam of birdsong.

Whooping cranes lived here too. Big Bear's people knew them as *otcak ka sâkowet*. In the morning cacophony rising from the fecund green marshes that filled the glacial hollows among these hills, the croaks and whoops of North America's largest birds mingled with the sounds of grebes, rails, coots, and geese in a discordant symphony of wild fecundity.

But they were easy to kill, and slow to reproduce. The cranes couldn't survive their encounter with the improvident hordes of newcomers bringing firearms and farming into the west. By the time I was born, whooping cranes were nearly extinct. Fewer than 20 migrated south to Texas each fall – from where, nobody seemed to know. I was less than 2 years old when forester George Wilson and biologist Bill Fuller finally reported they had found those last survivors nesting in the vast northern wetlands formed by the confluence of the Peace and Athabasca Rivers, an area already fortuitously protected within Wood Buffalo National Park.

Whooping cranes might no longer nest in the settled regions of central Saskatchewan and Alberta, but their migratory path still took them through Nêhiyawak country, where a landscape of farms and fences has replaced so much of the original wild.

Just a few months earlier, Gail and I had spent a rainy October day searching this very countryside, north of Blaine Lake, in hopes of seeing cranes. To our surprise and wonder, we found them: a pair of gleaming white adults and an ochre-coloured youngster feeding quietly along the edge of a grain field. They were utterly glorious – both as living relics of the Pleistocene and as inspiring testimony to the ability of people not just to exploit but to restore. The birds we found were part of a population that has now recovered to well over 500 individuals, thanks to the efforts of many.

We parked a few hundred metres away to keep from disturbing them and watched through a spotting scope for half an hour as the elegant white birds alternately foraged along the field edge and poised upright, watching for danger. Eventually, we drove away, leaving them to their journey, returning to ours.

It was early summer now, however, and those cranes were several hundred kilometres farther north, raising their young in remote boreal wetlands. When my phone rang, I checked the call display and promptly pulled over into a field access so I could answer. It was a call from Alan Latourelle, chief executive officer of the Parks Canada Agency.

"Are you busy?" he asked.

I told him where I was. I might even have mentioned the cranes.

"Well, I'm phoning to offer you the post of superintendent in Banff National Park," he said. I could hear his grin; he knew I'd be floored by the offer.

"Banff?" I said. My first reaction was less one of excitement than of dismay; the adrenaline rush took the wind out of me. Applying for that job had been a long shot; now it was on the brink of becoming a reality. In a flash of horrified self-awareness, I was suddenly certain I was not up to the challenge of managing Canada's oldest, busiest, and most complicated national park. Whatever had possessed me to apply for it?

For that matter, whatever had possessed Alan to offer it to me?

He assured me he had chosen me personally from the final shortlist. He didn't tell me what he saw in me that I didn't, but I was pretty sure he was seeing things that weren't there.

Alan seemed a bit taken aback when, after a brief discussion, I told him I'd call him back in the morning with an answer. I wanted to talk it over with Gail first. He must have assumed that conversation would already have taken place. But I'd actually applied for two different vacancies – one in Jasper and one in Banff. It was the Jasper position that Gail and I had talked about most, given my certainty they would want somebody more seasoned for Banff. Alan was always a gracious man, though; he sounded only mildly exasperated as we finished the call.

I sat in the car and looked around at the quiet land. Far away, a plume of dust showed above the aspens where a truck was travelling a lonely farm road. Red-tailed hawks circled overhead, and out my window I could hear the song of a vesper sparrow – *pîyesîs* to Mistahi-maskwa. Like the whooping cranes, that song would have been part of how Big Bear knew himself barely a century and a half ago – before this was Canada. Before there were parks. Before a newcomer people had to invent the concept of conservation because of the mess they were making of the Indigenous homelands they had appropriated with the confident certainty that their God meant them to do so.

The man history remembers as Big Bear died in the white man's prison. But the biggest part of him – that part of his identity that rose from the land, vegetation, skies, and waters – lives on. The newcomers appropriated it, ploughed it, riddled it with roads, but we failed to destroy it. That vesper sparrow's song was in a way an anthem of survival – and the whooping cranes Gail and I had watched a few months earlier were living emblems of possibility: of second chances. This early summer day I sat alone in that wounded landscape, contemplating what would be the last big step in a conservation career through which it felt like I'd pretty much blundered my way for the previous three decades. If Banff was next, what was the meaning of that, and of the fact that Alan's call came to me here, in so storied a corner of western Canada?

***

The road to Banff began not in Waskesiu but in Waterton.

When we had moved to Waterton we doubled that little village's elementary school population – Lisa Lenz's little class went from three to six with the addition of our three children. So small a school was almost unheard of in a province that had been ruthlessly cutting public service budgets for almost a decade, but somehow the Waterton school had managed to survive as an outlier. It was exceptionally good luck for our kids – they had the full attention of a passionately engaged young teacher. Lisa was so committed to her little charges that she used to come looking for them outside regular school hours to share evening adventures too.

The kids thrived both academically and socially for two happy years. Inevitably, however, the school got shut down and its students had to enroll in Pincher Creek schools, almost an hour's bus ride away. We stuck with my family's tradition and put Corey, Katie, and Brian into St. Michael's Catholic school. It didn't work out well for anyone.

At the same time, my work was evolving into something less rewarding than it had been during the initial years. At first, Bill Dolan, the manager of resource conservation, and my boss, had let me focus my energies on conservation strategies and cross-border initiatives, but he and I both knew the job was supposed to be more focused on ecological monitoring and reporting. By the late 1990s, Bill had taken on more of the collaborative work I enjoyed, and I was back doing work not unlike what I had done almost two decades earlier with the Canadian Wildlife Service. By now I felt capable of more than that, but it was all Waterton had to offer.

When Jasper advertised a vacancy for a new position – ecosystem secretariat manager – I brought the poster home and Gail and I talked it over. If we moved to Jasper, the kids would be home for lunch from school and spared the two hours of bus travel each day. High school was drawing near, and we didn't like the idea of having them out of our sight and under the influence of strangers as much as they now were. We knew Jasper well and had friends there, having lived there before. There were more job opportunities for Gail. I was keen to challenge my own abilities again.

I applied for the job and, after an intense interview and selection process, I got it.

It wasn't completely a happy move – Waterton was a close-knit community, and we were leaving good friends behind. Corey, now in his teens, was bitter about being torn away from his Pincher Creek friends. But we'd weighed the pros and cons, and Gail and I had no doubts that this was the best choice for all of us.

In Jasper my job was to coordinate environmental monitoring, most of which was actually done by biologists reporting to Brian Wallace, the manager of resource conservation; to ensure that projects and initiatives that triggered the Canadian Environmental Assessment Act or Parks Canada's own internal policy requirements were subjected to rigorous environmental assessment; to develop conservation strategies for thorny challenges; and to provide environmental advice to the park superintendent. It was a delightful bundle of responsibilities. And I saw our kids more often too.

Gail soon got a job with the Friends of Jasper National Park, a nonprofit cooperating association. She loved the job and the people she worked with.

Much as we missed the Crown of the Continent, it was good to be back in the familiar Athabasca valley at the edge of those wild, far valleys I had come to know so well a couple of decades earlier. Back in 1979, my brother Greg, fresh out of high school, had come to visit me for a week. He had never left and now, in 2000, was the town's fire chief. So I had a hunting buddy again too. High school brought all the predictable teenage issues, but at least they arose in the same town in which we lived, and could be dealt with as they came up.

But I was no longer a staff biologist; I was a manager, close to the top of the bureaucratic food pyramid. I had spent most of my life distrusting people in authority. On more than one occasion, I'd had to live with what seemed like wrong-headed decisions made by managers. And now I was one of them. It was a weird and conflicting position to find myself in; it was as if I was no longer seeing the same me in the mirror. I wasn't quite sure who I saw there, but I was pretty sure he was getting out of his depth.

***

When I had first discovered the Rockies in the early 1970s, it had been a time of change. The original trails, made by and for horse people, were being taken over by backpackers. There was conflict in the woods, mostly related to muddy trails. The equestrian users didn't really notice the mud their horses churned up. The hikers did, and their preferred solution was to get rid of the horses. Horse people saw the hikers as elitists and interlopers.

Hiking into the Skoki area of Banff one day, I had met a group of riders coming out. It was a beautiful day and we were all feeling good, so we stopped and visited for a while. But pretty soon I was swatting flies.

"I'd better get going," I said, finally. "These horse flies are getting annoying."

The guide gave me a long, cold glare. "We call those 'hiker flies,'" he said. I'd inadvertently reminded everyone of the gulf between us. And with that we all headed off on our separate journeys into the future of mountain recreation.

Most of those early conflicts got resolved. In Banff, Parks Canada shifted recreational horse use from the wetter Main Ranges of the Rockies into the better-drained Eastern Slopes, where the soils are better able to resist wear and tear. Starting in the mid-1970s, the parks also started hiring dedicated trail crews to reroute and repair trails, many of which had never been properly planned or built in the first place.

But by the turn of the 21st century another recreational conflict was arising, this one involving mountain bikes. Mountain biking originated in the 1970s when enthusiasts in California and Colorado started adapting traditional road and town bikes for use off-trail. As interest grew and spread, bicycle companies began designing bicycles specifically for trails and rough terrain, incorporating lighter materials, shock absorption systems, specialized gears and tires, and other innovations. By the 1990s, interest in mountain biking had spread beyond the initial faddists and was becoming mainstream.

Mountain bikes might be increasingly popular, but that didn't mean they were welcome in the national parks. Parks culture had long been a conservative and traditionalist one, rooted in the wilderness purism of John Muir, James Harkin, George Bird Grinnell, and others who had originally conceived and promoted the national park ideal. These were meant to be places of recreation, certainly, but it was meant to be a kind of recreation rooted in awe of and appreciation for nature. Bicycling didn't fit that ideal: it was too fast and too technical. On a mountain bike the park became less a place for connecting to nature and more a setting for testing one's gear and skills. Cyclists move rapidly and relatively quietly – conflicts with bears and other wildlife seemed inevitable.

In Waterton, I had been among those who worked to limit the reach of this new technology into the park. Mountain bikes there had been restricted to paved roads and short reaches of only a couple of park trails.

Jasper, however, had a large resident population who had always treated the park as their playground. Whereas residents of other park communities like Waterton, Banff, and Field were almost all there because of the national park, Jasper had a long history as a railroad town. A significant number of its residents loved the place but had no real attachment to national park ideals. As a consequence, the community had a significant subculture that saw Parks Canada as an annoying landlord with way too many silly rules. Circumventing those rules was almost a local sport.

Unfortunately, the town of Jasper is situated in the heart of the most ecologically important part of the national park. It sits at the confluence of three major valleys – the Athabasca, Miette, and Maligne river valleys – and partially blocks long-important travel corridors for large wildlife. Its low elevation and connection, via Yellowhead Pass, to the mild interior valleys of BC also gives it a montane climate – warm, dry summers and mild, often snow-free winters. That makes it an important wintering area for deer and elk and, by extension, their predators. That montane climate combines with abundant streams, wetlands, and old glacial features to create a biologically diverse complex of habitats that sustain many other kinds of plant and animal life.

In the 1800s, it made sense to put a town in so central and biologically rich a location. By the 21st century it had become pretty clear that had been an unfortunate error, given that the primary responsibility of Parks Canada is to protect nature. The most ecologically vital part of Jasper National Park was now also its busiest and most heavily developed.

Still, there were corners of the surrounding landscape that the road builders and trail makers had missed, and these now served as vital refuges for warier wildlife species like wolves, grizzly bears, and moose. When I arrived in the park, biologists and planning staff were hard at work on what they called the Three Valley Confluence initiative. They were mapping out the best remaining wildlife patches and planning how to keep wildlife free from disturbance there, in part by relocating trails.

That should have been easy. There were very few officially designated trails along the lower flanks of Signal Mountain, the mouth of the Miette River, or the aspen forests and willow wetlands behind Patricia and Pyramid Lakes. It wasn't easy, however, because park wardens had discovered a growing network of unauthorized bicycle trails penetrating even the most secret of places, all built surreptitiously by the town's hard core of renegade mountain bikers.

Ron Hooper tasked me with figuring out how to resolve that problem, but I was also conscious of my own personal bias; I still didn't really believe that mountain bicycling had any place in parks devoted to quiet enjoyment, education, and the protection of wildlife. On the other hand, my pragmatic side conceded that if mountain biking was here to stay, it would need to be managed.

The Canada National Parks Act had been amended, in 2001, to clarify that ecological integrity must be the first priority in making any decisions involving the parks. That amendment was intended to bring an end to the era of "balance" debates over what were often perceived to be dual (or duelling) mandates of use and protection. Henceforth there was meant to be no debate: any use must be consistent both with visitor education and with protection of ecological integrity.

Changing a piece of legislation is a pretty straightforward

process. But changing organizational culture in light of that amendment is a lot more complicated. And persuading local communities with deeply held traditions of use and abuse is even harder. Parks Canada senior managers, to their credit, adopted a series of measures to drive the changes home. No sooner was the ecological integrity clause added to the act than a team of scientists, educators, and human resource specialists from across the country was convened to develop an ecological integrity training program. I'd been assigned to that team and helped deliver the training. It was an ambitious approach to rewiring the organization.

Concurrently, the top brass prepared a pitch to the Treasury Board for new money. Much of the new investment was in science capacity; if you're going to manage for ecological integrity, you'd better have people on staff who can monitor, measure, and report on it. Some of the money was reserved for showcase projects. The idea was to challenge parks staff to come up with ways to engage their local communities in restoring or protecting ecological integrity while enhancing the ability of people to use and enjoy their parks.

Applying for some of the ecological integrity project money seemed like a good idea. In discussing how to get those unofficial bike trails out of sensitive areas in the Three Valley Confluence with my staff and colleagues, it had become clear we needed to understand the motivations of the people building the trails and then come up with an approach that made them feel like winners, rather than driving them further underground.

This was the kind of problem I liked, the kind we'd worked on during my best years in Waterton. I asked around, got a few names of local bicyclists, and started inviting people out for coffee. The questions I posed to each of them were always the same: Why are people building those trails? What would the ideal trail network look like to you? And if we invited you to help get trails right, what mistakes should we avoid?

Perhaps the most interesting, and certainly the most passionate, bicyclist with whom I met was Loni Klettl. The daughter of an old-time park warden, she had been born in Jasper and never left. She worked as a restaurant server but lived for the outdoors, and was fully invested in the view that Jasper was, first and foremost, a place for Jasperites to play. She seemed sure the wildlife would be just fine. Loni told me she owned 11 bikes and one old truck that she used primarily to deliver herself and her bike to trailheads.

Other hard-core bicyclists declined to meet with me; they didn't like Parks Canada and they didn't feel accountable to anyone but their peers. But Loni was quite forthcoming. She explained that the motivation for building clandestine trails was based on stories Jasper's cycling community had heard. They believed bicycling had been shut down on some trails in Banff and elsewhere after hikers and horse users had complained about sharing the trail with bicyclists. I detected a fair bit of conspiracy thinking in those tales, as usual, but perception is everything in human affairs. The Jasper bicyclists had concluded that if they built their own trails they could stay out of sight and out of conflict, and avoid getting shut down. She also said that the official trails in the vicinity of the town were no longer fun to ride – they were so heavily used by horse riders and hikers that they had become wide and dusty, and they didn't have the banked corners and fun downhills that bicyclists like.

Loni agreed – if we could find the money, and if we were honestly committed to keeping mountain biking as an accepted use of the townsite-area trails – that she would help to champion a project to redesign the official trail networks and close down the most problematic of the unofficial trails. We'd call it the Jasper Trails Project. It would benefit both wildlife and recreationists by concentrating use on well-designed trails, outside of important wildlife movement corridors and sensitive habitats.

Loni's support was vital, because she was well known and popular in the community and a recognized champion for biking access. A few coffee meetings later, the park biologists, planning staff, and I sat down with spreadsheets and worked up a project plan. We would create a team made up of local bicyclists, the Parks Canada trail crew, wildlife biologists, and GIS mappers to identify the best and worst places for trails, and then reconfigure the trail network. The estimated cost came out to about $1.7 million over four years.

I headed off to a national meeting to pitch the project to Alan Latourelle and his executive team. Much to my surprise, they approved it.

**

I had to hand the project over to others, however.

Parks Canada had been going through a series of organizational upheavals since the 1980s. I had fled the Calgary office in the midst of the first strategic planning exercise, and managed to stay on the sidelines during the second, while I was in Waterton. I found myself back in the land of flip charts and sticky notes soon after arriving in Jasper. While other staff went to work organizing the Jasper trails project, I found myself attending frequent meetings on what was meant to be a "Sustainable Business Plan" for the mountain parks.

The problem was that the mountain parks spend more than their share of Parks Canada's budget. That can lead to resentment from smaller parks that need funding too. It was park managers who were mismanaging the budgets, so it was those same park managers who were put in charge of finding the economies that would get us back in the black.

Some of the managers were old game players from way back who saw the whole project mostly as a defensive exercise. They liked spending oodles of cash and didn't want to give anything up. If possible, they hoped to tilt the table so that a few more coins slid their way. I was a new manager, and one used to feeling and thinking like an outsider. And I've always hated debt. So I took the whole thing seriously and soon started making enemies – mostly in Banff, which was the biggest offender in the mountain parks block and the one with the canniest old boys' club.

One big inefficiency was redundancy at the management level. The managers of resource conservation – formerly called chief park wardens – were responsible for protecting park resources. To this end, they had been put in charge of specialist staff as Parks Canada gradually built its professional capacity. But many of those managers had only technical diplomas and had risen to their positions from the ranks of old-school wardens who weren't scientists but practical, hard-working outdoors people. The public service's rigid hierarchical rules said that scientists had to be managed by university-educated managers. So the powers that be had come up with a costly workaround: they created new work units called Ecosystem Secretariats whose managers would have science degrees. Each park now had an additional highly paid manager simply to compensate for the fact that some old guard managers couldn't keep up with the new science responsibilities being added to their portfolios.

I argued that we could save a lot of salary dollars by getting rid of the ecosystem secretariat managers and putting all the science responsibilities back where they belonged, under the resource conservation managers. Then it would just be a matter of succession planning; when the old former chief park wardens retired, they could be replaced by staff with more advanced science educations. There was no lack of likely candidates available by now anyway.

I won that debate. But in the process, I did myself out of my own job.

Fortunately, Jasper's manager of resource conservation, Brian Wallace, was getting ready to retire. Ron Hooper saw me as a logical replacement, since I was already classified at the same level and had worked for years with many of Jasper's science staff and park wardens. The idea was that I would just slide in, as Brian slid out.

Nothing, however, is ever easy in a bureaucracy. Years of organizational changes and repeated shocks as Parks Canada had to adjust to a changing world meant that morale was fragile, particularly in resource conservation. Several years earlier, frustrated with the number of bighorn sheep and elk dying on Highway 16 – the transcontinental Yellowhead highway that transects the park – Jasper wardens had purchased speed radar equipment and started enforcing highway speed limits. Although this was notionally the responsibility of the RCMP, they had been told repeatedly that speeding in wildlife zones was a low priority for the Mounties because the accidents rarely resulted in death or injuries to humans. The police were spread too thin to waste time saving sheep when their priority was to save people.

Once park wardens in Jasper, and then Banff, began pulling over motor vehicles for speeding, the risk profile of their job changed dramatically. Every drug dealer, murderer, rapist, and terrorist who drives between Alberta and BC drives through a national park. Wardens were no longer dealing with campers and hikers; they were potentially dealing with dangerous criminals. Every vehicle stop was another toss of the dice.

Mounties wear body armour, carry handguns, and are trained in high-risk incident management. Some park wardens began to lobby for similar gear and training. Senior managers resisted; in their view, campers and hikers should not have to feel intimidated by armed officers telling them not to pick the flowers.

When the arming issue first erupted in Banff and Jasper, I was still wearing a park warden uniform in Waterton. Most of my colleagues, like me, had no interest in being equipped with handguns and taking on the responsibilities and risks that come with lethal force. But wardens are a culture within a culture. Already aggrieved by changes that had reduced the amount of time park wardens spent on backcountry patrols – work that had long been central to their sense of who they were – many wardens felt undervalued and underappreciated by senior managers in Parks Canada. When a park warden in Banff teamed up with a Labour Canada investigator to challenge senior management on the decision not to issue handguns to wardens, the issue became an us-versus-them conflict. Wardens who had initially opposed arming went over to the pro-gun side simply because that was their team.

That conflict boiled for almost a decade, and it got ugly. The Parks Canada CEO tracked the revolution by monitoring email exchanges among the wardens, many of whom were naive enough to think they could expect privacy on work-assigned email accounts.

226   The Road to Banff

Those exchanges got pretty nasty, and it wasn't long before the CEO – an otherwise objective thinker – began taking the whole thing personally. He pointed out – quite legitimately – that when senior managers make a decision that they have legitimate reasons and legal authority to make, staff have an obligation to faithfully implement that decision. But he also seemed unwilling to look behind the anger and name calling in those emails and respect the legitimate fears that drove them. He came to view warden tribalism not as one of Parks Canada's greatest strengths, but as its biggest problem. It was, in fact, both.

By the time I moved to Jasper, the conflict was almost beyond resolution. Wardens were no longer authorized to stop vehicles on major park highways, but that had ceased to be the issue. They enforced laws; that meant they confronted lawbreakers. They felt they needed the ability to defend themselves, and to many of them that logically meant they should carry handguns, like other law enforcement professionals. But the government had made it clear they weren't going to get those guns.

Ultimately, faced with the need for some sort of compromise, senior managers decided to create a dedicated law enforcement unit of about 100 staff nationwide. They would be called park wardens and issued with guns and protective gear, but their only duty would be to enforce regulations. The remaining resource conservation staff would cease to have the power to enforce park laws and instead would be responsible for fire management, conserving park resources, research and monitoring, and protecting visitors from dangers like avalanches, climbing accidents, and animal conflicts. The old warden service was finished.

The changes were a painful compromise that made nobody happy, but there was no alternative. In a candid moment, Alan Latourelle told me that he had had to fight a rearguard defence to protect Parks Canada's role in law enforcement before a Cabinet committee that had been leaning towards handing that role over to the RCMP.

"They don't want an armed public service," he said. "If arming is necessary, then their inclination is to have one agency responsible for all law enforcement, and it wouldn't be us. I couldn't let that happen."

Alan had fought for and won a Solomonic solution: he split the baby down the middle. But the old park wardens wanted that baby whole; they saw the solution as punitive. Several of those who had fought hardest failed to qualify in the screening tests for the new positions. That came as no surprise to me. One of them, when I interviewed him for one of the new armed positions, said that as soon as the wardens were armed he hoped somebody would shoot the CEO. Afterwards, when – having been rejected for a job he felt he'd been doing for years – he demanded a post-board interview, I gently pointed out to him the simple truth that no organization in the world would issue a firearm to somebody who had made a statement like that.

He sat for a moment, staring at the table, then slowly nodded. It was a heartbreaking moment; the conflict, clearly, had broken him. He retired soon after.

**

That was the environment when I was being considered for the position of resource conservation manager in Jasper. It wasn't helped by the fact that Brian Wallace was retiring under stressful circumstances. Brian was a man most of us admired. He had worked his way from the bottom to the top. He started as a farm boy with a lot of horse sense but not much post-secondary education. The only job he could get in Jasper was driving truck for the highways crew. But in his spare time he tagged along with park warden friends on climbing courses, took snowmobile and fire training sessions, and missed no opportunity to learn and refine his outdoor skills. After a few years he finally managed to get hired on as a junior warden. He worked in the backcountry, became a skilled climber who participated in some of the diciest rescues in Jasper history, fought fires, and then, as the warden service moved into the business of prescribed burning, lit them. Brian was a hard-working man who had built his career from the bottom up. Easygoing, smart, and a natural leader, he had an immensely loyal following.

Brian and I were friends, but it was an uneasy friendship. I felt inferior to him, and he felt inferior to me, each for different reasons. But each of us had essential qualities the other valued. Having worked so long and so hard to reach the level of chief park warden, it wasn't easy for Brian to step away, especially with a university-educated biologist breathing down his neck. And that tension wasn't lost on the work unit he managed. For all that I had friends there, there were conflicted loyalties at play – along with a prevalent sense that I lacked sufficient depth in the old warden service to be parachuted in as their manager.

Brian's final project was to manage the removal of an array of microwave and other long-distance communications paraphernalia from the top of Pyramid Mountain. On the day of his retirement party at the Maligne Horse Range, I stood out in the meadow and looked across at that iconic peak, restored once again to its original profile, and thought it a fitting monument to a good man's long career protecting one of Canada's greatest national parks. But it was a bittersweet reflection, because I knew he was leaving reluctantly and probably associated me with many of the changes that were sweeping him away.

Having eliminated my own job and taken over the job of a valued colleague, I didn't last much longer in Jasper. Many of the staff for whom I was now responsible were old friends, but this was different; I was being judged under an intensely critical magnifying glass, and my biggest flaw was that I wasn't really one of them. Unlike Brian, I hadn't come up through the warden ranks. I'd served as a warden briefly in Waterton, in mid-career, but it was more as a visitor than a lifetime member of that culture-within-a-culture. Gaby Fortin, the western Canada regional director and a former warden, refused to sign off on my appointment. Instead, I served as an acting manager for the next year. It was clear that he, too, saw me as an outsider.

Well, to be honest, so did I; I always had.

So I was more than a little relieved to see, one day, an announcement that there would be a competition for park superintendent positions in Waterton and Prince Albert national parks. Those positions, in relatively small parks, were classified at a level not much different from the one I held in Jasper. I applied, and after yet another difficult interview and reference process, was accepted. In my conversation with Gaby, he assured me that, since I was first on the list, the Waterton job was mine for the taking.

It came as a bitter blow to find out Gaby was wrong. Existing superintendents, if they want to transfer, get first dibs on any vacant positions. Rod Blair, superintendent of the Northern Prairies Field Unit, wanted out. He asked for a transfer to Waterton. That door slammed shut, and suddenly my only option was Northern Prairies – a job I had never even imagined. What did I know about Prince Albert National Park?

If the move to Jasper had been hard on the kids, it was the move to Waskesiu that was hardest on their parents. Gail had to leave a job she loved and move to a place she'd never seen before. We would be leaving our youngest son, only 17, behind in Jasper and we would be many hours away from our other children, who now lived in Edmonton and Lethbridge. We knew almost nobody in Prince Albert National Park. It felt like we'd lost all control over our fate; the stress became so intense that one day Gail and I melted down and had a furious row, something we had never done before.

On top of all that, the job offer was conditional on my learning French. Park superintendents are senior executives in an agency that serves all Canadians, and Canada is, constitutionally, a bilingual nation. So, in the midst of all the stress and unhappiness that had landed on Gail, I had to leave her for five months to travel to Gatineau and immerse myself in a language of which there was a very good likelihood I would never have a need. I was 52 years old, only a few years away from my own retirement. While I understood the rationale for the language requirement, it seemed an awfully strange time to pull me away from work I was good at and spend half a year teaching me a language virtually none of my staff or stakeholders were likely to use.

That year was one of the most challenging I've ever experienced. The loneliness was crushing, especially knowing that Gail was stuck back home dealing with the family's teenager issues and making all the arrangements for a move she didn't want to make. As one who had always taken pride in my communications skills, having my ability to communicate stripped away and having to start again from scratch was deeply destabilizing. And I knew how much that training was costing; there was guilt and frustration tied up in the angst as I grimly battled my way through conjugations, grammar, and vocabulary in the sullen, sweaty heat of a long Quebec summer. I lost 15 pounds, became deeply insecure, and learned just enough French to embarrass myself in conversation.

But I got it done, and we moved to Waskesiu, retaining our Oldman River property as our Alberta anchor. Something would come up eventually; we'd get back home.

Something did: Banff.

13. Imposter in the Executive Suite

The Banff National Park administration building is an imposing edifice designed to communicate bureaucratic authority. It sits at the top of a slope in a gated park, and the superintendent office windows offer a view straight down Banff Avenue to the towering bulk of Cascade Mountain two kilometres away. It's a big office, attached to another large office housing an executive assistant who intercepts those hoping to meet with the big boss.

I felt profoundly out of my depth in such a lofty perch and portentous role. I might be in my fifties now, but I was still the skinny little 13-year-old kid I'd been in Grade 10, surrounded by bigger, more confident teenagers. The first time I looked out that window at the traffic and crowds below, and the patient mountains beyond, it wasn't panic that I felt but it was something like that; a sort of sense of impending doom.

My first phone call was from the general manager of the Sunshine ski resort, inviting me out to lunch. Well, that didn't take long. I met him at a restaurant on the Banff Springs golf course and we had a pleasant conversation. It was clearly meant to be a bonding moment. He grabbed the bill before I could tell the server we wanted separate ones. I felt angry and compromised but kept that to myself.

The following day he called again. He'd forgotten to ask: There was a bit of misunderstanding between his staff and some of the park wardens. Would I mind straightening them out? It wasn't a big deal, really. I said no.

There were no more lunch invitations. Maybe I could do this job after all.

232   Imposter in the Executive Suite

***

But it wasn't much fun. Banff is by far the most complicated national park in Canada. It is the first and the oldest, so everything that happens there is loaded with symbolic importance. Mistakes and successes are magnified simply by virtue of the fact that Canada sees them as evidence of what its government really intends, where protected heritage is concerned. Thanks to the railroad, the Trans-Canada Highway, and the proximity of Calgary with its crowds of well-heeled outdoor recreationists, it is by far one of the most heavily developed and busiest parks in the world. More than five million people – and their cars – visit the park each year. All of that adds up to a lot of money, and money motivates greed. The power of the tourism industry in Banff is immense.

Years before I arrived, when Alberta was rolling in more oil royalty revenues than the provincial government knew what to do with, the government decided to invest in economic diversification. One part of that was to make grants and loans easily available for tourism business operators. Parks Canada wasn't ready for the resultant development boom. Faced with national concern over the rate at which the park was being paved over and turned into a monster resort, the federal government had commissioned a panel to look into the ecological health of the Bow River valley. The panel found that the park was, indeed, in big trouble. The montane habitats of the Bow valley, critical to the wildlife ecology of the whole park, were on the verge of being clogged with tourism infrastructure.

In response to the panel's report, Parks Canada developed a new management plan that directed the removal of unnecessary facilities from the Bow valley, put a firm cap on commercial growth in the townsite, and invoked a number of other measures aimed at dialling back overdevelopment and restoring ecological health. My predecessor as superintendent of Banff, Jillian Roulet, had done a lot of the heavy lifting involved in implementing that plan. The work had burned her out. When we met for the handover of responsibilities, she looked tired and cynical. She warned me that the job would use me up. I was quietly sure she was wrong. She wasn't.

In response to the new restrictions on commercial growth, some tourism operators got together and formed the Association for Mountain Parks Protection and Enjoyment. AMPPE presented itself as a grassroots group representing the interests of ordinary Canadians whose fun was being ruined by all these new rules. In reality, it was a front for businesses that wanted as few restrictions as possible on their ability to exploit public assets for profit.

AMPPE hired Julie Canning as its executive director and sent her into battle. Julie was bright, well-spoken, and assertive. When I first met her, while I was still in Jasper, she had been out of her depth and overconfident. She had frustrated and annoyed Ron Hooper and me, but had little real impact. Now, however, several years later, she was a seasoned lobbyist.

As executive director of Banff–Lake Louise Tourism (BLLT), a destination marketing organization, her job now was simply to attract more credit cards to Banff on behalf of her board of directors. The problem was that Julie kept defaulting to conflict with Parks Canada, even though her job was now to collaborate. That led to my first test in my new job. It didn't go well.

I learned later that the business community wasn't happy about Alan's choice for his new park superintendent. They felt I was "too green." It wasn't lack of experience they were talking about. It may have been that initial hostility that led to Julie's warlike mien when we met again.

When I moved my files into the superintendent's office and my new team started briefing me, I learned that the park's resource conservation staff had developed an aggressive plan to protect the town of Banff from wildfire. West of the town of Banff all the way to Lake Louise and beyond is a continuous blanket of densely crowded, aging lodgepole pine. When that valley catches fire – and it will; they always do – the conflagration could well prove uncontrollable. The park was building a fireguard on the west side of Sulphur Mountain to prevent fire from climbing the slope and raining embers on the town below. Now they had a plan for a prescribed burn in the valley bottom to create a gap in the dense white spruce forest west of Vermilion Lakes. Banff was known internationally as a leader in the use of fire in risk reduction and ecosystem renewal. It was a good plan.

But Julie didn't like it. Fires create smoke. Nobody likes smoke. She complained to everybody except me that Parks Canada was going to drive tourists and their dollars away. She even complained to the *Calgary Herald* – a strange choice since in doing so she herself was essentially warning tourists off in advance.

I stayed out of the fray, because it was an operational issue for which Ian Syme, the manager of resource conservation, was responsible. But I also made it clear that I trusted his fire management staff to get it right. That might be why I arrived at work one day, barely a week into the job, to find a letter waiting in my inbasket. Julie, in her capacity as executive director of BLLT, had written to me – and cc'd the regional director for western Canada's national parks – to complain that our plan for a prescribed burn was going to cause grievous harm to Banff's tourism industry.

I was furious. She hadn't even tried to create a dialogue or build a relationship with me; with that cc she'd gone straight over my head. It was like an act of war, a particularly strange one given that, as superintendent, I sat on the BLLT board of directors, and, as such, was essentially one of her bosses.

The phone rang an hour later. It was, finally, a call from Julie Canning.

The first thing she said was, "Kevin, we have a problem."

"Yes, we do, Julie," I said. "And you are it."

It didn't get better after that. Finally, before I could say anything more to regret, I hung up on her.

I sat staring at the phone, horrified at myself, remembering that long-ago time when I had put my axe through a speaker one night beside the Castle River. That hadn't turned out well, I told myself, and neither was this likely to.

I went upstairs to where Ron Hallman, the executive director for the mountain national parks, had his office. It would be better if my higher-ups heard about this incident from me first. I told him the whole story. Ron stared at me blankly. I could see him thinking – probably something like: "Oh my God, what have we hired?"

At length, however, he said, "Well, let me know when you've got it straightened out."

Ron was a very good manager.

It was Cliff White and Ian Pengelly, the park's senior fire staff, who saved my bacon. They had been in the fire business long enough to understand the importance of stakeholder relations, and they weren't interested in power struggles. On their own initiative, they arranged to take Julie on a helicopter flight over the Bow valley. They showed her the continuous fuel load carpeting the valley. They showed her the area they planned to burn. They explained the precautions that were built into the burn plan. They talked about the consequences to the tourism industry should we fail to head off a catastrophic wildfire.

Julie went silent on fires and smoke after that trip.

As it happened, the prescribed fire never happened. It's called prescribed fire for a reason; there is a very specific prescription that has to be met before anyone can light up a drip-torch. The fire team monitors moisture levels in the soil and vegetation, precedent and predicted weather, and other variables that can influence fire behaviour and intensity. The prescribed conditions never arrived, so the burn never went ahead. Julie, on the other hand, had burned her bridges – for nothing.

***

A fundamental conflict built into Parks Canada is that it is responsible for both the ecological integrity of living systems and the cultural integrity of historic resources, most of which are buildings and structures. But living systems are dynamic; there is no place in nature for stasis. Nothing is meant to last; everything is meant to decompose. Life is not about objects that last; it is about cycles of destruction and renewal.

The things that threaten our historic artifacts are actually the things of life: dry rot fungus, weather systems, leachate from bat droppings, carpenter ants, fire. Defending built heritage means waging constant war on...ecological integrity. So part of Parks Canada is devoted to promoting and protecting the forces of nature that destroy and renew and destroy again, while another part is devoted to fighting those same forces. Cognitive dissonance is hard-wired into the organization's "heritage" mandate.

One rarely comes away from a conflict between those two priorities unscathed. That was certainly the case when I took on a challenge that my predecessors had – perhaps wisely – been kicking down the road for a couple of decades.

Arthur O. Wheeler was founder of the Alpine Club of Canada and a well-connected promoter of Canada's mountain national parks in the early 20th century. As such, he became a darling of the mountaineering movement and of the Dominion Parks Service that ran the young parks system. In a development-focused and pragmatic era, the national parks were on shaky footing because a lot of parliamentarians, reflecting the attitude of their electorates, saw them as frivolous and wasteful. They didn't generate income, they left idle land unused, and they cost the public treasury a lot of money. In the world view of these newcomer people, nature was simply a bundle of economic resources meant to be used, not cherished.

James Harkin, the idealistic but politically savvy bureaucrat in charge of Canada's national parks, knew that aesthetic arguments and conservation rationales wouldn't win over those cynics, so he worked hard to build a case for the national parks founded on their health benefits and their value in attracting tourist dollars to Canada. In that regard, allies like Wheeler were indispensable. It was normal for influential white males in that era to reward other influential white males with perks. Wheeler did very well by Harkin: he was granted a large lease watered by hot springs at the base of Sulphur Mountain. There he built a small resort cottage and surrounded it with gardens. It was a unique and beautiful property.

But time and the forces of nature have never been particularly kind to the things people build. After Wheeler died in 1945, his summer home fell into disuse. For all its attractiveness, it was an isolated spot with dangerous road access. It didn't get a lot of sun, especially in winter, tucked as it was under the looming shadow of Sulphur Mountain. As tourism developments incrementally filled the adjacent valley floor, the springs and forests around the lonely cottage became increasingly important for wary animals like wolves, cougars, and grizzlies trying to make a living in an increasingly busy landscape. The abandoned house fell into disrepair. The original lease lapsed, and the property became an unencumbered part of the national park again.

That was the situation when, during the 1980s, Parks Canada and the town of Banff were faced with the dilemma of how to accommodate the park's growing population. A building boom, fuelled by generous capital grants and loans made possible by Alberta's booming oil economy, had created a need for staff accommodation. The town had no room for new housing. Town planners and developers soon became focused on the Middle Springs area, on the western edge of the town, downslope from Wheeler's abandoned estate.

Finding a good place for new housing development had been a challenge; getting approval to actually develop it was another. Parks Canada was already under attack from environmental groups for its failure to keep a lid on commercial growth. The media were being fed a constant stream of images and rhetoric showing how Parks Canada was failing in its duty to keep Canada's oldest national park unimpaired for future generations by allowing developers and their local politician friends to urbanize the place.

Middle Springs faced an uphill battle for approval – as well it should have. Commercial development in Banff was almost totally out of control.

238 Imposter in the Executive Suite

But the housing need was real too. The development got approved, but only after a comprehensive environmental assessment that set a number of conditions to try and mitigate the impact of filling some of the best remaining habitat in the montane heart of the Bow River valley with yet more asphalt and buildings. One of those conditions was that the new development would be fenced in. The adjoining narrow corridor of forest on the uphill side would be permanently out of bounds to recreational use, leaving it for the exclusive use of the wildlife who were losing so much habitat to development. That corridor included the Wheeler property. The environmental assessment prescribed that the old house be removed and the site reclaimed.

Wheeler was a historic figure of national prominence. He had not just promoted alpinism in the mountain national parks but had also done pioneering survey work along the Continental Divide, founded national organizations that promoted national park ideals and tourism, and left his name all over the history books. Tearing down his house risked being seen as tearing down his legacy. It wasn't the kind of thing for which park superintendents like to be blamed.

When I arrived in Banff two decades later, the house was still standing – mostly. The roof had partly caved in. Plastic tarps partly covered the gaping hole. Bats had occupied the attic and bushy-tailed wood rats lived in the walls and under the caved-in floor. The place reeked of guano and was stained with fungus. Bureaucrats might have been reluctant to get the job done, but Nature was deconstructing the place in its own slow, inexorable way. But the out-of-bounds site also hosted occasional illegal bush parties and trysts. That created a liability risk, because the building's increasing instability meant it might easily collapse on someone.

My naive view was that a deal is a deal, and that it was time to stop the dithering. Most of my management team agreed that it was past time to get the job done before somebody got hurt in there. Closing the area might be an inadequate effort to mitigate the impacts of a large housing development in one of the most ecologically significant parts of a national park, but turning a blind eye to trespass made that effort even more inadequate.

When we announced that this can would no longer be kicked down the road, the reaction was fast and furious. Local artists and cultural heritage champions banded together to fight the demolition. Instead, they wanted the cottage restored to its original condition and the site opened to public use, as a sort of shrine to Wheeler's legacy. They were relentless, determined and – to a degree – right. The house and grounds had great historic value. That, however, should have been recognized two decades earlier before a legally (and morally) binding decision was made to sacrifice them for housing. In fact, the problem went back even further, to when Wheeler's descendants and champions, and Parks Canada, allowed the house to fall into disrepair in the first place.

Arguably, the real origin of the problem was the original decision to give Wheeler such a patronage award in the first place – at the expense of the public interest and the unique ecological values of the property.

***

When I finally set a firm date for removal of the house, the defenders went over my head to the minister of environment, Jim Prentice. That sort of thing happens a lot in Banff, but usually the minister's office wisely stays out of the crossfire and simply sends the lobbyists back to the park superintendent. In this case, however, Prentice's staff felt it warranted his attention.

It was 2010 and the eyes of Parks Canada's senior executive cadre were fixed even more intently on Banff than they usually are, because this was the 125th anniversary of Banff National Park and, consequently, of Canada's system of national parks. Just as in Harkin's era, Parks Canada's senior administrators faced the ongoing challenge of persuading skeptical politicians of the importance of spending public money on places that couldn't be logged, mined, or otherwise exploited for profit. And just as in those earlier times, tourism and recreation were the selling point. So the anniversary was seen as an opportunity to build more buzz that would attract more visitors to an already desperately overcrowded national park. The powers that be informed me and my colleague Pam Veinotte, who was superintendent of a field unit that included the western part of Banff National Park, that we would be hosting a big celebration.

Jim Prentice would be there. I got a message from the office of Parks Canada's chief executive officer that Prentice wanted me to meet with him about the Wheeler house. The stakes suddenly felt a lot higher; I finally understood why previous superintendents had chosen to leave that matter in their pending files.

The minister met me at the Banff Springs Hotel. He had half an hour, and he wanted to see the house. Prentice, a smart, results-oriented guy, was all business. We got in a car and headed down the hill to the junction with the Sulphur Mountain drive. Steve Malins, Banff's cultural heritage specialist, had given me a binder of photographs, interior and exterior, of the house. I hadn't asked him to prepare it, so I was both grateful for and impressed by his initiative in doing so. I handed it to Prentice, and he leafed through it as I drove.

As we drew near, I directed the minister's attention through the trees to the brief glimpses of the house visible there and explained that I was a bit reluctant to turn into the grassed-over and gated access road, given the traffic hazard at that corner. Prentice looked up from the binder, then nodded and said, "That's okay. I think I've seen what I need."

We turned around at the Upper Hot Springs parking lot, and I delivered him back to the hotel. He shook my hand and told me his office would get back to me the following week. As he walked away, I felt a bit bewildered. I couldn't tell whether things had gone well or poorly.

On the assumption that Steve's binder, with its images of rotting walls, fallen-in roofs, and mounds of guano, had done the job, however, I called John Rose, the park's asset manager, and told him he should have the demolition contractor on site the following

Wednesday morning. At nine in the morning I got a call from Ottawa; we could proceed with whatever we had decided to do. I hung up and called John Rose. Fifteen minutes later he called me back to let me know that the house was now a pile of partly rotted wood and the crew was starting work on cleaning up the site.

I was now confirmed as the devil incarnate in the eyes of some good people who were completely correct on the historical value of what was now gone forever. The conflict between protecting nature from development, on the one hand, and protecting built history from nature on the other, had been resolved in favour of nature. The heritage advocates saw my decision to finally get that job done as proof that Parks Canada simply didn't value history. It didn't, of course, prove that at all; if anything, it showed that development pressures had once again won at the expense of the national park's heritage values – both cultural and ecological.

But perhaps not quite. That very same week Skoki, a young wolf from the Bow valley pack wearing a radio collar that enabled park biologists to monitor his travels, used the Wheeler estate and the wildlife corridor of which it was a part to squeeze past the teeming town of Banff and escape into the peace of the Spray River valley, en route to the Kananaskis valley. There Skoki became the founding father of a new wolf pack. His sensitive nose was doubtless assailed by the alien odours of domestic dogs, people, lawn fertilizers, and engine exhaust as he wended his watchful way past the Middle Springs housing development and through the mildew-scented opening where the old house had stood. But he made it safely.

If there was any lingering bad taste in my mouth from the whole episode, it was the silence of the environmental groups who were always more than ready to challenge Parks Canada in the media over what they saw as failures to stand up firmly enough for ecological integrity. I've rarely felt so alone and unsupported as I did during the darkest hours of that debate, because friends and allies were nowhere to be found. Once I became a park superintendent, environmental organizations I'd long supported chose to treat me as an adversary. Not once did they ask for a meeting with me, write

242   Imposter in the Executive Suite

the minister, or speak up in the media in support of the decision to finally complete the restoration of that Sulphur Mountain wildlife corridor.

In the midst of my angst and self-pity, however, I remembered how I had chosen to attack Rory Flanagan in the media instead of picking up the phone and calling him. Those crows had come home to roost. I could almost hear Rory's laughter.

***

For all the frustrations of being the guy holding the lightning rod in Banff National Park, there were some profound rewards too.

Sykes Powderface was a handsome man in his early seventies with a sly sense of humour and a seemingly bottomless well of wisdom. He lived on the Stoney Reserve and was respected as an Elder of the Iyarhe Nakoda First Nations. I had gotten to know him through Cliff White, Banff's chief scientist, when Cliff introduced me to what he described as the Stoney Natural Resources Council – a group of Elders and Knowledge Keepers from all three of the Iyarhe Nakoda First Nations. Cliff and Dennis Herman, the park's Indigenous liaison officer, had spent years building what was now a strong, congenial relationship with the group.

Sykes joined me one afternoon for a short hike around Johnson Lake. It had been quite a few years since he had last been there and he was curious about an old cabin tucked away in the lodgepole pine forest not far off the trail. It had been built originally in 1910 by a reclusive Englishman by the name of Billy Carver who lived there alone, working in the nearby Bankhead coal mines from time to time, until failing health forced him into a retirement home in 1932. Sykes remembered visiting the cabin when he was young. He said his family used to trade bighorn sheep meat for fresh vegetables with a Chinese market gardener by the name of Gee Moy, a friend of the old hermit.

"Where did you get the sheep?"

Sykes flashed an ironic grin at the park boss walking beside him.

"Oh," he said, gesturing vaguely, "up in those mountains. Where they live."

***

Howard Douglas had been one of my early predecessors. From 1896 to 1911 he served as superintendent of Banff (then called Rocky Mountains Park). In his 1906 annual report he channelled prevalent beer parlour wisdom when he wrote:

> Twenty years ago, the eastern slope of the Rocky Mountains from the Kicking Horse Pass to the boundary line (international), was filled with game. Moose were frequently seen, elk and black tail deer, white tail deer, bighorns and goats were plentiful; now some of these have totally disappeared and the remainder have been so thinned out as to make this hunting ground practically valueless.
>
> The Stoney Indians are primarily responsible for this condition of affairs. They are very keen hunters, and always have been, and they are the only Indians that hunt in this section of the mountains. For years, from their reserve, south to Chief Mountain, they have systematically driven the valleys and hills and slaughtered the game. ... In season and out, winter and summer, in lambing and fawning time, in fact as long as any game is in sight, they shoot. There is no stop; no rest for the hunted beasts. The old haunts are deserted and sheep runs are falling into disuse, and the greatest game country the sun ever shone on is fast becoming a thing of the past.[7]

Never mind the hundreds of coal miners then living in the Bow valley or the countless Calgary and rural hunters who came west each year to fill their larders. "Indians" were the problem, and Howard Douglas was determined to fix that problem. He declared the Stoney no longer welcome in the park. The park wildlife would be safe at last.

Sykes told me that his people had no love for the national park. Their story of the place centred on the years after the park was expanded in 1902 to include the Kananaskis drainage, most of the Ghost, and the Bow valley east as far as Seebe. Based on Douglas's loathing of the Stoney, the Canadian government stationed police at the park entrance gate. Indigenous visitors were turned away lest they do harm – even though they had lived in harmony with the place for many generations. Ironically, the wildlife abundance that Douglas was so determined to protect was partly the result of a Stoney tradition of setting fire to south-facing mountain slopes to keep back tree growth and provide better forage for elk, sheep, and deer.

In spite of that bitter experience, the Iyarhe Nakoda are big-hearted people. Sykes and other Elders and Knowledge Keepers had agreed to support Cliff White's efforts to understand the original stories of the place. They met regularly with park biologists to discuss wildlife conditions and to share their own stories. Cliff told me about one trip he and Dennis Herman had helped organize to get some of the Elders back into the remote northern part of the park. It was a difficult horseback trip, not least because some of the Elders were well past their prime. None had ever been there before. But again and again, one or the other would point out a landmark or valley and tell a story about the place. They knew where they were going before they even got there, because they still had the old stories of the home from which they had been evicted.

That walk with Sykes left a deep impression on me. Cliff felt that the relationship had progressed to the point where the Iyarhe Nakoda First Nations might be ready to consider a more formal kind of collaboration. I consulted with John Snow and others on the reserve. They were willing to talk to the Chiefs and float the idea of a new relationship.

The Chiefs, it turned out, were interested.

***

The wind was calm and the temperature mild on the morning

of November 25, 2010. A thin band of mist hung just above the ranks of lodgepole pine that blanket the lower slopes of Mînî Hrpa (Cascade Mountain), thinning and finally dissipating as the low sun finally emerged above the dark bulk of the low mountain that the Iyarhe Nakoda call Eyarhey Tatanga Woweyahgey Wakân and the Siksikaitsitapi call Iinii Istako. Both Indigenous names reference the shape of the mountain, which looks like a sleeping buffalo.

The maps call it Tunnel Mountain, after a railroad tunnel that never got built: another one of those newcomer names.

The grassland that carpets the flats where Forty Mile Creek spills into the Bow River valley is a mix of Columbia needle grass, rough fescue, and other native mountain grasses. Not long ago, at least as the mountains know time, bison grazed those grasses. The bison were long gone, but today there were a few elk on the flats when I arrived. The elk didn't linger long, because the place was busy. Trucks and cars were parked along the edge of the old Banff Indian Days grounds and people were milling around. Most of the activity was centred on a large ceremonial teepee to which Dennis Herman directed me when I arrived, all spiffy in my park superintendent outfit.

Pam Veinotte was there too. Pam was superintendent of the Lake Louise, Yoho, and Kootenay field unit of Parks Canada, which meant she had responsibility for operational management decisions affecting the western edge of Banff National Park. Although my position had the lead on management planning and other strategic initiatives, Pam and I had adopted a collaborative approach. Although only mine was required, both our names were on the signature page of a new park management plan.

One of the things the plan committed Parks Canada to do was to restore plains bison to the park after a century and a half of their being absent.

Bison are keystone species. Their trails, grazing patterns, wallows, droppings, even the soft, warm underfur that birds use for lining nests, all give shape and character to the ecosystems of which they are part. In their absence, those ecosystems lose shape and become something poorer. Bringing back the bison would be a kind of reconciliation with the land. It would breathe a new kind of life and meaning into this place that was originally set aside, after all, to preserve the nature of Canada.

Today was time for another sort of reconciliation – or perhaps it was part of the same thing. A month earlier, Pam and I had signed a memorandum of understanding that finally brought an end to the exclusion of the Iyarhe Nakoda People from their ancestral home. Drafting that memorandum had been a complicated task, since we'd had to involve lawyers whose task it was to protect the status quo even as we were determined to move past it. But we'd got it done. Today we were here to join in ceremony with the Chiefs who had also signed that paper: Chief David Bearspaw of the Bearspaw First Nation, Chief Bruce Labelle of the Chiniki First Nation, and Chief Clifford Poucette of the Wesley First Nation.

This was the Stoneys' day, so I swallowed my discomfort at learning that Pam would not be allowed in the ceremonial teepee. When I ducked under the flap, all the faces arrayed around the circle were male. This was a sacred ceremony, an occasion of deep significance to the leaders who had gathered here, only a few of whom I had actually met before. Quiet voices spoke, some with deep solemnity and others with animated passion. Pipe holders reverently unwrapped stone pipes and handed them to intense young men who packed them with tobacco and lit them. As the pipes came around the circle, we bathed ourselves in the sacred smoke.

The ceremony completed, we rose and stepped out of the tent shadows into the bright light of a November day. An old, wizened lady standing just outside the tent stared at me curiously and I nodded awkwardly back at her, unsure of what to say or why I would say it. Children were racing around under the trees. I felt out of my depth; I couldn't share the emotion I could feel around me because I had never fully belonged to, nor been excluded from, this place. Or any place, really. I was also painfully aware that, even though I knew it well and my personal identity was deeply attached to parts of the park – the Cascade River valley in particular – I could never really know these mountains in the same way as those Elders did.

I could only hope at least that the kids playing under the trees would some day know it in the same way. They belonged here, after all. These mountains had formed their bones, their language, and their people's songs.

***

A year later, I retired from Parks Canada.

And eight years after the Stoney People were finally welcomed home, the bison came home too. Over a hundred now range freely through mountain valleys that had almost forgotten them. Old wounds are healing. The spirits of the place are returning.

14. Spirits and Stories

1967

Shunda Creek, dark-watered and secret, curled itself in against a grassy bank under the broken shade of an old spruce forest. Tree roots hung from the undercut bank into the deep bend. It was a perfect place for trout but also a perfect place for losing hooks. As I looked for gaps in the tangle where I might be able to tease my lure into those fishy-looking shadows, I heard a rhythmic thumping sound. A flicker of motion, and a coyote appeared, trotting along a trail on the far bank. As it drew abreast of me, it turned its head and looked into my eyes without breaking stride. We held each other's gaze for a long moment and then it looked away, intent again on whatever it was that had sent it hastening through the late afternoon forest.

Something had passed between us. I had no idea what it was.

1976

Hiking alone over Verdant Pass in Kootenay National Park, I emerged from timberline forest into a wide avalanche path through which the trail angled down into the creek valley. It was a late morning, and the wilderness was bright and calm in the early July sun. Unlike most other slide paths in the area that tend to be choked with alders and other shrubs, this one was quite open – mostly grasses and low greenery. I could see the occasional flicker of water where the creek danced in the sun, far below. Suddenly I stopped dead in my tracks, paralyzed by total, abject terror. It was like those rare nightmares you wake from, unable to move. It felt like some kind of bitter hostility was focused on me.

"Something's going to happen," I said after a few moments, mostly just to hear the reassuring sound of my own voice.

But nothing did. I looked all around. No wild predator hiding behind a bush; no rocks or trees poised to fall. Nothing. Just a lonely valley, walled by sunlit peaks. And the inexplicable terror that had brought me to a halt.

I took a step. Nothing happened. I took a couple more steps, watchful, looking in all directions. Nothing. A few more steps and the feeling was gone. I went a short distance and looked back. It was just an avalanche meadow. White-crowned sparrows and MacGillivray's warblers were singing. I could hear creek chatter down below.

A couple of kilometres further I came to the Parks Canada warden patrol cabin tucked back in the woods off the trail. I'd picked up the cabin key from the Kootenay Crossing Warden Station, so I let myself in, opened the shutters, and pumped up the Coleman stove to make tea.

As I stepped out to sit in the sun, steaming cup in hand, I heard footsteps approaching. It was Jim, another of the summer park naturalists, heading out for an overnight trip to Talc Lake. I called to him. He stopped for a visit over sandwiches and tea.

Before I could tell him about my experience, Jim said, "You know, I had a really weird thing happen a ways back up the trail."

The hair prickled on my neck.

"Like what?"

"You know that big slide path this side of the pass? I was just about back into the trees where the trail comes off the bottom of it when it was like, just, a feeling of doom or something. I thought there must be a cougar stalking me or something. But there was nothing there that I could see. Really spooky."

1979

John Kansas and I had finished a winter field trip and were heading back into Jasper on the old 93A highway. I had started a few minutes ahead of him and was on a straight stretch near the Edith

Cavell road junction when something large and white crossed the road a few hundred metres ahead of me. A mountain goat? I sped up and then coasted to a stop where its snow tracks showed on the frozen asphalt.

Picking its way up the road embankment was a snow-white wolf. It paused at the top, at the edge of the trees, and looked down at me over its shoulder.

It was a beautiful animal. I knew John would be along shortly, and I wanted him to see it too, but it was only a few steps from cover and there wouldn't be enough time. I cranked down the window and howled.

The wolf turned and stared at me. Then it lowered itself down on its haunches and howled back. Its eyes were bright and attentive. I howled again. It did too.

Still no sign of John. A long moment later the wolf stood, turned, and, without another glance, loped slowly away into the silent, snowy woods.

We had conversed. I had no idea, however, what we had said.

The wolf might have known, but it was gone.

1986

In Jasper, hiking on Cinquefoil Ridge, a heavily grazed knoll at the south end of Talbot Lake, I wandered over towards where several bighorn rams were grazing, stopping at a respectful distance to snap some photos. Then, as traffic streamed past on the Yellowhead highway below, I sat down and dug my lunch out of my day pack.

The sheep grazed a bit longer and then began to pick their way up the hill. One passed a couple of metres from me, slowed, and then lay down, angled away from me. Another stopped just below me and bedded down too. The others settled down on the other side of me. The nearest ones looked at me lazily, so near that I could see that strange, buttery void in the centres of their oval pupils. Then they looked away, relaxed, chewing their cuds, each facing in a different direction, content to have me in their herd today.

Humbled, awed, I took my cue from them and laid back, resting my head on my pack, staring across the valley at Mount Desmet, feeling the minutes stretch into timelessness. They'd chosen to accept me into their world.

When I finally stood to go, the rams watched lazily, still chewing their cuds.

Down at the highway I looked back. They were still there, where I had so briefly been.

2014

Hunting elk one November morning in the upper Oldman foothills, I set out in darkness and was three kilometres in before there was enough light in the sky to turn off my headlamp and head up into the woods. The Douglas fir trees were dark and close there, however, and I had to turn my headlamp on again.

The way was steep and littered with downed branches. The winds blow hard in that country, and they keep the timber trimmed. A web of faint trails cut by the hooves of mule deer, elk, and cattle twisted through the litter and undergrowth, and although I had chosen a route that would connect me to a major elk trail, I missed it in the dimness. Slipping on ice patches, stepping over branches and around logs, I pushed myself uphill, racing daybreak for the open slopes on the ridge top, where I hoped to find elk still feeding before their daily retreat into the timber.

Panting, I stopped to turn off my headlamp and slid it into my pocket. Pale sky showed through the tree stems a short distance above, and I wanted my breathing to be calm before I emerged onto the bunchgrass slopes where the elk might be. Taking advantage of the breather, I looked down into the trees. There, in an open glade, was the broken stub of an ancient Douglas fir tree. Most of the tree lay prone where it had broken off, but the first four or five metres still stood: deeply grooved bark festooned with lime-green wolf lichen and the paler, olive-coloured *Alectoria*. The top was shattered. A woodpecker had drilled nest holes just a bit down. It stood utterly still, dead, yet full of life and memories, where it had grown through all the long centuries before I had been born. The trees around it hadn't even been there for most of its life; it had doubtless been one of only a smattering of similar trees in the open grassy landscape that existed here before the 20th century brought an end to Indigenous burning and wildfires.

I had given up the warm comfort of my bed and worked hard to get here at first light. I should be going; the elk might be just over the rim right now. But the old fading giant held me there. My sense of hurry now felt like something shameful, like I wasn't giving this place enough time, in the presence of one who had given it centuries. The glade seemed lost in some ageless moment, holding itself in, pregnant with potency and patient with waiting. There was something here to be learned, something about time and place and meaning...There was a great deal to be learned. If one knew how to hear a tree.

Eventually, however, I turned and went hunting. The elk weren't there.

I took my regret home, but it wasn't a hunter's regret. It was more like the regret a son might feel for a conversation he never had.

There are languages I don't speak, even now. Not for lack of trying.

***

What do I know?

So much less than I might once have thought. I was born into blindness and deafness, surrounded by white noise I mistook for meaning. I learned the wrong names for the places in my world. My education and religious institutions isolated me from the kinds of relationships with other beings that could have made me more fully human. I chose a life in biology to learn my way into intimacy, but the very nature of that science built up barriers. When animals and plants offered me understanding, I didn't know the language being spoken. And the things I did know, the things I was sure of, the stories of a life I still find myself reflecting upon with grateful nostalgia – they weren't true. At the very least, they were only partly true. Even when there is light in the treetops, the understory is full of shadows.

***

Catholic families such as ours were experts on sin, but not on avoiding it. Our religious tradition taught that we could simply erase it and move on, by partaking of the sacrament of Penance. That comforting thought, invented by the male clerics who ran the institutional Church, helped assert their control over congregations. By their interpretation of the Christian Bible, it was only they to whom their God had granted the power to absolve us from sin. Emerging from the shadowed hush of the confessional, having counted off my lies and petty thefts to the shadowy figure on the other side of the wooden grill, I never felt sanctified. It was a bit like wiping the crumbs off the table while trying to hide the stain in the cloth. Some sins were simply too egregious to confess; I suspect those ones rarely are. That was especially true when, as in the case of my family, there was a high standard to meet and a public reputation to uphold.

Even so, it came as a shock when Mom told me, one day in 1994, that Dad's youngest brother, Frank, had been arrested for sexually abusing young girls. The first allegations had emerged five years earlier, but now it had become a legal matter that would be dealt with transparently, instead of through hushed proceedings behind the screen of a church institution seemingly more concerned with protecting itself than protecting little children.

When Frank had been ordained as a Catholic priest, the feeling of pride among his siblings was palpable. Their father had spent years training to become a priest himself but had eventually left the seminary and married. In a way, Frank's ordination was a completion of his own father's unfinished business. We knew him now as Father Frank.

Of all our adult relatives, it was Frank and Gerry, my dad's only sister, who were most closely tied to our chaotic little clan. They shared an apartment near our Calgary home. Gerry was a gentle, self-conscious woman who often stepped in to help my mother when Dad was away. She had a car and could take Mom shopping or to church. I remember many weekends when I went to stay with her – a privilege that came with television and exotic treats like raw honeycomb, grape jelly on toast, or powdered chocolate in my milk. At home there were no such luxuries – with ten children to feed and clothe, Mom and Dad had no money to spare.

Gerry never married. She devoted her life, when she wasn't working as an accountant for an engineering firm, to the service of family and church. On the weekends when I stayed over, there would inevitably be one or two masses to attend on Sunday because Gerry was the church organist. Other times, it would be evening choir practice. I didn't like her church because it was new and bright, with modernistic stained glass in the windows, as unwelcoming in its own way as the cathedral-like dimness of our inner-city Sacred Heart Church. You could hide in the shadows at Sacred Heart; at Holy Name my only way of avoiding grownups was to sneak into the storage closet where extra chairs were stacked and sit there, listening.

On the weekends when I stayed with Gerry, I would share a bed with a grown-up – Gerry when I was very young, and later, as the years progressed, Frank. Gerry's room faced the front and was lit by street lamps and the flash of passing headlights. Frank's was in the back and had only one small window. It was a dark place. I would lie quietly beside the large, warm lump that occupied most of the bed and listen to the stillness. This wasn't home, but I could comfort myself by knowing it was family.

When awake, Frank was cold and controlling. He compensated for his own weaknesses by exerting power over his brother's children. We didn't see him that way, because he was so much a part of our lives. It just seemed normal that he would mock and belittle us, and that he made up unreasonable rules and then punished us for breaking them. The water-filled squirt gun beside his plate at Sunday dinner, with which he drenched any kids of whose behaviour he disapproved, seemed normal to us; it was what we knew.

What we didn't know was that Frank's issues went a lot deeper than just bullying. Like too many other Catholic priests, Frank was a pedophile. He took pleasure in grooming, dominating, and sexually abusing pre-adolescent girls. As a priest, he had access to many of them. Their parents trusted him because they saw him as a man of God. He moved from parish to parish, leaving wounded children in his wake, their trust in others, their sexuality, and their self-image shredded by the things they had experienced at the hands of a man their parents held in high esteem. I think of those nights I spent sleeping next to him and try to imagine the twists my own life might have taken had he been as interested in boys as he was in girls. He wasn't yet, fortunately. I was lucky.

But I also had sisters. They weren't so lucky.

And, really, nothing was normal.

***

Frank went to jail for three years – a much shorter sentence than what he had inflicted on his victims. My sister Margaret, who had spent her young life trying to protect our other sisters from his abuse by enduring it herself, became an alcoholic to cope with the pain and self-loathing she had accumulated through those lonely childhood years. She chose men who treated her poorly. Only when her doctor, after she was admitted to the emergency ward, told her that she was going to die and leave her children motherless did she turn to Alcoholics Anonymous for help. She fought her way back to sobriety. She divorced an abusive husband and found a job in a home for recovering male addicts. She excelled there; she understood them, after all. Then, with several woman friends who each had their own life stories, she helped found a refuge for families fleeing abusive or dangerous relationships.

Margaret went from being a victim to becoming a survivor, and then a leader, turning the misery of her early life into a source of power to help others find the kind of hope that came so late to her. She is a very fine woman. But I was never kind to Margaret when we were young. She seemed so needy and so vulnerable. I didn't know then what I know now. We've become close, but I cannot look at my sister without a feeling of guilt for all the times I failed her.

There was a time when I was unreservedly nostalgic for what I remembered as an idealized childhood, before I understood the degree to which it was a dream edifice built upon a bog of betrayal. Much as I wish I could, I can't un-know that. If the Bible from which we were taught as children is to be believed, it was eating from the tree of knowledge that banished humankind from the Garden of Eden. That metaphor rings true in more than one way.

Child sexual abuse hurts more than just the victimized children. The poison seeps through and affects the whole family, turning its story of itself into lies and illusions. The guilt might belong to the abuser, but it ultimately infects everyone.

Frank could have been stopped, if anyone had cared enough, and dared enough, to look into the shadows. It's not as if there weren't clues. It's not as if Margaret never asked for help. But we were a good Catholic family, and he was a priest, and so there were rocks that nobody, it now seems, was prepared to look under. That's how abuse thrives; otherwise good people simply choose not to see it.

Long after Dad's death, when an aging Frank suffered a stroke, Gordon took on the burden of being his uncle's caregiver because as the oldest son he felt it a duty he owed his father. Frank had pleaded guilty to abusing seven girls. Gordon once asked him how many victims there had actually been. The response, seemingly without shame: "I lost count."

There is only so much that can be said. Then words fail.

***

Dad had been diagnosed with leukemia, then Hodgkin's lymphoma. He lived with his cancer for 13 years. During periods of remission he enjoyed time with grandchildren and trout streams, hunted pheasants and elk, and became my confidante and friend. But by January of 1991 his time was up. Rather than go into hospice care he chose to come home from the hospital to die. He lay in the metal bed in the girls' bedroom at the back of the house on Sharon Avenue and sipped liquids through a straw. A clear plastic bag was pinned to the side of the mattress and hung flaccid below the covers, slowly filling with a frightening black liquid. My sister Patricia, who had trained and worked as a registered nurse, tended to that awful thing with a resolute calm. We boys tended to look the other way rather than acknowledge its existence, as the males in our family usually did with anything unpleasant.

Even so, Mom drafted her sons to help too, when we were around. I stayed over one night when the end was near, and Dad was drifting in and out of lucidity. In the early hours I heard the hall floor squeak – betraying him as it had betrayed his offspring so many furtive nights in those long-ago childhood years. I found him in the bedroom doorway, his tubes bundled up in his hands and an urgent look on his face. I never was good at reading Dad's mind, but if I had been asked to put a thought bubble over his head at that moment it would have read, "I've got to get away from this."

But he couldn't. None of us could.

A devout Catholic to the end, he had prepared himself spiritually for his imminent death and then waited with a sort of transcendent glow for his release and ascension. But his God made him wait. The glow passed and gave way to the desperate fading misery of a dying old body.

That old body might have been wasted and weak, but this was still Dad, the patriarch of our family of six sons and four daughters, the firm and unwavering moral authority whose dominance I had sometimes challenged but never really questioned all my young life. Yet now I found myself holding his once-powerful shoulders and bracing against him, staring desperately into his even more desperate eyes until reason seemed to reassert itself, and he let me turn him around and guide him back to his room. I raised the covers for him as he lowered his wasted, pyjama-clad body back down, pulled them up to his chin and, in response to a peremptory motion from him – a brief reassertion of his lifelong authority – held his water glass so he could sip slowly from the straw. He gave me a grim but grateful smile – lucid again – and closed his eyes.

I watched his lined face – those lines etched by wind and sun along countless miles of trout streams, pheasant coverts, deer trails, and elk ridges over seven good decades – and saw that the lines just spoke of aging now. He was shrinking into himself. I eased quietly out of the room and closed the door until it was just ajar, so I could hear if I was needed again. Mom was at the other end of the hall, in the front bedroom she had shared with him through four decades of married life, where their children had been conceived. I hoped she was getting some sleep at last.

The house was utterly still. I felt woefully alone amid all the ghosts and memories, with two aging parents and my own sense of utter inadequacy when faced with the profound duty of attending at a death. The question burning in my heart, the critical bit of unfinished business that lay between me and my father, didn't make it easier. Because there was a conversation I needed to have with him, but now was not the time. And that meant there would never be a time.

***

A week later, I was at Kananaskis Village, in one of the mind-numbing and ultimately useless strategic planning meetings that Parks Canada was going through at the time, when I got the phone call from home.

My mother's quiet voice: "Your father just died."

I hung up the phone and drove home down the Kananaskis valley, where Dad had once taken my older brother and me hunting for elk. It hadn't been his idea. Gordon and I were in our teens and eager to try big game hunting. Dad had only ever hunted birds, in farm country, with a shotgun. He didn't like the idea of his boys carrying rifles around other people's homes. So when he finally succumbed to our pestering, he decided to take us hunting in the Kananaskis, where there were still very few people.

We didn't have a clue what we were doing, but we bought our

tags, borrowed some guns, and went hunting. Our trump card was meant to be Dad's friend, Joe Quinn, who accompanied us. Joe had hunted deer before, albeit in the Maritimes. We spent a long day dispersed through the pine forests on the slopes above Grizzly Creek. Dad saw a cow elk, briefly, ghosting through the timber. Gordon and I saw nothing. Joe tracked and missed a white-tailed buck. Then, en route back to the car, in response to an eerie sensation between his shoulder blades, he turned around to see a cougar crouched and staring at him, the tip of its tail lashing.

That was the three rapid gunshots I had heard. At the car, I found Dad and Joe preparing to set off down the hill. Joe looked pretty pale. Dad had his borrowed .303 rifle in hand, but Joe's gun was missing. We found it down in the woods beside a dead cougar, where he had apparently thrown it after emptying it in panic.

Dad and Joe were cut from the same Depression-era, waste-not, want-not cloth, so the four of us set to work gutting the cougar, tying it to a pole, and slowly hauling it up the steep wooded hill to the car. It was huge. Dad later told me that the big cat became like the Ancient Mariner's albatross to poor Joe. He had never wanted to shoot it, he didn't really want the hide and head, but he couldn't just throw it out. That would be too disrespectful. His family probably still has it, glaring with glass-eyed reproach from the wall of some room.

I remembered that and other hunts. Dad's khaki-coloured overalls and the work boots that he finally bought for big game hunting when it became clear that the rubber hip waders he wore for bird hunting just weren't going to cut it. The peaked red cap, jammed on a greying head, sweat-stained around the rim and tilted sideways so that the lining flap would cover his bad ear. The three red canvas jackets he bought at Ribtor for himself and the boys in accordance with the hunting regulations of the day. His bad moods, and his frustration when we didn't stick with the plans so carefully worked out in advance of each hunt. We boys never did. The long drives from Calgary out to the various hunting grounds we found over the ensuing years, and the long, tired drives home.

Sometimes he would reminisce, mentioning names of people I'd never met and places that held important parts of his past; things he thought worth sharing. Those were good drives, when it felt like he was bringing us into a sort of historic continuum, imparting family lore that, while we could never truly absorb the meaning or depth it held for him, still meant he wanted that part of his story to become part of ours.

My long drive home this day, however, was surreal; the familiar flashed past the windshield with a totally unfamiliar sense of loss and the end of remembered things. I turned the corner onto the street I'd grown up on and saw an ambulance parked in front of our home, rendering everything suddenly hard and strange. I had never seen an ambulance there before. Its presence made everything irrevocable.

As I pulled up, two attendants were pushing a wheeled gurney down the driveway. I watched as they lined it up for loading. Dad's dead foot slid briefly out from under the sheet that covered his body. It was shockingly white. It simply lolled there, loose, unattached to purpose or thought or instinct or anything alive at all. Then it was gone. The gurney was loaded, the doors closed, and the men got in the ambulance. It pulled away and turned slowly around the corner onto 17th Street, and seemed simply to cease to be.

I sat in my car, reluctant to go in and face whatever there was to face in the suddenly haunted family home, looking at the hedge my dad had trimmed so many times, the lawn that had once been a potato patch, the house he and my mother had bought almost 30 years previously. Everything around me was familiar, but distant, as if a lifeline had been cut. Or a heartline. So much of my life was on that street, in that yard, in that house. But even more of his had been, I suddenly realized. And the part of mine that had been him was gone forever, rolled away lifeless on a folding metal gurney, by strangers.

He was gone. His brother, Frank, lived on. There would be no answers to those last, most urgent questions I had hoped to ask. I will take them to my own final resting place.

***

But that summer I went fishing with him. It was a time of introspection and reframing of my own life narrative. In reflecting on our most recent visits, it occurred to me that, although Dad might be gone, the streams we fished were still here. So I loaded up my gear and drove up into the headwaters of the Elbow River. When I pulled off to park, I felt a sense of bemused pleasure at the sound of the gravel crunching under the tires; that was a sound I remembered from countless trips with Dad. Outside, the air was cool with morning shadow, not yet loaded up with the midday pungency of pine resin, but I knew that was coming. Dad and I had breathed it many times together.

The creek gurgled quietly against its cobbles and burrowed into the branches of a half-submerged sweeper at the downstream bend, its dark, cold water both alien and inviting, ready to freeze my feet until the very bones ached, but at the same time beckoning me downstream where there were pools I remembered well, and trout to be caught. I strung my fly rod, tied on a fly, made sure the car was locked, and headed down a cattle trail into memory.

Dad was there ahead of me. He was in the willows that crowded down into the water and the overhanging spruce trees that snagged at my drifting fly, in the sudden tug and struggle of a cutthroat trout and the way the sun caught the coral stain of its belly when I lifted it out of the creek and teased the hook from its mouth. My hands soon smelled like Dad's old creel had always smelled. When I hooked an unusually large trout I almost looked around to see if Dad was watching. Perhaps he was.

I felt a heavy sense of loss, fishing in Dad's most recent favourite creek without him, balanced with a strangely reassuring sense of his presence. This had, after all, been part of him. An important part of him. We'd fished here together but, other times after I had moved away, when I would sometimes phone home, Mom would say he was out fishing. He had been here.

He wasn't gone. This place was a part of him and it was still here. In returning to it I was reuniting with him. Maybe I was only now finally learning to see it properly. Perhaps one can only truly know a place through the spirits that linger there, and the stories they inhabit.

***

That was 1991. Mom lived on, sharing a history with the man she had married in 1947 but also emerging from the decades of service to which she had willingly subordinated herself as the Catholic mother of a large brood of demanding children. The house that once echoed with our squabbling, laughter, play, and complaints was quiet now; the heavy footsteps of her husband no longer echoed in the hallway. When grandchildren came to visit, they confided in her but no longer needed to be shy and fascinated around the stern but kindly old man with the bushy eyebrows and crinkly face.

It became a woman's home, that initial emptiness giving way to a new ambience as the furnishings and wall hangings evolved to reflect her tastes, rather than the practicality and frugality of the family years. Eventually, the house became too much for her, though, and she sold it and bought a condominium; then that, too, became too much and she sold it and moved into a basement suite in the home of one of her children.

It had seemed like a good idea when she and my brother and his wife started discussing that move. It turned out an unfortunate one, because they chose a new, unfamiliar district, far from the friendly wooded streets of her home neighbourhood and from her friends. The walk to a strange bus stop was too much for an increasingly fragile and fearful woman, and so she lived in the stillness and loneliness of a basement suite through her final years. Her children planned to visit often but seldom did.

When I retired from my final posting in Banff, I made a habit of visiting her weekly. Each Thursday morning I did the hour drive into the city to take her grocery shopping and then to lunch at a little bistro not far from her home. One day she asked, her voice uncertain and desperate, "Do you think I might be losing my mental faculties?"

She wasn't, but she was reading her reactions to aging and isolation as evidence that she might be. Some of her children had started hinting at the possibility, interpreting her loneliness, boredom, and depression as signs of mental failure. It wasn't her mind that was failing her.

We talked and talked, mostly about the past. I sought her advice. She sought mine. It was a ritual we both looked forward to, for different reasons, and only rarely interrupted. But I always left. One cold afternoon as I prepared to head home, my aged mother looked up at me with eyes weary of solitude and said, "Oh, Kevin. I wish your father was still here."

I wish they both were.

I wish we had lived the life I thought I remembered, and that we could reminisce, with undiminished pleasure, about those family years. But it turns out we were all lonelier than we knew, or should have been.

***

The revelation of my uncle's moral betrayals brought an end to my recurring attempts to shoehorn my spiritual beliefs back into the rigid and patriarchal structures of the Catholic Church. It wasn't as if he was the first black-frocked pedophile to show up on my radar screen, after all. Our parish priest in Field had been charged with similar offences. At least three of the priests who had taught me at St. Mary's High School had been convicted of molesting boys. The news media was full of such tales. The church I had been raised to revere had proved itself to be an institution that sheltered and protected sick and twisted men.

It was also an institution that had no place for women except in subordinate roles – as submissive mothers, chaste nuns, or cheerful church volunteers. In declaring itself to be the one, true church,

Catholicism turned up an arrogant nose at deeper, more ancient spiritual traditions and justified the invasion, enslavement, conversion, and oppression of entire nations.

All of which I knew, and had gone through all manner of mental contortions trying to rationalize in my effort to stay connected to the comforting religious culture of my childhood. But there can only be so many worms in an apple before it becomes clear it is no longer food but compost. Many others, of course, have had different journeys than mine, and still hold fast to their Catholic faith. I respect their choice. Actually, I envy them, because I remember how good it felt to be part of the institutional Church, but there can be no way back for me.

And yet the teachings of Jesus remain the basis of the moral code by which I interact with other humans. I still see the beauty and power of the Judeo-Christian creation myth, especially the story of the Fall. The teachings in the books of the Christian Bible don't belong to any institution, and certainly are not the exclusive domain of the Catholic Church. Those teachings are ancient stories that reveal some spiritual truths, obscure others, and were inevitably adapted and interpreted to serve the purposes and prejudices of their all-too-human male authors. The Church I left is a man-made bureaucracy. It built its power over centuries by professing to own those teachings. It doesn't. Too often in the course of history, it has betrayed them.

The Church did not protect my family. It protected the man who betrayed us, along with many other similar men. Worse, it called them priests and gave them all its power.

***

For all that there is wisdom and morality to be found in the ancient scriptures, they came to us from farmers and fishermen who lived long ago in a hard, dry place on the far side of the planet. Their teachings, curated and reinterpreted by generations of ostensibly celibate male clerics, were brought to this place by men who saw nothing in this landscape that aligned with their view of what is normal and right, and who felt they had nothing to learn from the people or the places they found here. They brought a god reshaped in their own image and set to work reshaping the land in their image too.

Mike Bruised Head described some of the effects of this smug religiosity on the Siksikaitsitapi in his PhD dissertation at the University of Lethbridge:

> With other institutionalized religions, they steam-rolled our spirituality, and now we're fighting back, young people and those who have been disconnected from their Indigenous ways. Because we have not found ourselves, a lot of us, in other European religious institutions. It is lacking that connectivity to the land. A lot of these institutions of prayer do not even mention land. They don't even mention water, animals, birds.[8]

In the Christian creation myth, God spends six days creating everything that exists, and at the end he looks at all that he created and proclaims it "very good." He doesn't say it was a rough draft, or that there are elements he regrets, or that he'd have done better if he'd given himself more time. He says that it is very good. It is his Creation. He loves it all.

That part makes sense to me, even if much of Genesis seems clearly to have been written by men, for men, to justify the cultural aggression of a desert agrarian/pastoral people.

The Indigenous Nations of North America have their own very different creation stories, but one point of agreement is with the existence of a Creator. Indigenous myth, however, offers more humble versions of the relationship of that Creator to us humans; we are seen as being not above but equal to all other living things. We are meant to honour and sustain good relationships not just with one another, but with everything the Creator put into this world with us. They are our relations, not our resources.

The faith that my great-uncle brought with him to western Canada set mankind aside from everything else and gave us licence to use and abuse it as we wish. Rational science and technocracy perpetuated that assumed right to exploit the nonhuman world for knowledge and power. We brought that culture of abuse to this continent, and like the abuses that Frank perpetuated on his victims, it continues to thrive because of our refusal to see it for what it is.

And here we are.

***

A few kilometres downstream from the Oldman Dam, in the heart of the Piikani Reserve, a massive concrete structure intercepts the river and diverts most of its flow into a canal that feeds water into the Lethbridge Northern Irrigation District. There is nothing to stop fish from entering the canal, so they do. In the autumn, when the diverted flow gets cut off, hundreds of fish become stranded as the canal goes dry.

Harley Bastien grew up beside Old Man's River, as he knows it. Having been raised into Niitsitapiisini – the Blackfoot way of life – he could not leave those fish to die through no choice of their own. They are his relations. Each autumn for three decades he has organized Trout Unlimited Canada volunteers to rescue the stranded fish and release them back into the river where they belong. That's where I met him in the fall of 2022 when I signed up to help out. He was too busy to visit just then, so we reconnected several months later in Fort Macleod, where we met over coffee, and he told me a story:

> My time growing up in the Oldman started at quite an early age. We'd go up there to the Paint River – the Castle River – and we'd go up in that area and we used to pick owl eyes, what they call today "huckleberries." And when we'd go up there, we'd go up in two, three, four vehicles, with my grandmother. There'd always be one adult male would come and carry a gun just for safety.
>
> We'd pick here and then we'd move over here; we had

our places where we'd pick. Probably been using those sites for thousands of years. Probably my great-ancestors picked those very same patches that I picked.

My grandmother was always in charge of the berry picking and there were rules when we went up there. The first rule was, we had to be quiet. We couldn't talk loud, and no dogs were brought up there. And the next rule was, we only picked so much, and then we moved on. The reason is we left some for the animals. We didn't take them all just for ourselves. Because those are our relatives, and they gotta eat too. And we're visitors to their home, so we'd also bring up tobacco and say a prayer and give thanks.

This one time when I got older, me and one of my cousins found a couple of branches and we were way over here on the side, and we were sword fighting. One of the older girls came running up and she said, "Grandma wants you guys."

So we went over there and she said, in a stern way, she pointed at me and she said, "You should know better. You're supposed to be quiet here."

And I was getting a little bit lippy by then, you know, 12 years old or so, and I said, "Well, why? There's nobody around here."

And she said, "First thing, put those sticks away and you get back here."

So we just dropped them on the ground and she said, "That's not where you found them. You bring them back where you found those sticks."

So we put them back, and she said, "The reason why we've got to be quiet is, lots of spirits live here in the mountains. And if we disturb those spirits, they will get mad and they will leave. Then the mountains will become sick. When the mountains become sick, all the land will become sick and the animals and the plants and the people will cry out to the Creator, but it will be too late."

Today, that story is just clear as could be. That's what she was talking about. That's what traditional Blackfoot wisdom and knowledge and respect is based on. Today in the mountains it's a free-for-all. You got everyone…just going hog wild out there.

I go out there to what they call the trunk road – we call it Napi's Split Rock – to harvest teepee poles every fall for my teepee camp. I go up there every September and in 15 years I might have seen five deer up there. I might have seen a few magpies. The odd raven fly by. They don't live there no more. People have run them right out of there.

And this is the thing: in the Blackfoot way, everything has a spirit. Not only human beings have spirits. Some human beings, I don't even believe they have a spirit. Science has no spirit. Why? Because science can't measure what they can't see. So that's the downfall and that's the problem with science: it's got no spirit.

Something that doesn't have a spirit is a dead thing.

When the newcomer peoples – my ancestors among them – came here, they didn't know the names of the places. For the most part they saw the people who already dwelt here as uncivilized and superstitious. They certainly didn't look for or recognize the spirits of this place.

Instead, those more recently arrived people considered themselves separate from both the land and other peoples. They looked at the land as a bundle of resources to be claimed, commodified, traded, and turned into profit and power. They saw Indigenous Peoples as incomplete humans — as obstacles, or sometimes as cheap labour. Even the most visionary among them were motivated by the calculus of capitalism and the smug assumptions of their Judeo-Christian religions, not by love of place. Their love was reserved not for what was already here, but for what they might be able to make of it.

One of the most influential, and visionary, of the newcomer

270   Spirits and Stories

people was a stocky bureaucrat named William Pearce. Appointed as inspector of Dominion Lands Agencies, he controlled the "development and allocation of all land, forests, mineral and water resources." From 1874 to 1904 he served as Ottawa's main guy in what was then known as the Northwest Territories.

At Pearce's urging, the government of John A. Macdonald prohibited homesteading and settlement in the mountains and foothills. Instead, government policy reserved those forested valleys and bunchgrass hills to protect the water supply for the hopeful hordes of settlers arriving to build new lives, now that Treaties 6 and 7 had made land available for them.

Water was not sacred in his view of the world. It was simply an economic resource. Protecting it made pragmatic sense. He would have scoffed at the idea that there were spiritual values involved.

That hard-headed watershed protection policy nonetheless kept the Eastern Slopes largely intact, even while railroad companies carved irrigation ditches across the plains, towns grew up around river fords, miners dug for coal, and land companies speculated. When massive fires burned through the headwater forests in the late 1930s, the government of the young province of Alberta turned to Ottawa for help. Together the two levels of government established an Eastern Rockies Forest Conservation Board to protect their water supply from fire and other threats. When Peter Lougheed's government came into power in the 1970s, full of ambitions for even more robust economic growth fuelled by windfall oil profits, the new government established an Eastern Slopes Policy and a Coal Development Policy that, again, ratified William Pearce's original view: the Eastern Slopes of the Rockies were too valuable as a water-producing headwaters region to allow other resource values to compromise them.

But they did anyway. It was inevitable that a culture built on a view of Creation merely as a bundle of resources would fret at restrictions on its ability to exploit those protected lands. Loggers, cattle producers, coal miners, and, of course, the oil and gas industry all established footholds in the Eastern Slopes through the latter half of the 20th century, in spite of the primacy of watershed protection.

As the province prospered, more people could afford outdoor gear and longer holidays. There were few places better to play than in those scenic headwaters. Our family became part of that.

The gravel roads that took our family to our camping and fishing paradises were originally built for fire protection, but the vehicles we encountered and the work camps we passed were there for other reasons. We might have come to love jealously the places we found during those long days afield, but none of us gave any thought to their spirits. Perhaps those spirits were already gone. Perhaps they began to fade into their own shadows when the old names – Niitsítapi names that derived from deep, long relationships with these places – were replaced by names that had nothing to do with them at all.

My family knew Chief Mountain, but not the Blackfoot's Ninaistako. We knew the Devil's Head but not Wetikwostikwan, its long-time Cree name. We visited Lake Louise, named after a foreign royal, not Hora Juthin Imne, which is how the Stoney had known that lake for centuries. Calgary had long ceased to be Kootsisáw, as the Tsuut'ina knew it, and was named instead after a place in Scotland.

Pointing out the parallel trails grooved into grassy sidehills by range cattle, Dad told us those were the trails of the mythical Sidehill-Gouger, an animal with shorter legs on one side than on the other, forcing them to walk in endless circles around the hills. He said dense thickets of young lodgepole pine were Paul Bunyan's toothpick farm. He didn't tell us Napi stories because he didn't know any. Very few of the more recently arrived people carving up the landscape, toting away its resources, and returning to camp, fish, and hunt did. But they knew stories about some guy named Moses who once lived on the far side of the planet.

Little wonder we made a mess of it. Even many of us who came to love it still don't know it as well as we might. Through all those years of experiencing it, bonding to it, fighting for it, we know the stories we made there but few or none of the stories that already lived there in forgotten names, silenced songs, and the sacred traditions of people who could have taught us but were instead relegated to reserves and their children sent to be reprogrammed in residential schools.

That's the view looking backwards from here. The future is what we will make of it. That future will be shaped by our stories about the land and one another. J. Edward Chamberlin, in the introduction to his book *If This Is Your Land, Where Are Your Stories?*, tells of the source of his book's title:

> It happened at a meeting between an Indian community in northwest British Columbia and some government officials. The officials claimed the land for the government. The natives were astonished by the claim. They couldn't understand what these relative newcomers were talking about. Finally one of the elders put what was bothering them in the form of a question. "If this is your land," he asked, "where are your stories?" He spoke in English, but then he moved into Gitksan, the Tsimshian language of his people – and told a story.[9]

We all have stories. They tell us where we are, who we are, and what we imagine to be possible. The story of my home place – the western plains and Rocky Mountains – can be read on the landscape and in its lakes and rivers. Too much of it has now been written over, with far too heavy a hand, in an alien language of domination and dismissal.

***

When we lived in Waterton, our children's teacher, Lisa Lenz, used to take her students to the story tree, a wind-gnarled poplar at the edge of Waterton Lake where they could look across at the mountain I now try to know as Sakiimaapi but that the maps call Mount Vimy. Vimy is in France. Sakiimaapi has always been here.

While she read them stories, they felt God's breath on their faces, though they didn't know that's what it was. On weekends we often drove north, past Pincher Creek and Cowley, to our property beside the Oldman River. There was another story tree there, but I can't recall ever telling stories beside it. Mostly, we wondered about the stories it must know.

We came to know that old female poplar as the goose tree, because one year a pair of geese nested in the broken-off top. We might as easily have called her the raccoon tree, the owl tree, or the yellow-bellied marmot tree after its later residents, but the geese got there first. The goose tree is an ancient black cottonwood. Admittedly, ancient is usually less than 150 years for a cottonwood, but the goose tree is much older than any of the other trees along our river trail. Squat, twisted, and half-dead, her main trunk has deeply grooved bark and deep holes where large branches have broken off in the past. The dead branches lie on the downwind side of the tree. Healthy younger branches spread leafy fingers into the sunlight on the river side.

Someday the river will take the goose tree away. Our property is only a kilometre or so upstream from slack water when the reservoir behind the Oldman Dam – the dam I helped fight against a third of a century ago – is full. Upstream from an impounded river the delta effect reduces the water's ability to cut downwards, so for the last 30 years the spring floods have been raising the riverbed and eating away at the sides of the valley. The river is now shallower and wider than it was when the goose tree was young, before the dam. Floods have almost consumed the bank where the tree stands. Part of a bison's skeleton has appeared in its exposed roots. That old tree may have been a sapling when the big animal originally washed up on what then would have been a gravelly point bar; I like to think it was and that the bison helped the tree become what she became.

The goose tree has been witness to other stories too. A few metres away is the first of a series of at least six teepee rings. There are two pits there too, each the size of a round bale. This would have been a good place for the occupants of those teepees – shelter from the wind, proximity to the river for water, and cliffs and coulees nearby that were almost certainly used for bison hunting. Only three kilometres downstream are several piles of rounded stones high on a bluff overlooking the reservoir; they appear most likely to have marked drive lanes for bison hunts.

The goose tree wouldn't have witnessed those hunts, of course. Nor, likely, was she alive when the pits were in use. But those teepee rings? Perhaps. The smoke from cooking fires and the sound of singing almost certainly wafted through her leaves when she was young.

The old trail from the south Porcupine Hills fords the river beside the goose tree. Gordon Johnson, a weathered, gentle-spoken realtor who first introduced us to this place, told us that the original ranchers who settled in the hills crossed the river here on trips to the train siding at Cowley when they needed provisions or had livestock to sell. The goose tree would certainly have witnessed those trips, just as she has felt the vibration of our family's footsteps on countless hundreds of walks along the river trail. She's known every spring flood for the last century and a half, including the big ones in 1995, 1997, 2005, and 2013 that washed out so many of her kindred and brought new silt and seeds from upstream to change the character of her surroundings.

She's known and survived droughts like the one in 1984 that sealed the fate of the downstream river by triggering the announcement of the Three Rivers dam. An earlier drought, in the mid-20th century, was so severe that the Waldron Ranch, 20 kilometres upstream, was unable to buy Alberta hay for winter cattle feed. The ranch managers arranged to have hay shipped in by rail from Manitoba. They didn't know the imported hay was full of leafy spurge, an exotic weed from Europe that is nearly impossible to eradicate. By the time we bought our property in 1993, spurge from that disastrous introduction had spread all down the Oldman River, well beyond Lethbridge and Medicine Hat. I wonder if the old tree sensed the difference in the soil once leafy spurge arrived, with its milky sap and deep root systems. Spurge soon displaced almost everything else. For the first few years I used herbicide to try and eradicate the spurge, but the weeds won. The herbicide didn't kill the goose tree either, fortunately. The old tree must have hated that chemical stink.

Lately, there is less spurge because I released four species of flea beetle that feed exclusively on that weed. The beetles, too, are from Europe. As are my ancestors. The goose tree is witness to new, exotic stories now, unlike when those old cooking fires sent blue smoke wafting through its foliage. I suspect it's all the same to the old tree; she accepts what comes. She holds a thousand stories, none of which will ever be told aloud. But you can feel them when you lean against that weathered bark. They are the stories of a place – this one place beside the Oldman River, in the lee of the Rockies, under the chinook arch. Some of those stories have people in them – the older peoples, and the more recently arrived.

I sometimes rest my head against the sleepy old giant, close my eyes, let the river chatter and leaf flicker fill my senses, and listen. I try to listen with my spirit, not my ears; I try to hear what the tree's spirit holds. I think it works, at least a little; I think I can feel her stories seeping into me. I hope so. We need better stories than the ones we've been telling ourselves.

Stories can lead us home. I used to think I knew where that was. Now I listen and hope to learn.

15. Home

Gerry seemed dwarfed in her wheelchair. A stroke had left her twisted and shrunken. She watched with a helpless smile pasted to her lopsided face while Gail's and my children quietly played in front of the television. Our kids were shy and quiet, unsure how to react to this fading old woman or the rigid, aloof man who was now her caregiver. Their relationship with my aunt and uncle was founded on a very few visits, over a much shorter span of time than mine had been.

Those visits had come to an end soon after Frank got out of jail. He had appeared on the doorstep of our Waterton home briefly a couple years earlier to stand in the doorway and recite, seemingly by rote, a declaration about his pedophilia being a mental affliction that couldn't be cured but which could be treated. No expression of regret, no apology; he framed his sentences in the passive voice, as if to distance himself from any moral responsibility. He took no questions, ignored our awkward invitation to stay for a meal, and departed.

The following spring I found a paper-wrapped package at the post office. It was addressed to Katie in Frank's distinctive, scratchy handwriting. I opened it. Inside were three chocolate Easter eggs, each with one of our children's names written on the box. My anger at what I saw as an opening gambit to groom Gail's and my daughter startled me with its intensity. I photocopied the wrapping with the address on it and sent it to Frank with a stern letter warning him off. I cc'd the Calgary Police, the Catholic bishop, and Frank's psychiatrist. Nobody responded.

We had a daughter to protect, so the simplest thing was to cut the predator off. However, after Gerry suffered her stroke, Frank had taken on the responsibility of caring for his older sister. If we wanted to see her, we would need to see Frank. Gerry had been a kind and generous aunt for many years, and I knew she'd be longing for contact. Finally, in 2003, Gail and I decided we would visit her in spite of him.

It was difficult communicating with Gerry, because she had lost her ability to speak. She also had lost her ability to hide her emotions, always an important survival skill in my family. When I tried to express my gratitude to her for something she had once done for me, her face distorted and tears flowed. The evening was full of discomfort, on all sides.

***

"Kathleen!" Frank stood in the kitchen doorway. We all looked up. He gestured peremptorily with his hand, which held a dish towel. Obediently, just as I had been with the same uncle when I was her age, our young daughter got up from the floor and followed him into the kitchen.

Gail and I exchanged glances. I got up and went to the kitchen door. Frank was leaning over the sink, handing sudsy dishes one at a time to Katie to be dried and put away. She looked tiny and trusting; he loomed. Frank felt my presence in the doorway and turned to look at me. The expression on his face was smug and mocking, in a "Made you look!" way. Rather than let my reaction give him any satisfaction, I simply leaned against the door frame and watched until the last dish had been dried and put away.

"Come on, Katie," I said. "We'd better be heading back if we're going to get home before dark."

My cheerful, idealistic little 8-year-old daughter followed me back into the living room, where Gail, having heard me, was already organizing the boys. I felt quietly angry, and a knot of bitterness was building inside me; he had poisoned another family occasion with his mind games. I didn't let any of that show, hoping the kids would remember their visit to their aunt without the darkness attached. That was easy; I'd grown up, after all, concealing emotions around the stern men of my family. But I also felt cheated, on Gerry's behalf. We might be able to escape, but she was trapped with that ruined body and this cold, controlling younger brother. Our visit had been important to her, but it would be the last. My daughter had to come first. Other daughters hadn't.

Gerry died a year later. For her sake, I hope she was right and that there was indeed a reward awaiting her on the other side of death. She deserved better.

***

Everything I've ever loved deserved better.

The Bible by which my elders ruled their lives allots to each of us a lifetime of three score and ten years. Mine have elapsed, and still I carry on. It's a long time. A lot can change in that span, and a lot has. Some changes have been for the better: more whooping cranes and bison in the wild, more women in positions of authority, more truth and reconciliation. I wish I could say the good things outnumber those that have changed for the worse, but that would be objectively untrue. We live in a grim time of consequences – a time of climate chaos, biodiversity crisis, land loss, worsening social conflict, and perpetual wars.

What went wrong? It's a question I take down to the Oldman River almost every time I return to our family retreat there. The river offers no answers. "This one's up to you," it says. "I have my own work to do. And it doesn't help that you people keep making it more difficult."

Religion and rational science, each in its own way, were meant to make things better. They continue to make things worse. If they are the source of the problems, then counting on them for solutions seems a bit questionable. Something even more fundamental must be flawed.

Biologist Lorne Fitch likes to tell the story of two Alberta cowboys who tip back a few too many beers one night at the Longview saloon. When it's time to leave, one finds the other crawling around on his hands and knees by the lone streetlight at the far corner of the parking lot.

"What are you doing?"

"Looking for my keys."

"But the truck's parked over there."

"I know. But the light's better over here."

∗∗∗

The Judeo-Christian Bible insists that humanity is separate from, and superior to, the rest of living nature. Catholicism and dozens of other *isms* instruct us to substitute dogma for thought and to surrender power over moral judgment to ordained clerics. Western rational science has ordained a whole other cadre of priests whose word we are also meant to accept without question. Science may profess to be evidence-based and objective, unlike religion, but it starts from the same assumption: that human superiority grants us an unquestioned right to objectify, isolate, and interfere with everything else in the nonhuman world. Far more often than not, Western science studies life not as a way of honouring and deepening our intimacy with Creation, but with the intent to control and use it.

The book of Genesis instructs man to "subdue the world." Science gets the job done. We sometimes seem determined to subdue it to death. What a profound insult to its Creator.

Religion at least acknowledges the existence of a spiritual world, even if it keeps that world just out of our reach, with stiff rules for admission, but science scoffs at the whole notion. In the theology of secular science, that which can't be measured or explained does not exist.

That these *ologies* exist in service of humanity is a particularly sad irony, because they have contributed to the undoing of humanity. Contrary to their basic assumptions, humankind does not exist separate from the rest of Creation. We exist *because* of the rest of Creation. When a new combination of DNA comes into being, that's just instructions for how to build one's relationships.

The individual becomes whole only through its connections with others – first with its mother, then its family, then with schoolmates, pets, neighbours, and surroundings, through a series of increasingly complex interactions in a steadily expanding world. Those relationships enable the full expression of one's DNA potential; they are what make us real beings.

Eternal life is, in fact, a thing. If we are made by the world in which we live, then only a part of us dies when our body ceases to function. The rest continues on. All the places we knew, birds and animals we encountered, the sound of rain and rivers and the smell of sage and spruce sap, the hard grey pellet snow that precedes a winter blizzard, and the golden light that spills out at evening from beneath the chinook arch – as long as those survive we are, in fact, assured of the eternal life promised by our religious institutions. Those things are all part of our spirits by the time our physical clock runs out.

Priests and preachers tell us that we need to die and leave this world to attain heaven and find eternal life. In truth, we're already where we were always meant to be. The existence into which we were born is all we'll ever get. And it's enough. We weren't banished from Eden; we banished ourselves by cutting ourselves off from the magic and miracle of being one with everything.

The key to that lost garden has been in our hand the whole time. When one sees that one's identity and purpose is a product of, not separate from, everything else that exists, then the whole notion of exploiting the world in which we live begins to look a bit like serving up one's own hand for dinner. It doesn't make a whole lot of sense, when that's the hand that holds the key whose loss we mourn.

But none of that is how we think. If it were, there would still be hope for woodland caribou because we could no more let that part of ourselves go than cut off an ear. If it were, we would agonize over the idea of damming rivers or using them to carry pollution away, because we would feel the consequences in our souls. If this were how we thought, we would enter our national parks with humility and awe, as postulants seeking enlightenment, not as consumers of social-media-worthy moments or outdoor recreationists looking for something to conquer. If it were, we would treat each other with kindness, because we would see one another as part of ourselves. We'd know that respect for our relations – all our relations – is self-respect.

**

Frank's uncle, Victor, served as an Oblate teaching brother at Brocket for many years. He found many reasons to complain about his Piikani charges, one being the way in which they would retreat off into the hills to participate in the Sun Dance. Victor saw the Sun Dance as a pagan ceremony, one that diverted the Piikani from pursuing their destiny as Christian farmers. The Canadian government had outlawed it, but that made no difference. Victor knew where his students went when they failed to show up for school. He felt offended. He believed he was there to help them, after all.

Like Frank, Victor assumed the right to make decisions for people he assumed to be his inferiors. In Frank's case, it was young girls over whom he exerted his power regardless of how they felt and the damage that would result. Victor's effort to force a Christian education on Blackfoot children was a different sort of abuse founded on the same kind of unquestioned right of power. Victor, were he still here, might be offended at the comparison, but the fundamentals were the same: a sense of natural entitlement and an assumption of superiority granted to men, by men.

The smug self-assurance of the senior forestry and water resources staff who summarily sentenced woodland caribou to extirpation and who plugged Napi's river with a cold, dead dam reflects the same pathology: lack of humility; failure of respect.

In every case, unwarranted suffering and perverse outcomes resulted.

Abuse, whether of land, rivers, children, or other peoples, results from men asserting power and authority that were never theirs to assume. The abuse of power involves a self-justifying sense of entitlement and the failure to respect what we think of as the other. Freeing ourselves from the normalization of abuse demands much more than better rules or better processes – it requires an entirely different way of thinking about who we are and how we relate to the world that forms and sustains us. It means questioning everything that passes as normal, and challenging any authority that places any human purpose outside or above those different from ourselves.

As I write these words, Frank is well into his nineties, bedridden and alone, waiting for death without the comfort of family. His little victories over helpless children are far behind him now. For whatever perverse reward he got from them, he lives now with consequences he brought on himself. None of us grieves with or for him. Through his failure to form right relationships when he could, he sentenced himself to an eventual death in solitary confinement.

Through our failures to form right relationships with other beings, we collectively sentence ourselves to isolation too – from the spirits of our home place, from teachings we could have shared, from the certainty of a future that works; from all our relations. From our best selves – our whole selves.

As I write these words, the basin behind the Three Rivers dam is nearly empty of water. Instead, it is choked with silt eroded from headwater landscapes that are being clear-cut for their timber, carved into erosion gullies by motorized recreationists and considered for coal strip mining. A changing climate brings less snow and more torrential rains, and so the river brings more mud and less water to a reservoir that was built to end water insecurity. The hubris that built that dam displaced ranching families, cut bull trout and other fish off from their spawning grounds, silenced the spirits and swamped the sacred sites of the Niitsítapi – and failed to add a single drop of water for the irrigators who had lobbied a willing water elite to build it. In fact, the first water licence the government issued for that reservoir – back when it stored more water than mud – was to itself, for evaporation. On years when it fills, the Oldman reservoir loses 2,000 Olympic-size swimming pools worth of water to evaporation. Gone with the wind: all those relationships betrayed, and the water too.

There are many kinds of abuse that hurt the world we live in, but most could be avoided if we saw every person, every animal, and every place as a loved and respected relation, and if we put our responsibility to honour those relationships first in all our decisions. But our religious institutions and objectivist, rational Western sciences tell us we don't need to. And so, too often, we choose to live as outsiders, and to consider that normal.

The language of truth and reconciliation too often implies the superiority of the abusers by assuming that trauma and harm were visited only on the Indigenous Peoples our systems have systematically abused for so long. In truth, we whose people arrived here more recently did just as much harm to ourselves, but the hard-wired hubris of our culture blinds us to it. The journey to healing and health requires reconciliation not only with Indigenous Peoples but with lands, waters, other living beings...and our own souls.

As treaty people, we should have started this journey together in 1887, at Blackfoot Crossing. We didn't, and so the need becomes more urgent, and the challenge more daunting, with each passing season.

***

Wolf Willow is the name we gave to our cabin by the Oldman River. The name derives from the native bushes growing along our access road. They rattle in the chinook wind and glisten a dusty silver-green under the foothills sky. Each June the wolf willows fill the prairie with a cloying and pungent odour unique to this part of the world. Wolf willows abound in the understory of the cottonwood forest that lines the river. In the understory there are trails that lead out to the water's edge, up onto the prairie, or into the deeper woods. Or perhaps the trails come from those places into the understory. They can get you lost, unless you mean to be there. They can get you found too.

***

Ever since we built it in 1995, not long after we bought these 56 acres beside the Oldman River, Wolf Willow has come to centre our family's existence. The cabin is full of memories and mementos. But it's the rest of those acres that I think of when I'm away. Regardless of what might happen elsewhere, what happens on these acres is our responsibility. Gail and I started out thinking we owned land. Gradually, we've come to see that we took on relationships and responsibilities; if anything, the land now owns us.

Barn swallows built a mud nest on the cabin porch soon after we built it. For two summers they shrieked in alarm and dove at us every time someone stepped outside. Then the young would hatch and beg for food from dawn to dusk. It was a relief when the fledglings took flight in early July and the nest was finally empty.

But then one year they didn't come back. We haven't seen a barn swallow at Wolf Willow since. Those graceful birds that were everywhere in my youth are now classified as a species at risk.

In the long summer evenings other kinds of swallow – tree, cliff, bank, and rough-winged – swirl overhead or sail in graceful arcs above the fescue grassland. When potato bugs found our garden, so did the rough-wings. I had never thought of swallows as birds that feed on the ground, but each summer evening anywhere from four to ten rough-winged swallows quietly descend on the garden to alight among the potato plants and pick insects from the soil.

Lately, bank swallows have become rare. I don't know why. I suspect pesticides, since they are scarce now everywhere. They were along every foothills creek when I was a kid with a fishing rod, but according to Environment Canada survey data their numbers have declined by 98 per cent over the course of my lifetime.[10] Cliff swallows are fewer now at Wolf Willow too, because the river, in the years since the dam, has begun undermining and collapsing their nesting cliffs. They've gone in search of something more stable.

The cliff swallows might find stable nest sites, but they won't find a stable climate. When snow falls in late March after a brown winter, or afternoon thunderstorms bring relief in July, Gail and I reassure each other that things are back to normal. But things will never again be normal, if there ever was a normal. In Jasper, during the late 1980s, national park interpreters were directed to treat climate change only as a hypothesis. That seemed ironic, since one of our most compelling stories involved the retreat of the Athabasca glacier. When the first white explorers found their way into the Sunwapta Pass area where today's Icefields Parkway runs, they had to continue by way of the higher Wilcox Pass because the main valley was blocked by glacier ice. Wooden markers indicate where the receding toe of the Athabasca glacier was at different points during the ensuing century and a half. Today it is a kilometre west of the parkway; the whole glacier looks deflated. Most of the ice mass has melted out and drained off down the Athabasca River to Wood Buffalo National Park, where, ironically, the Peace–Athabasca delta is drying up. Glaciologists predict there will be no glaciers visible from the Icefields Parkway by the end of this century.

Glaciers vanished from the headwaters of the Oldman River hundreds of years ago. I try to picture those northern rivers running as low and clear as the Oldman does each summer and I can't make the picture work. That's not how I know them. But that's what our grandson will see when he reaches my age.

Even without glaciers, the Oldman is becoming a different river. As snowpacks in the high country dwindle, the summer flows diminish as well. Upstream from the Oldman reservoir the stream has grown wider and shallower, so the summer sun penetrates to the riverbed and heats the water faster. I used to sit beside the river during summer's long, calm evenings and watch the valley breathe. Lately, I put my lawn chair in the middle of the river instead and feel warm water caressing my legs. I no longer fish the river in summer, not because the fish aren't there – so far, trout have been able to survive in spite of near-lethal water temperatures – but because those fish don't need added stress when their water world has become so nearly intolerable. I'm content to watch them rise for caddis flies while shadows work their way out from the cliffs and the cooling evening breeze comes snuffling through the cottonwoods to send me back inside and give the fish a few hours' reprieve until the sun returns.

There are fewer birds in the cottonwood forest now than there used to be. Back in 1970 I turned my back on birds for a while and tried out being a hippie. It didn't work. I should have paid more attention instead, because Breeding Bird Survey data analyzed by the Cornell Lab of Ornithology show that there are at least three billion fewer songbirds in North America now compared to when the Canadian Wildlife Service first hired me to count them.

Prairie songbird numbers have declined by two-thirds.[11] I thought those longspurs, kingbirds, sparrows, and others would always be as much a part of the world as they still are a part of me, but I was wrong. The long quiet pauses during the evening bird-song chorus weren't there before; they announce to me that I am a diminished person in a diminished world.

There is more than one way to lose one's hearing. When the sounds of life vanish on their own, that's the worst. Gordon Ruddy, a Jasper friend, wrote me a note one day: "I'm getting old enough to see that there are a lot of birds just missing. That some birds were plentiful, but are rare now. I try very hard not to get down. It's hard."

I know that grief. It's how I felt as I watched my mother's final breaths; the same sorrow washes over me sometimes even now when fishing one of Dad's old streams. The difference is this: we expected them to go, but we expected the world that made them to carry on.

Now we grieve a far greater loss.

***

Still, there is that yellow warbler who feeds busily in the sandbar willows across from my evening chair. He breaks into song from time to time, taking me back to the first time I heard that cheerful tune in the backyard of a long-ago Calgary home. Cedar waxwings perch on tilted trees at the edge of the river cliff and dart out over the water to pluck mayflies out of the breeze. Their soft voices offer a promise of continuity that I hope will be kept. Robins sing lustily; they seem more abundant than before.

And the river still flows. For all that it's a living thing, it's also a metaphor. If one's life experiences are lived stories about the meaning of things, a river is more than running water. It's where the stories and spirits in the land come together and find their voice. Especially, perhaps, this river: the Old Man's river – Napi's river. From where I sit, the water comes into sight up by the big midstream rock, swamper of canoes. It tumbles out of a long, boulder-strewn riffle, piles up in a big eddy near a sandstone cliff, and then sorts itself out before coursing down a long run to where I watch. It's constantly arriving, bringing stories from farther upstream where some of its waters rested in beaver ponds or spilled off mountain walls while other tributary streams carved slot-like shadows into conglomerate cliffs or wide, curving sinuousities through green fen meadows. It arrives confident in its knowledge of where it's been and busy with purpose, carrying those gathered waters, stories, and spirits down from the mountains where, even now, its waters are still in the process of being born.

Passing my chair, chuckling and whispering in the way that rivers do, the water pushes against the near bank before spilling into a downstream riffle and, a few dozen metres further, sweeping in against another sandstone cliff. The evening sun is golden there, unlike the shadows that enfold me. At the last, only the sparkling tops of waves show briefly through willows before the river is gone. That river must have endless faith, because those waters have no knowledge of where they are going, yet they flow unquestioningly towards that unknown destiny.

The river is always arriving and always departing, yet it's always there. We sit together each warm evening, and become part of the same moment, for all that we both have different ways of being. It's a relationship that only one of us thinks about. Perhaps I should think less, but that's my contribution. The river's contribution is faith.

***

What would be a better way of knowing the world, and our place in it? If we held the key that would get us back into Eden, how might we recognize it?

I was taught by priests who insisted they had the answers. I was instructed by scientists who were no less sure that they could tear the truth out of things. For all those smug certainties, today the glaciers are going missing, rivers are running low, the forests and plains listen in vain for their birds, and ghosts haunt the caribou woods. Those self-anointed guides appear to have gotten us well and truly lost.

When we first met, Gail trusted my woods sense; she would go anywhere I suggested. Then she developed a bit more experience with me. She would ask, "Are we lost again?"

"No," I would reply, indignantly. "We're just exploring."

So maybe we're not lost – just exploring.

Every misstep is a lesson; every new friend is the next teacher. Through the generous counsels of Dr. Leroy Little Bear and the late Narcisse Blood, the friendship of Elliot Fox and Lani Blackwater, Kansie Fox and Harley Bastien, and the writings of Dr. Mike Bruised Head and Betty Bastien, I've found other guides and better lessons. Summer evenings, I consult with the Oldman River. There are many trails out of the understory, once one begins to look.

I've come finally to believe that what we need is not more churching, cold science, expertise, or technocratic power. Instead, a good path forward demands humility, respect, kinship, reciprocity, gratitude, love, and, finally – because urgency demands it – fierce determination.

Humility
The gods we remade in our own image might tell us that we are the purpose of existence and that all else exists to be put in our service,

but they are wrong. Everything that was created was created equal. If there is purpose to Creation, look around. Everything you see is the expression of the Creator's purpose – not just the people. In George Orwell's *Animal Farm*, the pigs, having asserted dominion, declare, "All animals are equal, but some animals are more equal than others." The pigs were wrong too.

Respect

Respect is a corollary to humility. Everything that exists has its own inherent purpose and dignity. Robin Wall Kimmerer, in her book *Braiding Sweetgrass*, describes an epiphany she experienced when trying to learn her own Ojibwa language. She was frustrated by the strangeness of nouns that weren't nouns. They were infinitives. A flower was not an object; it was "being a flower." A swallow was not a swallow; it was "being a swallow." A hill was "being a hill." It was Jesuit Thomas Berry's writings that finally helped her see that her people's language relates to the world not as a collection of objects but as a communion of subjects. It is a language founded in respect for the way in which other beings exist, rather than on their utility.

I tried it out one day on the river trail at Wolf Willow. It was much more difficult than I had expected because the language and culture in which I had been raised forced my thinking into hardened patterns. My brain struggled to escape deeply worn ruts, but I persevered. The river was "being a river": moving sediment, pulling oxygen from the air and carrying it to the gills of fish, chattering and gurgling, reflecting the clouds and providing buoyancy to mergansers. Those mergansers were "being mergansers": providing warmth and food to the mites that live in their down, working as a team to herd and hunt sculpins and dace, startling me with their splattering retreat when I got too near. I stopped at the goose tree and rested my head against her, and I could feel her "being a tree" – being that specific tree, roots deep in the soil, leaves open to the sky, billions of chloroplasts pulling carbon from the air and energy from the sun to magick them into living carbon, sending her seeds into the wind in an annual profession of faith.

It was a world not so much transformed as rendered more deeply real. These were not resources awaiting their allocation in the marketplace; these were complex, meaningful beings whose very existence inspires respect – once one works to see them for who they are. It also had the effect of turning the world into a place where I can never again feel alone – because I'm not.

What if the government and the churches had chosen to see the people who lived here already not as "Indians" but as "humans being real people"? What if Frank had respected his victims not as sexual objects to be abused but as "children being real people" – feeling, imagining, caring, doubting, trusting, becoming – as whole, complex beings?

We would have had better stories, and less to reconcile.

Kinship

The fact that I never got to go to Woodstock, at that teenage stage of my life, was a bitter disappointment. Joni Mitchell didn't get there either, but she nonetheless wrote the song that came to define it, and wherein she reminded us that we are all stardust.

Indeed, we are.

Everything that exists in this world originated as stardust. The atoms that make up our bodies came from and return to the same once-inanimate earth planet that emerged out of...what? Priests and scientists assert answers, but we will never truly know. The guesses are fascinating, but they are guesses.

The air we breathe was exhaled by other living things. The air we exhale will be inhaled by others too. The food we consume was living tissue that died. It becomes our living tissue, and that will die too. If we don't cheat the earth, it will be consumed by others and live again in them. Life flows through us, not to us.

Everything that exists lives on in everything else. We are indeed stardust – one thing that assembles and reassembles itself through the magic and mystery of life, world without end. We are, literally, among our relations. We are kin to fungi, grizzly bears, hummingbirds and swallows, glacier lilies, minnows, limber pines, nematodes, and one another. Our family tree branches off into infinity and has its roots in stardust.

Things are not separate from us. They are family. If we actually thought that way, how might that affect our choices? Would we, perhaps, agonize over the decision to fire up a bulldozer and lower its blade? Would we clear-cut whole forest stands and flood whole valleys behind dams?

Reciprocity

Well, perhaps sometimes we would, out of necessity. As living organisms, we all need food and shelter, health, and security – all the biological necessities of life. In order to create shelter, we cut trees and mine minerals. In order to eat, we kill. No matter how we know or relate to a chicken or a carrot, we are going to end up eating it. In the event, that turns out good for us, and not so great for them.

If these are our kin, if we truly respect them, then the transaction by which they give up their lives to sustain ours requires that we enter into that transaction with reverence and love. We have to give back. It's neither respectful nor honourable to take what hasn't been earned or given, or what won't or can't be repaid.

True reciprocity goes beyond the self-serving conservation that pats itself on the back for having secured a future supply of whatever "resource" is being consumed. Logging companies that replant trees are not engaged in reciprocity; they are simply renewing their capital stock. Organizations like Ducks Unlimited were founded by hunters not so much to give back to the waterfowl they kill as to ensure that there will be more ducks to shoot next fall. Livestock producers who balance herd numbers with what their grasslands produce are, as often as not, merely managing an investment.

But true reciprocity exists. Volunteers gather on weekends to plant willows or construct beaver dam analogs along small foothill creeks as a way of giving back to wounded streams where, on other weekends, they might fish for trout. Ducks Unlimited Canada has evolved their approach from merely producing ducks to restoring wetland ecosystems that benefit not just waterfowl, but frogs, sandpipers, muskrats, and herons too. Some ranchers invest in species-at-risk plans for their properties and adjust their livestock management to give streams, prairie falcons, rare plants, and bears the ability to thrive there too. Urban dwellers donate money and time to conservation organizations. Rural people put up bluebird boxes or put out feed to help wildlife during hard winters.

Reciprocity is the pragmatic face of respect; it acknowledges that to live in the world, we must take from our relations. Giving back in as generous and meaningful a way as possible is how we manage that conundrum with integrity. Failing to give back is theft – a form of abuse.

Gratitude

Everything that exists came into existence somehow. There are those who are willing to tell us how that happened. They don't know. Nobody ever will; how could they? We're only humans, and we came late to the party. But somehow all this was created, and in coming into being, it became an ever-expanding, complex, and utterly incredible miracle. We emerge from the womb into a work of living art that would be inconceivable if it were not real, actually there, already waiting for us. And then we become part of it, and it becomes part of us.

If that isn't cause for gratitude, what is? Simply to exist: what a gift!

Whether we call the creative force behind this universe the Creator, God, magic, physics, accident – it doesn't really matter. Gratitude is due. Expressing gratitude reminds us of what we owe. It keeps us from the arrogance of assuming that anything is owed to us. Gratitude leads us back to reciprocity.

Love

To speak of *our* world, *our* family, or *our* land implies ownership, and that in turn could be taken to imply control. But ownership that grants control is a perverse social construct. In a world where everything is part of everything else, nobody really can be said to own anything in that way. We earn the right properly to use the possessive voice through love, not law. To the extent that my spouse and kids are "mine," that imposes a duty of care on me; it doesn't grant me licence. I own my family not because I bought them, but because I love them and they, in turn, love me. That bond of love allows me to call them "mine" and them to call me "theirs." We earn those possessive pronouns by nurturing what we love. We lose it by failing to do so.

The same should apply to land, livestock, water, and wildness. Ownership, if that concept has value at all, should never be seen as something that grants a right to abuse or destroy; it should be seen as imposing a duty of love and care. It should be founded on humility, based on reciprocity, and informed by respect. It isn't about power; it's about love.

Fierce Determination

If I dig for it, I can still find the fury that awoke in me when I saw Frank turn his sick attention to my daughter. I was already filled with grief from seeing the effects on my siblings from his abuse of power and betrayal of trust. Gail and I were determined to keep that poison from infecting any more of our family. We protected our daughter, and now she's grown. The fierceness of our determination to protect her arose out of love and anger, but we've left the anger, and Frank, in the past. The fierce determination remains: this must not happen again to anyone or anything we love.

Anger motivated by hatred does harm to all it touches. But anger fuelled by love can generate a fierce determination to defend that which is threatened, especially if it can't protect itself. We live in a time when countless beings deserving of love are under threat. There has never been a greater need to transform love, grief, and anger into fierce determination. If our relationships matter, at a time of so much peril, then they are worthy of that. In fact, they depend on it, and so do we. We are family. We share this home.

***

I struggle against despair. So much of what I loved is gone. My mother and father – but that was inevitable. My youth and so many memories of it – that, too, was inevitable. But all the birds. The free-flowing streams and quiet places. The caribou, curlews, and cutthroat trout. The burrowing owls that once nested in a much-smaller Calgary, and the river Gail and I floated in hopes that we could help save it. All are part of me, but all are diminished or gone.

Aging brings a decline in one's faculties – muscles grow weak, joints deteriorate, the mind begins to wander – but when the birds go silent that's a different kind of deafness. When places and species disappear, that's a different kind of blindness. The losses that haunt an aging naturalist in 21st-century Alberta are far more profound than just the normal costs of aging. These are losses that penetrate to the soul. It's like watching spirits die – the sacred spirits that welcomed us into the world and were meant to carry on after we depart. It's a darker kind of mortality when the death that draws near is not just of one's body, but of the best parts of a world that made one who he is.

This must be how the Niitsítapi felt when they awoke to the end of all things – to the knowledge that all that now remained of Iinii, the plains bison that centred their world, were bleached bones, empty prairies, and regret.

***

But I go down to the river in the evenings and I listen to the water – that mountain-born stream that Harley Bastien knows as Old Man's River because of its connection to Niitsítapi stories of that first and oldest of people, Napi. Quiet voices in that living water remind me that hope is not something we are given; it is something we must make for ourselves out of love and fierce determination. The river has not given up. Nor should we.

We make the stories we live, and then those stories make us.

Some of those stories shine, but many more are full of false starts, flaws, and failures. That's inevitable; we're human. Still, we awaken each day into the next set of possibilities. We can choose to steer away from hubris and towards gratitude. We can find our true selves again in this sweet, living place, and in each other. We need only find the humility and respect to listen – not just to people who live in different ways, but to the world itself: to the river and the wind, the trees and willows and grasses, to the birds and coyotes and chorus frogs, to the deep silence of winter nights and the thunder that comes over the hills on humid summer evenings – and to know ourselves as one with those beings – those teachers – and with one another.

The family is waiting for us to come home. They never left us; we left them. We're not doomed, just lost. Okay: exploring. We do belong here – but we are not in charge and it's never been all about us. It's always been about the whole of Creation, of which we are but one small part and without which we can have no real meaning, purpose, or hope.

We will never be the gods we try to make of ourselves.

When we come to terms with that humbling truth, we may yet find ourselves holding that long-lost key to the Eden from which we continually banish ourselves, and emerge at last into the light of a future in which things are no longer so broken and the spirits of this sacred place sing again – not just in all our relations, but in us too.

As it was always meant to be.

Notes

1 *Who Has Seen the Wind?* (Macmillan, 1947), 1.

2 Mary Eggermont-Molenaar and Paul Callens, *Missionaries among Miners, Migrants and Blackfoot: The Van Tighem Brothers Diaries, Alberta 1875–1917* (University of Calgary Press, 2007), 179–80.

3 Lindsay Amundsen-Meyer, "Nested Landscapes: Ecological and Spiritual Use of Plains Landscape during the Late Prehistoric Period" (PhD diss., University of Calgary, 2014), https://prism.ucalgary.ca/items/d3e3b28b-f6e7-46cd-9287-5a3eba1af49d.

4 Eggermont-Molenaar and Callens, *Missionaries among Miners, Migrants and Blackfoot*, 257.

5 Henry Stelfox, *Rambling Thoughts of a Wandering Fellow, 1903–1968*, edited and self-published by John G. Stelfox, 1972, 140.

6 Ninna Piiksii (Mike Bruised Head), "The Colonial Impact of the Erasure of Blackfoot Miistakitsi Place Names in Paahtómahksikimi, Waterton Lakes National Park" (PhD diss., University of Lethbridge, 2022), https://opus.uleth.ca/items/01429387-dc1a-4e5d-9c33-705d87f40ab3.

7 W.F. Lothian, "Chapter 7: Preserving Canada's Wildlife," in *A History of Canada's National Parks*, vol. 4, Parks Canada, 1981, http://parkscanadahistory.com/publications/history/lothian/eng/vol4/chap7.htm.

8 Ninna Piiksii (Bruised Head), "The Colonial Impact of the Erasure of Blackfoot Miistakitsi Place Names in Paahtómahksikimi, Waterton Lakes National Park."

9 J. Edward Chamberlin, *If This Is Your Land, Where Are Your Stories?* (Penguin Random House, 2004), 1.

10 "Bank Swallow (*Riparia riparia*): Recovery Strategy 2022," Government of Canada, https://www.canada.ca/en/environment-climate-change/services/species-risk-public-registry/recovery-strategies/bank-swallow-2022.html.

11 "The State of Canada's Birds," *NatureCounts*, https://naturecounts.ca/nc/socb-epoc/main.jsp.

Selected References

Bailey, R.E. *Proposal for the Alberta Water Plan: The Prairie Rivers Improvement Management and Evaluation Programme (P.R.I.M.E).* Alberta Department of Agriculture, Water Resources Branch, Edmonton, 1960.

"Bank Swallow (*Riparia riparia*): Recovery Strategy 2022." Government of Canada. https://www.canada.ca/en/environment-climate-change/ services/species-risk-public-registry/recovery-strategies/bank -swallow-2022.html.

Bastien, Betty. *Blackfoot Ways of Knowing.* University of Calgary Press, 2004.

Berry, Thomas. *The Dream of the Earth.* Counterpoint, 2006.

Bradley, C., A.A. Einsiedel Jr., T. Pyrch, and K. Van Tighem. *Flowing to the Future.* Proceedings of the Alberta's River Conference, University of Alberta Faculty of Extension, May 1989.

Chamberlin, J. Edward. *If This Is Your Land, Where Are Your Stories?* Penguin Random House, 2004.

Daschuk, James. *Clearing the Plains: Disease, Politics of Starvation, and the Loss of Aboriginal Life.* University of Regina Press, 2013.

Douglas, Howard. *Report of the Rocky Mountains Park of Canada for the Year Ended June 30, 1903.* Department of the Interior, 1904.

Eggermont-Molenaar, Mary, and Paul Callens. *Missionaries among Miners, Migrants and Blackfoot: The Van Tighem Brothers Diaries, Alberta 1875–1917.* University of Calgary Press, 2007.

Environment Council of Alberta. *Management of Water Resources within the Oldman River Basin: Report and Recommendation.* Government of Alberta, 1979.

Farr, D., A. Braid, and S. Slater. *Linear Disturbances in the Livingstone-Porcupine Hills of Alberta: Review of Potential Ecological Responses.* Government of Alberta, Department of Environment and Parks, 2018.

Fish and Wildlife Historical Society. *Fish, Fur, Feathers: Fish and Wildlife Conservation in Alberta, 1905–2005.* Co-published by Fish and Wildlife Historical Society and Federation of Alberta Naturalists, 2005.

Freedman, Bill. *A History of the Nature Conservancy of Canada.* Oxford University Press, 2013.

Geist, Valerius. *Mountain Sheep: A Study in Behaviour and Evolution.* University of Chicago Press, 1971.

Government of Canada. *Canada National Parks Act,* SC 2000, c. 32. https://laws-lois.justice.gc.ca/eng/acts/n-14.01/.

Government of Canada. *Parks Canada Agency Act,* SC 1998, c. 31. https://laws-lois.justice.gc.ca/eng/acts/P-0.4/.

Holroyd, Geoffrey, and Kevin Van Tighem. *The Ecological (Biophysical) Land Classification of Banff and Jasper National Parks, Volume III: The Wildlife Inventory.* Canadian Wildlife Service, 1982.

Jacobs, Jane. *Systems of Survival: A Dialogue on the Moral Foundations of Commerce and Politics.* Penguin Random House, 1992.

Kimmerer, Robin Wall. *Braiding Sweetgrass: Indigenous Wisdom, Scientific Knowledge, and the Teachings of Plants.* Milkweed Editions, 2013.

Klassen, Stan, and John Gilpin. "Alberta Irrigation in the Old and the New Millennium." *Canadian Water Resources Journal* 24, no. 1 (1999): 61–69.

Leopold, Aldo. *A Sand County Almanac, with Essays on Conservation from Round River*. Random House, 1966.

Lothian, W.F. *A History of Canada's National Parks*, vol. 1. Parks Canada, 1976. https://publications.gc.ca/site/eng/9.837433/publication.html.

Lothian, W.F. *A History of Canada's National Parks*, vol. 2. Parks Canada, 1977. https://publications.gc.ca/site/eng/9.837433/publication.html.

Lothian, W.F. *A History of Canada's National Parks*, vol. 3. Parks Canada, 1979. https://publications.gc.ca/site/eng/9.837433/publication.html.

Lothian, W.F. *A History of Canada's National Parks*, vol. 4. Parks Canada, 1981. https://publications.gc.ca/site/eng/9.837433/publication.html.

McClane, A.J., ed. *McClane's Standard Fishing Encyclopedia*. Holt, Rinehart and Winston, 1965.

Mitchell, W.O. *Who Has Seen the Wind?* Macmillan, 1947.

Naftel, William. "The Cochrane Ranche." Parks Canada, Occasional Papers in Archaeology and History No. 16, 2006. http://parkscanada history.com/series/chs/16/chs16-4j.htm.

Nelson, Joseph S., and Martin J. Paetz. *The Fishes of Alberta*. University of Alberta Press and University of Calgary Press, 1992.

Nestor, Jack J. "'To Convince the Red Man That the White Man Governs': John A. MacDonald and Canadian Indian Policy in the North-West." In *Canada and the Challenges of Leadership: How Canadian Prime Ministers Have Responded to Crises at Home and Abroad*, edited by Kelsey Lonie, Jonathon Zimmer, and Corey Safinuk. University of Regina Open Education and Publishing, 2023. https://opentextbooks.uregina.ca/primeministersandcrisis/chapter/__unknown__-3/.

O'Connor, Dermit. *A Review of the Literature on Blackfoot Use and Occupancy of the Crowsnest Pass & East Kootenays*. Report prepared for Blood Tribe/Káínai and Siksika Nation, 2020.

Olson, Wes, and Janelle Johane. *The Ecological Buffalo: On the Trail of a Keystone Species*. University of Regina Press, 2022.

Orwell, George. *Animal Farm*. Secker and Warburg, 1946.

Page, Robert, Suzanne Bayley, J. Douglas Cook, Jeffrey E. Green, and J.R. Brent Ritchie. *Banff-Bow Valley: At the Crossroads*. Report of the Banff–Bow Valley Task Force. Government of Canada, 1996.

Pannekoek, Frits. "Mistahimaskwa (Big Bear)." *The Canadian Encyclopedia*. Article published December 19, 2006; last modified September 13, 2016. https://www.thecanadianencyclopedia.ca/en/article/big-bear.

Parks Canada. *A Management Plan for Banff National Park*. Government of Canada, 2010.

Rosenberg, Kenneth V., A.M. Dokter, P.J. Blancher, J.R. Sauer, A.C. Smith, P.A. Smith, J.C. Stanton, A. Panjabi, L. Helft, M. Parr, and P.P. Marra. "Decline of the North American Avifauna." *Science* 366, no. 6461 (2019): 120–24.

Russell, Andy. *Grizzly Country*. Alfred A. Knopf, 1967.

Russell, Charlie. *Spirit Bear: Encounters with the White Bear of the Western Rainforest*. House of Anansi, 2017.

Salt, W.R., and A.L. Wilk. *Birds of Alberta*. Queen's Printer, 1966.

Stegner, Wallace. *The Sound of Mountain Water*. Doubleday, 1969.

Stelfox, Henry. *Rambling Thoughts of a Wandering Fellow, 1903–1968*. Self-published by John G. Stelfox, 1972.

Thunder, Jim. "Voices from Our Past: Crowfoot Valued Land More Than Government Money." Windspeaker. https://windspeaker.com/buffalo-spirit/voices-our-past-crowfoot-valued-land-more-government-money.

Tolkien, J.R.R. *The Lord of the Rings* (trilogy). George Allen and Unwin, 1954.

Van Tighem, Kevin. "Grey Ghosts: Alberta's Threatened Caribou." *Nature Canada* 19, no. 4 (1990): 22–27.

Wetlands Alberta. "Wetland Loss." http://www.wetlandsalberta.ca/wetland-loss/.

About the Author

Kevin Van Tighem, a former superintendent of Banff National Park, has written hundreds of articles, stories, and essays on conservation and wildlife that have garnered him many awards, including Western Magazine Awards, Outdoor Writers of Canada book and magazine awards, and the Banff Centre Mountain Film and Book Festival Jon Whyte Award for nonfiction. His conservation activism and nature writing have been recognized with the Canadian Wildlife Federation's Robert Bateman Award for advancing conservation through the arts, an honorary Doctor of Science from the University of Lethbridge, and the Blackfoot name meaning Rough Rapid Water. He is the author of *Bears Without Fear, The Homeward Wolf, Heart Waters: Sources of the Bow River, Our Place: Changing the Nature of Alberta,* and *Wild Roses Are Worth It: Alberta Reconsidered.* He lives with his wife, Gail, in High River, Alberta.